AF725681

Grandparents in a Digital Age

Grandparents in a Digital Age

The Third Act

Laura Tropp

LEXINGTON BOOKS
Lanham • Boulder • New York • London

Published by Lexington Books
An imprint of The Rowman & Littlefield Publishing Group, Inc.
4501 Forbes Boulevard, Suite 200, Lanham, Maryland 20706
www.rowman.com

Unit A, Whitacre Mews, 26-34 Stannary Street, London SE11 4AB

Copyright © 2019 by The Rowman & Littlefield Publishing Group, Inc.

All rights reserved. No part of this book may be reproduced in any form or by any electronic or mechanical means, including information storage and retrieval systems, without written permission from the publisher, except by a reviewer who may quote passages in a review.

British Library Cataloguing in Publication Information Available

Library of Congress Cataloging-in-Publication Data

Names: Tropp, Laura, author.
Title: Grandparents in a digital age : the third act / Laura Tropp.
Description: Lanham, Maryland : Lexington Books, an imprint of The Rowman & Littlefield Publishing Group, Inc., [2019] | Includes bibliographical references and index.
Identifiers: LCCN 2018044181 (print) | LCCN 2018046007 (ebook) | ISBN 9781498575799 (Electronic) | ISBN 9781498575782 (cloth : alk. paper)
Subjects: LCSH: Grandparenting. | Grandparents. | Internet--Social aspects.
Classification: LCC HQ759.9 (ebook) | LCC HQ759.9 .T76 2019 (print) | DDC 306.874/5--dc23
LC record available at https://lccn.loc.gov/2018044181

∞™ The paper used in this publication meets the minimum requirements of American National Standard for Information Sciences Permanence of Paper for Printed Library Materials, ANSI/NISO Z39.48-1992.

Printed in the United States of America

To Charles and Carol Tropp,
whose own "Third Act" was the inspiration for this book.

Contents

Acknowledgments

This book would not have been possible without the guidance and assistance of many people. I would like to thank my colleagues at Marymount Manhattan College for their support throughout this process. In particular, I thank Peter Schaefer, Jenny Dixon, Eileen Doherty, Katherine Wood, Katie LeBesco, and Sarah Nelson Wright.

Thanks to Lexington Books for their support of this book, and especially Lindsey Falk and Judith Lakämper for their commitment to this work. Thank you to the reviewers, who provided valuable feedback and made this a stronger book. Thanks to Meredith Jose for her constant optimism and helpful suggestions whenever I needed them and Jess Gorman for being my enthusiastic writing buddy. I also would like to thank all the grandparents I met throughout this process, in formal interviews, at train stations, at zoos, and on streets, who were delighted to share their stories.

In my home, books are always family endeavors. I thank Ethan, Maya, and Gillian for occupying themselves when mom was working on her book. I am in debt to my father, Charlie, for his devotion to the citations, references, and index. I am grateful to my mother, Carol, for her time engaged in the act of grandparenting so I could write about it. I owe much gratitude to my sisters, Jennifer and Deborah, for their wise counsel on all things child and research related. Finally, I thank Michael, my partner and faithful editor, whose constant support and dedication to this project made it possible.

Introduction

Age as Superpower

Kenneth Harmon is an elderly man and grandfather in Oklahoma, but he is more recognizable throughout social media as "poor Papaw." He received national attention when he made a hamburger dinner for his grandchildren and only one showed up. After his sad picture, which his grandchild posted on Twitter, went viral with over 180,000 retweets, the grandchildren hosted a follow-up barbecue. People drove from all over the country to eat with Papaw, take a picture with him, and buy an "I ate a burger with Sad Papaw" T-shirt.[1] Papaw's journey from an unknown, private grandpa to a celebrated public grandpa mirrors the power shifts of grandparenting over time. Depending on the group, the period, and the family, grandparents have been powerful patriarchs and matriarchs, reliable second parents, dependents, burdens, or community figures, like Papaw. This book investigates the history of grandparenting and the changing depiction of grandparent culture from "old" to "hip." The chapters that follow explore the development of the celebrity grandparent, the emergence of media technologies that allow for new communication and relationships between grandparents and their grandchildren, new rituals associated with grandparenting, the growth of the marketing of grandparenting as a new stage of life, and the impact on our culture of the commodification of grandparenting.

Prior to the twentieth century, within the United States the idea of the modern grandparent likely did not even exist. Many people did not live long enough to reach the grandparent stage of life. In fact, since death was likely in childhood and adult life was arduous, someone managing to survive to an old age was respected for just this achievement.[2] Those reaching the grandparenting age became the elder members of an extended kin group that sometimes lived together or nearby to help ensure the survival of the family.[3] Grandparents were dependent on the younger generation for eventual care and sustenance, and younger people relied on their grandparents for support, and in wealthier classes, inheritance. Early involvement in grandparenting not only helped to preserve the family; in some ways it was the final achievement of being a parent.

In the United States, as migration patterns changed, so did family life. People began to live longer, and extended families became more separated by distance. The matriarchs and patriarchs, once revered figures within a household, often shifted to the periphery of the family. Gone were the days when families were dependent on the eldest male to pass on property or when the female matriarch was an essential figure for caregiving and advice. Instead, experts began warning parents not to listen to an interfering grandma.[4] Across society today, the culture of grandparenting is changing once again as a variety of cultural, economic, technological, and social factors are giving rise to a new generation of grandparents. People are living longer, and grandparenting is occupying a longer phase in one's life. A *New York Times* article reports: "The number of grandparents in the United States rose to 69.5 million in 2014, up from 65.1 million in 2009, the [census] bureau reported last week. The youngest baby boomers turned 50 in 2014, and the country's 75.4 million boomers make up an exceptionally large pool of potential grandparents."[5]

Economic challenges have returned adult children, often with their own children, to their parents' homes. Conversely, the elderly, living longer and needing more care, are sometimes moving into the households of their children. Unlike the stereotypical image of the elderly grandparent knitting on a rocking chair, grandparents today are active; they engage in sporting activities, take teens shopping, and join their grandkids in the latest hobbies, such as video games or social media. In Philadelphia, for example, crowds cheered for the last person to finish a race because it was a world record for Ida Keeling, a centenarian. Her daughter Shelley oversaw her mother's race, including taking out her hearing aids to avoid distractions. In news coverage of the event, she discussed how she entered her mother in her first race when the elderly lady was in her sixties.[6] In this interesting reversal, instead of parents supervising their children in their participation of sports and other activities, children and grandchildren are managing their elders' activities. Another grandfather received national attention for his volunteerism by visiting and cuddling preemies in the hospital, stepping in for parents who could not always be there.[7] Instead of being cared for himself, he has transformed into a more universal grandfather figure for these babies and for the public, which embraced these stories about him.

The legacy of feminism also is reshaping grandparents, as some women who once balanced work and family with careers now have the chance in retirement to completely focus on their grandchildren. Millennials entering parenthood while working within the United States need the support of grandparents to solve childcare challenges. It used to be that kids would participate in "adopt-a-grandparent" programs to foster bonding with the aging community. Now, new parents sometimes "adopt" a grandparent in order to help raise their family. Many grandparents are absorbing some of the "second shift" caregiving as described by sociologist Arlie Hochschild.[8] Grandparents have switched from being the ones in need of pity and care to the ones providing caregiving and assistance. In post-industrialized nations, it is common for grandparents to help in aspects of childcare. They are picking up their grandchildren from school, taking them to baby exercise classes, and bringing them on vacations. Some grandparents describe this time as their "third act" or their "second phase of parenting." Others worry that grandparent abuse might become more of a problem. Some grandparents are feeling the need to assert their boundaries, pointing out that they are a grandparent and not a parental figure.[9]

Children have opportunities to establish relationships with grandparents that last long past their adolescent years. Claude Fischer, an expert in American cultural history, writes, "In 1900, about one in five 30-year-olds had any living grandparent; in 2000, about four in five did. Before, almost no 30-year-olds had *two* living grandparents; now about two in five do."[10] Grandparents are appearing in children's books where they are the stars. Grandparent playgroups are becoming more popular, and elementary schools have grandparent days so that young children can benefit from interacting with their grandparents. Colleges hold special Grandparent Visiting weekends, acknowledging not only the relationship between college-aged grandchildren and their grandparents, but also that grandparents sometimes help finance the cost of increasingly expensive higher education.[11] Many grandparents are a weekly or daily part of the lives of their grandchildren, in person or virtually. Newer technologies, such as Skype, Google Hangout, and FaceTime, allow grandparents who are far away to establish relationships with their grandchildren. Many grandparents also use social media and blogs to chronicle their experiences.

Though she preferred to maintain a low profile, recently one of the most famous grandparents in the United States was Marian Robinson, Michelle Obama's mother. When the Obamas moved into the White House, they brought her with them because they knew she would be helpful in raising her grandchildren. They echoed earlier intergenerational living patterns, which have never left some cultures. One does not need to live in the White House to have a close relationship with a grandparent. A Pew Research Study notes, "About 7 million grandparents lived with a grandchild in 2013, up from 5.8 million grandparents who did so in 2000, according to Census Bureau data."[12] Changes in real estate reflect the fact that retired folks are buying homes closer to their children so that they can help them by taking care of their grandchildren.[13] Intergenerational living is becoming popular enough for architectural firms to design houses around the concept, and tourism companies are designing multigenerational trips. While this trend of engaged grandparents who are a part of the everyday life of their children is re-emerging among a white, middle-class America, for some cultures, races, and classes, this type of grandparenting is not new. For example, African American grandmothers historically have played a primary role in raising their grandchildren and, during the antebellum period, helped them survive the institution of slavery.[14]

Marketers have realized the power of this new consumer group. Economists indicate that many American retirees today may be well positioned financially. As reported in the *New York Times*, "People on the leading edge of the baby boom and those born during World War II—the 25 million Americans now between the ages of 65 and 74—have emerged as particularly well positioned in the nation's economic timeline."[15] Emotionally laden commercials market products directly to grandparents, whether it is toilet paper, lunch meat, or consumer technologies. Johnson & Johnson created a campaign around "The Grandparents Frame," designed to easily send pictures to grandparents across the globe. A tearjerker Toyota commercial features parents and grandchildren presenting their grandparents with a surprise. A tree that was an important part of the grandparents' courtship had fallen, but the children had transformed it into a dining room table, to sit at the center of the family's life and heart.[16] The centrality of the grandparents in the family becomes the driving force in commercials like these. In the United States, with over 50 million grandparents, an average of $27.5 billion is spent each year on grandchildren.[17] Grandparents Day, declared by President Carter in 1978, was a day designated to acknowledge a hidden and vulnerable population. Today, it primarily is a day to spend time and money on grandparents.

Grandparents also are being targeted for their political power. In 2008, comedian Sarah Silverman made a video encouraging young people to persuade their Floridian grandparents to vote for Barack Obama. In 2016, a political action committee used Jewish grandparents in a social media campaign in which they warned their grandkids to vote for Hillary Clinton or risk being haunted from the grave.[18] Clinton herself singled out Abuelitas in an attempt to persuade them and their grandchildren to vote for her. International organizations use the grandparent figure as a way to universalize issues. When President Trump first issued a ban on immigration from several Muslim countries, an article in *Teen Vogue* by a young woman protested the ban on behalf of her grandma. In the article, which was shared widely, she wrote, "I may never see my grandmother again. Not because our relationship is strained or because she's fallen ill. It's not even a matter of distance. The next time I see my grandmother is directly dependent on our president, Donald J. Trump."[19] Elderly women have realized the power in using their grandmother image to surprise people and promote a political agenda. The Granny Peace Brigade protests military curriculum in public schools that they see as acting as a pipeline for the armed forces.[20] The use of the grandparent image activates the affection normally applied to grandmothers and transfers it to their cause.

Grandparenting is becoming its own life stage, where new rituals exclusive to grandparents are emerging, such as the grandmother shower or videos announcing a pregnancy specifically to a grandparent. As more grandparents live longer and spend more time in this stage, names that are now associated with aging are less appealing to many of them. Some celebrities have said that they associate traditional grandma names as too old and prefer names that offer a more youthful or glamorous image. Lionel Richie prefers G-Pa, while Goldie Hawn calls herself Glam-ma.[21] Language accommodates new words, like "Gigi" for great-grandmothers, who are living longer and becoming an increasing presence in families. As grandparenting becomes a life stage all its own, people want to learn how to be the best grandparents they can be. Grandparents used to be the experts that the family turned to for guidance; now, grandparents themselves can consult a slew of outlets for their own advice. There's a quick quiz that promises to answer "What Kind of Grandparent Are You?"[22] Grandparents can read articles like "10 Grandchildren Icebreakers" to help develop their relationship with their grandchild.[23] Today, competing books for grandparents-to-be inform them about different grandparenting styles. Books like *The Grandparents Handbook*, *GrandLoving: Making Memories with Your Grandchildren*, and *How to Be the Perfect Grandma* are just some options for finding the ideal grandparent purpose. Some grandparents have turned their grandparent lifestyle into a business, creating blogs like *Grandma's Briefs* and *GaGa Sisterhood*. Others have been thrust into the public eye performing unusual grandparent roles, such as the raging "Angry Grandpa" who regularly destroys consumer technologies, and Helen Ruth Elam Van Winkle, better known by her Instagram handle, "Baddiewinkle," whose fans love her sexy grandma image. Ari Seth Cohen, inspired by his own grandmother, has built his photography and film career documenting older people in glamorous poses.[24] Another young woman has found the inspiration for her clothing line from her great-grandmother's aprons, creating gingham mini-dresses.[25]

For those who are not already grandparents, a few experience the phenomenon of grandparent lust. As some couples postpone childbearing, would-be grandparents must wait until their children decide to have children.[26] Others not willing to chance missing becoming a grandparent take more extreme measures. Fertility centers are noticing more women coming in with their mothers who pay for the procedure to freeze their daughters' eggs.[27] In this way, family planning seems to be returning to the extended family. The pressure to provide grandchildren is so intense that blogs and advice columns now advise adult children how to tell their parents that they won't be grandparents.

Even the image of the grandma and grandpa is becoming hip. One may say that "old is the new black," as projecting old age becomes less about something to avoid and more about something to emulate. One study suggests that elderly people are more likely to feel content.[28] Surely, this does not mean ageism and stereotypes about the elderly have ceased to exist. However, views on aging are shifting gradually, and grandparents are playing a role in making that happen. Supreme Court Justice and Jewish grandma Ruth Bader Ginsburg is known among her fan base (yes, she has a fan base) as "The Notorious RBG."[29] The LeBron James Grandmothers Fan Club is described in *The Wall Street Journal* as some "rowdy grannies" who attend games together to bond, support, and root for him.[30] Traditional grandma tasks, such as knitting and cooking, are becoming "retro cool." One restaurant even promises to its customers rotating grandmas that do all the cooking.[31] Grandparents, once overlooked because of their age, are now using their age and experience to sell products and become a desired commodity themselves. People are showing an increasing fascination with the elderly people in their lives. As grandparents collect pictures of their grandchildren, grandchildren and great-grandchildren are exploring the worlds of their grandparents. Young people are re-creating pictures they found of their grandparents by matching themselves in the same poses and clothing. They post these pictures on social media, celebrating the traits they share with their grandparents.[32] Social media allows people to take their appreciation of their heritage out of the confines of their own homes and proudly display it for others to see.

The representation of grandparenting in popular culture is shifting as well. Once pictured as aging, depressed figures, grandparents are now valued as major players in the family.[33] *Wheel of Fortune* now features grandparent/grandchild teams, with one recently coming close to winning a million dollars.[34] An episode of *MasterChef Junior* featured grandmas (or VIGs) as judges.[35] Programs such as *Downton Abbey* and *Game of Thrones* display powerful geriatric patriarchs and matriarchs. Films like *Grandma*, *Dirty Grandpa*, and *Bad Grandpa* have propelled grandparenting from supporting characters to starring roles. Grandparents can be heroes and adventure-seekers, like the magical nana who always saves the day in the video shorts *Nina Needs to Go* on the Disney Channel, or Grandpa Rick, who takes his grandson Morty on crazy adventures in the Adult Swim cartoon *Rick and Morty*.

Grandparents are becoming more visible in television and film with travel programs such as *Grannies on Safari*, cooking programs like *My Grandmother's Ravioli*, a cooking show where the host interviews grandmothers around the country for their most treasured recipes, and *Grandma at 30*, about the mothers of teen moms entering grandparenthood while still relatively young themselves. Grandparents also are major characters in popular sitcoms, including both characters named "Pops" in *Blackish* and *The Goldbergs*. While some grandparents are portrayed as determined to play an important part in their grandchildren's lives, reluctant grandparenting also appears in several films and television programs, like John Stamos's character in *Grandfathered*, the family surprised by the sudden arrival of a baby in *Raising Hope*, and the grandmother saddled with a "bad" teenager in *Georgia Rules*. The relationship between a granddaughter and her grandmother is a central theme in the Amazon children's program *Just Add Magic*. Some representations pose the grandparent figure as a threat, like Ellen Barkin's matriarchal figure managing a household engaged in illegal activities in the TNT program *Animal Kingdom*. In M. Night Shyamalan's 2015 film *The Visit*, the director turned a brother and sister's visit with grandparents into a theater of horror. Road trips and other adventures with grandparents are the basis of films like *Grandma*, *Bad Grandpa*, *Dirty Grandpa*, *Willy Wonka and the Chocolate Factory*, and *Little Miss Sunshine*. Grandparents, once hidden away, the brunt of jokes, or otherwise marginalized, now play critical roles in these fictional families. Many shows derive their humor from juxtaposing scenarios in which grandparents do not conform to deeply held stereotypes about the elderly.

New studies tout the benefits of both being a grandparent and having a grandparent. When Hillary Clinton campaigned for president, she announced that she had a "grandma glow."[36] A study of grandparent mortality rates found that grandparents who provided childcare for their grandchildren were one-third less likely to suffer a mortality hazard.[37] Another study suggests that babysitting regularly for a grandchild can lower the risk of Alzheimer's disease and lead to a smarter brain.[38] Research continues to examine the grandparent brain and explain the evolutionary functions of grandparents, such as the necessity of grandmothers who can care for children, allowing mothers to birth more children.[39] While parents often have been blamed or lauded in the past for their influence over their children, it's the grandparents' turn now. New studies question whether living with grandparents can increase rates of obesity and if grandparents can affect their grandchildren's social class.[40]

It is clear that people are reevaluating, admiring, and rediscovering grandparents. Yet, despite the pervasive images of grandparents, some of which present empowered figures, grandparent representation in popular media continues to mimic many of the stereotypes commonly associated with aging, encouraging people to laugh at versus laugh with these figures. Though the grandparent image is evolving, the value society places on youth rather than the aged presents many challenges for grandparent representation.

While culture industries generate and encourage a new grandparent lifestyle, the commodified ideal of the grandparent image is often white and middle class. Those who can afford to buy into this lifestyle often belong to this demographic group, while the rest are left behind.

Shifting conceptions of grandparenting also necessitate debate over the meaning and consequences of these changes. Elderly people have to manage relationships with their children, their grandchildren, and, in some cases, their great-grandchildren. Some grandparents are engaging in a type of co-parenting and need to negotiate with their children regarding their caregiving. Courts have offered conflicting rulings about what rights a grandparent should have when parents contest custody of their children, particularly when divorce affects the family. Many grandparents that do not fit the idealized image receive little visibility in our culture, including those who are denied access to their grandchildren and others who assume a parental role. For many, grandparenting is a privilege that not everyone gets to have. It also illuminates how the elderly are viewed in our society.

The subtitle of this book, *The Third Act*, recognizes grandparenting as a new stage of life that is distinct from parenting. In order for this stage to exist, people have to live long enough to experience it. This book incorporates concepts from life course research, which studies aging by incorporating history, demographics, social structures, and cultures to understand generational and familial patterns.[41] This research emphasizes that life transitions are important to examine, especially now as economic and cultural influences are changing expectations of life events. For example, the rising trend of adult children returning to their parents' homes mimics earlier periods of living arrangements with grown children. A more intensive parenting style is leading to parents remaining tied to their adult children's lives; as these parents become grandparents, relationships with their grandchildren may appear different from those of previous historical periods. In some ways, this may resemble relationships in the nineteenth century, when parents and children spent more time together during the course of their lives.[42]

Other research, such as the work of Gunhild Hagestad and Peter Uhlemberg, addresses ageism and age segregation among the elderly population.[43] These studies document how society tends to signal aging, and that intentional and unintentional separation into age cohorts often disserves the elderly.[44] For example, the chronology of aging became more important in the nineteenth century as families moved from agrarian life to industrial areas. Aging became more noticeable, and perhaps even problematic.[45] In relation to life course research, grandparenting is an interesting topic to study as it can occur at different ages and is a stage of life often introduced without any real choice or control. As grandparenting becomes more of a life stage all its own, it likely will influence how people think about aging. Grandparenting, instead of something that just happens to people, is now experienced with more awareness and deliberation. Grandparenting, in fact, may serve as a "superpower" that helps to transform the experience of aging.

The title of this book, *Grandparents in a Digital Age*, reflects how grandparenting is changing in a digital environment. More than how grandparents are embracing, using, or critiquing new technologies (although many grandparents certainly discussed those experiences with me), the following chapters explore how grandparenting is changing in an age that is shaped by new characteristics, values, and priorities. New media change our symbolic environment, including how we see social groups like the elderly. Our digital era, with its emphasis on images, fame, individualism, and accessibility, has the power to change how we see grandparents and how grandparents see their own world. Even those who choose not to use new technologies are still part of a digital society that has been reconfigured around them. In *Technopoly*, media scholar Neil Postman writes that new technologies bring with them a Faustian Bargain. "A bargain is struck," he writes, "in which technology giveth and technology taketh away."[46] Digital cultures allow some grandparents to gain attention and power, but others will remain invisible, even as a commodified grandparent figure emerges. The primary aim of this book is to explore how grandparenting in the digital age is different from earlier periods, changes how people think about and treat grandparents, and transforms how grandparents themselves navigate this reconfigured life stage.

Grandparenting is underexplored to this day, requiring more research on all types of grandparents in many cultures and countries, which is too large a task for any one book. This book limits discussion to grandparents largely within U.S. culture, and since it examines the representation of grandparents in traditional and digital media, many of the examples presented here conform to dominant representations, which are often white, heteronormative, and middle class. It is important, though, to acknowledge that there is no monolithic grandparent experience; the pages that follow make an effort to affirm marginalized groups, highlighting voices that are heard less often in grandparenting discourse, including minority grandparents and those of lower income classes. My research for this book incorporates multiple methods, and I talked with grandparents and parents to learn about the joys and challenges their evolving relationships have generated. In finding subjects to interview, I searched across the country to be sure that different regions, classes, and ethnic and racial groups were represented. I sent requests for interviews to senior organizations, blogs, and Facebook accounts that reach the grandparent population. Many grandparents themselves recommended other grandparents I could interview.[47]

In its examination of representations of grandparents in popular culture and the struggle that media have had in creating "better" representations, the book questions how grandparents are adapting to life in the digital age and how their changing presence influences our understanding of families. In addition, through interviews with marketers and business owners, I investigate the branding and commodifying of the emerging grandparent market. Despite these goals, I make no claim that I have documented the experience of all grandparents. As I argue in this book, there is no one group of grandparents. They exist in all different age brackets and have little choice in the decision even to become grandparents, some longing for that status and others dreading it.

Chapter 1 reviews the history of grandparenting in the United States. This chapter explores evolutionary and sociological theories about the changing functions of grandparents as patriarchs and matriarchs. I examine the "grandmother hypothesis" that posits the evolutionary value of grandmothers, along with the impact that industrialization and migration patterns have played in changing grandparent roles. The chapter compares grandparenting traditions within different cultures and classes. Finally, the chapter surveys trends emerging today that signal the rise of a new age of grandparenting.

Chapter 2 shares the voices of grandparents across the country to document the changes in expectations of aging and grandparenting. From taking their grandchildren on safaris to hiking up mountains, grandparents today don't necessarily slow down during this period of their life. Based on interviews with grandparents and current data gathered by researchers, this chapter examines how new aging practices influence grandparenting. Grandparents describe how they define themselves and the challenges they encounter as they grandparent, and how they push against boundaries and stereotypes often associated with grandparents.

Chapter 3 explores the contrast between invisible and visible grandparents as some try to emulate the emerging idealized grandparent lifestyle. Legal battles often result from power shifts related to grandparents' rights. Some grandparents never get to have the grandparenting experience. The chapter investigates notions of grandparent privilege by using life stories of grandparents whose own experiences run counter to popular expectations of grandparenting. Meanwhile, political activists and politicians often play "the granny card" to shape public perception.

Chapter 4 examines the grandparent figure in popular culture, including images of the reluctant grandparent, the nagging grandparent, and the second chance at being a parent. It looks at the popular plotline of the grandparent road trip and the images of the grandfather as an adult child. The chapter uses examples from television programs and films to see how representations of grandparents reinforce attitudes about aging, but it also shows how power may be redistributed to grandparents as newer representations emerge.

Chapter 5 turns to the representation of grandparents in reality television, YouTube, Instagram, celebrity culture, and within political movements, such as the "Raging Grannies." These arenas become places where grandparents can reinvent images of the elderly, reclaim a new image for themselves, or gain popularity, intentionally or not, for being a grandparent. However, becoming a grandparent poses a new challenge for celebrities, who often reposition their public image in this new role but also are pressured to retain a youthful appearance to be seen as valuable.

Chapter 6 considers the growing commodification of grandparenting as a new stage of life and the emergence of grandparents as a new demographic and psychographic market. How do businesses market to grandparents, and how are grandparents marketed to others? How is the concept of grandparenting itself branded? The chapter studies the burst of advertisements that use the grandparent image and includes interviews with people who are involved in marketing to grandparents. The chapter also documents new rituals and trends, including within fashion and entertainment, that foster connections between grandparents and their grandchildren.

The purpose of this book is not to offer advice on how to live as a grandparent. Having said that, in these pages are useful reminders of the cyclical nature of families and that current challenges may not always be new. I argue that the ability to grandparent a certain way reflects the luxury of privilege—grandparents with more power and wealth can offer gifts to their children and grandchildren beyond love. One goal of this book is to highlight groups of people and types of caretaking that have been less visible in society. This book offers insights as to how new technologies, as well as cultural, economic, and social forces, are defining a new stage of life. These changes impact how we think about grandparenting, and by extension the elderly, in our society.

NOTES

1. Char Adams, "Happy Papaw! Over 100 People Show Up to Cookout for 'Sad Grandpa': 'I Had a Burger with Sad Papaw,'" *People.com*, March 26, 2016. http://people.com/celebrity/happy-papaw-dozens-show-up-to-cookout-for-sad-grandpa/.
2. Dale Dannefer and Karie Feldman, "Age Integration, Age Segregation, and Generation X: Life-Course Perspectives," *Generations* 41, no. 3 (October 2017): 21.
3. Ursula Adler Falk and Gerhard Falk, *Grandparents: A New Look at the Supporting Generation* (Amherst, NY: Prometheus Books, 2002), 23–25.
4. Ann Hulbert, *Raising America: Experts, Parents and a Century of Advice about Children* (New York: Alfred A. Knopf, 2003), 70.
5. Sharon Jayson, "More Grandparents Than Ever," *New York Times*, March 20, 2017, https://www.nytimes.com/2017/03/20/health/grandparents-population-census.html?smid=nytcore-ipad-share&smprod=nytcore-ipad.
6. Derk Call, "100-Year-Old Sets World Record at Penn Relays," *Runner's World*, May 1, 2016, https://www.runnersworld.com/masters/100-year-old-sets-world-record-at-penn-relays.
7. Jason Duaine Hahn, "Sweet 'ICU Grandpa' Cuddles and Soothes Babies Too Sick to Go Home at an Atlanta Hospital," *People.com*, September 29, 2017, http://people.com/human-interest/sweet-icu-grandpa-cuddles-and-soothes-babies-too-sick-to-go-home-at-an-atlanta-hospital/.
8. Arlie Russell Hochschild and Anne Machung, *The Second Shift* (New York: Penguin Books, 2003).

9. Shaon Jayson, "Need a Babysitter? Don't Count on Grandma," *New York Times* (Well blog), August 9, 2016, https://well.blogs.nytimes.com/2016/08/09/need-a-babysitter-dont-count-on-grandma/.

10. Claude S. Fischer, "Grandparents Today," *Boston Review* (blog), October 19, 2015, http://bostonreview.net/blog/claude-s-fischer-grandparents-today.

11. Farran Powell, "What Grandparents Should Know about Paying for College," *US News*, November 2, 2016, https://www.usnews.com/education/best-colleges/paying-for-college/articles/2016-11-02/what-grandparents-should-know-about-paying-for-college.

12. Jens Manuel Krogstad, *5 Facts about American Grandparents* (Washington, DC: Pew Research Center, September 13, 2015), http://www.pewresearch.org/fact-tank/2015/09/13/5-facts-about-american-grandparents/.

13. Harriet Edleson, "Grandparents Who Move to Be Closer to Granchildren," *New York Times*, June 26, 2015, https://www.nytimes.com/2015/06/27/your-money/grandparents-who-move-to-be-closer-to-grandchildren.html?action=click&contentCollection=Health&module=RelatedCoverage&region=EndOfArticle&pgtype=article.

14. Jillian Jimenez, "The History of Grandmothers in the African-American Community," *Social Service Review* 76, no. 4 (December 2002): 525, http://doi.org. 10.1086/342994.

15. Dionne Searcey and Robert Gebeloff, "America's Seniors Find Middle-Class 'Sweet Spot,'" *New York Times*, June 14, 2015, http://www.nytimes.com/2015/06/15/business/economy/american-seniors-enjoy-the-middle-class-life.html.

16. Alexandra Jardine, "Toyota Echoes 'This Is Us' In a Nostalgic, Heartwarming Holiday Spot," *AdAge*, November 29, 2017, http://creativity-online.com/work/toyota-rs/53331.

17. Liberty Reverse Mortgage and Sacramento State University, "Grandparents Spend $27.5 Billion per Year on Grandkids," report cited by *Grandboomers.com* (web page), accessed October 5, 2017, http://www.grandboomers.com/page/grandparents-spend-275-billion.

18. Ann-Christine Diaz, "Jewish Grandparents Promise to Rise from the Dead and Haunt Their Grandkids If They Don't Vote for Hillary," *AdAge*, September 22, 2016, http://adage.com/article/campaign-trail/jewish-grandparents-promise-rise-dead-haunt-grandkids-vote-hillary-clinton/305980/.

19. Mona Khalifeh, "Trump's Ban on Muslim Immigrants Could Mean I May Never See My Grandma Again," *Teen Vogue* (web page), January 30, 2017, https://www.teenvogue.com/story/trump-ban-muslim-immigrants-see-grandma-again.

20. Joyce Chu, "These Grannies Are Helping to Plug the School-to-Military Pipeline at Its Source," *The Nation*, May 11, 2016, https://www.thenation.com/article/these-grannies-are-helping-to-plug-the-school-to-military-pipeline-at-its-source/.

21. "Celebrity Grandparent Names," *Grandparents.com* (web page), accessed April 5, 2017, https://www.grandparents.com/family-and-relationships/grandparent-names/celebrity-grandparent-names.

22. "What Is Your Grandparent Style?" *mom365.com* (web page), July 24, 2017, https://www.mom365.com/mom/for-grandparents/grandparents-style-quiz.

23. Carol Baicker-McKee, "10 Grandchild Icebreakers," *Grandparents.com* (web page), accessed February 20, 2018, https://www.grandparents.com/grandkids/you-and-your-grandkids/talking-to-grandchildren-icebreakers.

24. "About Ari Seth Cohen," *Advanced Style* (blog), accessed February 7, 2018, http://www.advanced.style/about.

25. Rachel Felder, "A Clothing Line Based on Her Great-Grandmother's Aprons," *New York Times*, January 30, 2018, https://www.nytimes.com/2018/01/30/fashion/paris-starn-99-opening-ceremony.html.

26. Anne Tergesen, "The Long (Long) Wait to Be a Grandparent," *Wall Street Journal*, March 30, 2014, http://www.wsj.com/articles/SB10001424052702303775504579395501172676002.

27. Elissa Gootman, "So Eager for Grandchildren, They're Paying the Egg-Freezing Clinic," *New York Times*, May 13, 2012, http://www.nytimes.com/2012/05/14/us/eager-for-grandchildren-and-putting-daughters-eggs-in-freezer.html.

28. Lura L. Carstensen et al.,“Emotional Experience Improves with Age: Evidence Based on over 10 Years of Experience Sampling,” *Psychology and Aging* 26, no. 1 (March 2011): 21–33, http://doi.org/10.1037/a0021285.

29. Alli Maloney, “How Ruth Bader Ginsburg Became ‘Notorious R.B.G.,’” *Women in the World* (web page), November 3, 2015, https://womenintheworld.com/2015/11/03/how-ruth-bader-ginsburg-became-notorious-r-b-g/?refresh.

30. Ben Cohen, “LeBron James’s Biggest Fans: A Gang of Rowdy Grannies,” *Wall Street Journal*, June 8, 2015, http://www.wsj.com/articles/lebron-jamess-biggest-fans-a-gang-of-rowdy-grannies-1433779319.

31. Gillie Houston, “Grandmas Do All the Cooking at This New York Restaurant,” *Food & Wine*, October 10, 2016, http://www.foodandwine.com/news/grandmas-are-swapped-chefs-new-york-restaurant.

32. Inga Ko, “25+ Times People Recreated Their Grandparents Photos, and the Result was Amazing,” *Boredpanda* (blog), accessed December 12, 2018, https://www.boredpanda.com/recreating-grandparent-photos/.

33. Tom Robinson and Caitlin Anderson, “Older Characters in Children’s Animated Television Programs: A Content Analysis of Their Portrayal,” *Journal of Broadcasting & Electronic Media* 50, no. 2 (June 2006): 287–304, https://doi.org/10.1207/s15506878jobem5002_7.

34. “Wheel of Fortune Family Left Stunned after Almost, but Not Quite, Winning $1 Million,” *Fox News* (web page), November 17, 2017, http://www.foxnews.com/entertainment/2017/11/17/wheel-fortune-family-left-stunned-after-almost-but-not-quite-winning-1-million.html.

35. *Master Chef*, “Top 16 Compete: Part 1,” Season 4, Episode 7, FOX, June 2013, directed by Brian Smith, written by Franc Roddam.

36. Sandra Sobieraj Westfall, “Hillary Clinton Shares Advice for Granddaughter Charlotte,” *People.com* (web page), October 3, 2014, http://www.people.com/article/hillary-clinton-granddaughter-charlotte-advice.

37. Sonja Hilbrand et al., “Caregiving within and beyond the Family Is Associated with Lower Mortality for the Caregiver: A Prospective Study,” *Evolution and Human Behavior* 38, no. 3 (May 2017): 397–403, https://doi.org/10.1016/j.evolhumbehav.2016.11.010.

38. Katherine F. Burn et al., “Role of Grandparenting in Postmenopausal Women’s Cognitive Health: Results from the Women’s Healthy Aging Project,” *Menopause* 21, no. 10 (October 2014): 1069–1074, https://doi.org/10.1097/GME.0000000000000236. Unfortunately, too much grandparenting (as defined by five days a week in this study) will actually lower cognitive performance.

39. Kirsten Hawkes, “Human Longevity: The Grandmother Effect,” *Nature* 428, no. 6979 (March 2004): 128, https://doi.org/10.1038/428128a.

40. Vanessa Moulton et al., “The Influence of Grandparents’ Social Class on Children’s Aspirations,” *British Journal of Sociology of Education* 38, no. 4 (May 2017): 500–517, http://doi.org/10.1080/01425692.2015.1093407.

41. Tamara K. Hareven, “Aging and Generational Relations: A Historical and Life Course Perspective,” *Annual Review of Sociology* 20 (August 1994): 438, https://doi.org/10.1146/annurev.so.20.080194.002253.

42. Hareven, 446.

43. Gunhild O. Hagestad and Peter Ulenberg, “The Social Separation of Old and Young: A Root of Ageism,” *Journal of Social Issues* 61, no. 2 (June 2005): 343–360, http:/doi.org/10.1111/j.1540-4560.2005.00409.x.

44. Richard Settersten Jr. and Gunhild O. Hagestad, “Subjective Aging and New Complexities of the Life Course,” *Annual Review of Gerontology and Geriatrics* 35, no. 1 (February 2015): 239–252, https://doi.org/10.1891/0198-8794.35.29.

45. Dannefer and Feldman, “Age Integration,” 21.

46. Neil Postman, *Technopoly: The Surrender of Culture to Technology* (New York: Vintage Books, 1993), 5.

47. Every parent and grandparent who agreed to be interviewed for this book was offered the option of a pseudonym to preserve their anonymity. Though many preferred to have their real names used, I have changed the names of those who did not.

Chapter One

The Grandparent Shift

The idea for this book came from a conversation with my young daughter. She came home from school one day with a concerned expression on her face and a chart she had been working on in school. At the top of her chart were two columns that said "immediate family" and "extended family." Her confusion came because she was not able to neatly characterize our family. As an intergenerational family, our household includes her maternal grandparents. We had moved in together several months earlier, purchasing a house where we could divide up the space to our liking. On that school day, she was puzzled because her teacher had told the class that immediate family meant those who lived with her and extended family were those that were part of her life but lived outside her home. Her teacher had used grandparents as an example of extended. The current definitions of family did not match her living arrangements. Though she understood that her grandparents were not the same as her parents, they were not extended relatives in her eyes, either. My daughter's confusion and my quest to help her make sense of the chart led me to explore the shifting understanding of grandparents historically and today. Grandparents have moved back and forth between integral family members, extended kin, custodial figures, and those who just pop in to shower their grandchildren with toys and luxuries. Economic, cultural, and political conditions have guided the changing characteristics of grandparenting in the United States and continue to shape the emergence of grandparenting as a cultural practice today.

POWER, GRANDPARENTS, AND EARLY HISTORY

A study on behavioral epigenetics found that our grandparents and great-grandparents who experienced trauma or other adversity may leave "molecular scars" in their genes that are passed on for generations.[1] In fact, the legacy of grandparents has been researched across a variety of fields beyond the genes they have passed on. Historically, grandparents have had a sociological and cultural impact, in addition to the genetic influence, on our lives.

Much of our early history of family involved extensively networked tribes, clans, and kin. A glance at the Bible reveals a lineage of families led by powerful patriarchs and matriarchs. The power and loyalty that kinship holds is still a common theme within popular culture today, as played out in real-life families like the Kardashians and fictionalized families such as the Sopranos. The grandparents in these families can vary from playing central roles in the lives of their family to being minor players who are sometimes manipulated by other family members maneuvering for control. The idea of a "grandparent" who performs roles familiar to us today would not make sense to families of the past. In earlier times, grandparents either were ever present in the family group, relatively unnoticed, or present only in memory because they had not survived to see their grandchildren.[2]

It's difficult to delineate the history of grandparents, as they often were not thought worthy of a separate topic of study. Grandparents were traditionally understood as close kin to be valued. If they were not living with a family intergenerationally, they likely were in close proximity to them. Perhaps their very necessity made them hard to distinguish from other family members, as one tends to take for granted that which is always there. Many historical figures have had formative relationships as or with their grandparents, but few have thought to comment on those relationships. Sigmund Freud, for example, studied the relationship between parents and children in his work on psychoanalysis, but he barely mentioned the role of grandparents. However, there is evidence that Freud himself was greatly affected by his role as a grandparent and suffered depression after the death of his grandchild.[3] Too often in the past, the image of grandparents in both research and popular culture concentrated on their parental role, exploring their relations with their children rather than their grandchildren. When relationships with grandchildren were explored, the grandparents often were cast as meddlers.[4]

One reason for the lack of research on grandparents prior to the twentieth century may be the mortality rates among adults. Conventional wisdom holds that not until the twentieth century could most people count on growing old.[5] Some scholars caution against jumping to that conclusion. In her research on early humans, Rachel Caspari found that there was a leap in survival within Upper Paleolithic Europeans that helped to increase adult longevity. Caspari argues, "Initially a by-product of some sort of cultural change, longevity became a prerequisite for the unique and complex behaviors that signal modernity."[6] It is likely that the older adults, who often became grandparents, contributed to transmitting knowledge across the group, ranging from what plants to eat to the rituals developed within the culture. One set of research that examined records from the Vernon region of France in the late eighteenth and early nineteenth centuries supports the idea that grandparents may have played important roles in earlier periods of time. Vincent Gourdon writes, "The twentieth century was not the first during which grandparents were family actors."[7] During this time, children may have known their grandparents for a brief period, though they were more likely to know their grandmothers than their grandfathers.[8] Studying historical records of housing and inheritance, Brian Gratton and Carole Haber articulate three key phases of the history of grandparenting. In the first phase, before the mid-nineteenth century, grandparents had more power because of the property that their children stood to inherit from them. By the second phase in the early twentieth century, grandparents had less power, as younger generations sought to establish their own households and saw elderly people as a drain on their resources or even a potential threat. By the third phase after World War II, grandparents were seen as sources of companionship but did not hold much in the way of family power.[9]

Historically, grandparents' power existed through what they had to offer the family, in terms of both money and knowledge. In the ancient Roman period, the oldest man in the household was considered the ruler of the family, both legally and in terms of family structure. Because of this, grandfathers were the ones with the most power and status.[10] Many grandparents would hold on to property until their death because their access to property and wealth guaranteed them a certain level of respect and care.[11] This is interesting to contrast with today's adult children encouraging their parents to spend their money now and enjoy life rather than waiting to die and leave an inheritance to them.[12] One way grandparents enjoy their wealth is by distributing it to their children's offspring. According to the AARP, "The vast majority (96%) of grandparents . . . spend money on their grandchildren."[13] Many grandparents today no longer use their wealth as leverage for caring and connection, and when they do, they often are seen as malevolently manipulative.

Scholars do disagree on how much respect grandparents were given in different historical periods. Some argue that those who mostly had access to resources and power were revered.[14] However, before the modern era, grandparents were valued because they possessed wisdom from age and could pass on the knowledge and myths of their culture to younger generations.[15] Anthropologist Margaret Mead once said, "Everyone needs to have access both to grandparents and grandchildren in order to be a full human being."[16] Historically, grandparenting was required to achieve a respected elder status; becoming old without children or grandchildren made someone a source of suspicion and scorn from the tribe. This view survives today in some traditional cultures, like the Tiriki and Irigwe in Africa.[17] In some communities, grandparents have stood between grandchildren and certain death. There is a community in the Ache of South America where orphaned children are killed if grandparents do not step in to claim responsibility.[18]

It is also likely that grandparents played an important evolutionary role in the past. People often make fun of the elderly enjoying early bird dinner specials, and older people sometimes lament the way their sleep is disrupted during the night. One study suggests that these behaviors have evolved to be genetically programmed to occur as people age. Grandparents were helpful to tribes as the early morning watchmen, being able to warn others of potential threats.[19] Grandmothers in particular played an important evolutionary role as caretakers that allowed their extended family to grow.[20] Grandfathers, whose reproductive capacity lasts longer than females', would take two or more wives in some cultures that permitted multiple marriages.[21] Women, with more limited reproductive windows, likely evolved to serve other functions. Sarah Hrdy, who studies motherhood across animal and human kingdoms, has noted that humans are cooperative breeders, a species in which individuals outside of the immediate family help to raise children. Hrdy writes, "Unlike mothers among other African apes, who nurtured infants on their own, these early hominin mothers relied on groupmates to help protect, care for, and provision their unusually slow-maturing children and keep them on the survivable side of starvation."[22]

Anthropologist Kristen Hawkes has argued that, instead of assuming that societal care of the elderly population explains longevity patterns, it might be actually the elderly themselves who are responsible for the welfare of the larger group. Hawkes argues, "Developments in evolutionary life-history theory suggest that, instead of help *for* older members of the population, it is help *from* postmenopausal grandmothers that accounts for the age structures of human societies."[23] Hawkes labeled caregiving by the elder female population "The Grandmother Hypothesis." With grandmothers helping to provide food and care to their grandchildren, they could assist mothers in shortening birth intervals, leading to more frequent reproduction.[24] Some scientists hypothesize that grandmother involvement allowed childhood to last for a longer period, longevity to increase, and brains to become more complex.[25] Thus, assisting in childcare helps invest in the future of the family, and by extension the tribe.

Scientists have continued to study the benefits that grandmothers provide in the lives of their daughters, influencing future generations.[26] In some traditional societies today, it is routine for mothers to pass on their infants and toddlers to granny caretakers so that they can devote their energy to providing sustenance for the family and preparing to birth the next child.[27] A study in Ethiopia determined that grandmothers involved in the lives of their daughters would result in a more likely survival for the grandchildren. The grandmothers would visit their daughters' households and assist them by taking over demanding chores, leaving the mothers to have time to focus on more intensive childcare.[28]

Historically, helping the survival of their kin probably was not grandparents' only goal. They also wanted to curry favor with the family. David Coall and Ralph Hertwig write, "During the prolonged post-reproductive period, grandparents may have the opportunity and the motive to boost their own fitness by investing resources in their children's and grandchildren's survival and reproduction."[29] Grandparents may also be engaging in what some scholars label the "rational grandparent model," in which grandparents plan relationships with those grandchildren whom they hope will help care for them in their last years. Others may simply develop reciprocal levels of affection with their grandchildren.[30] Sarah Hrdy compares the past with the present: "Just as in modern America, where children telephone grandparents more times each month if they possess significant heritable resources, old women in foraging societies are more valued when the food they gather is an important component of the diet."[31] Building relationships could lead to future assistance when they need care.

In the modern era, these relationships serve similar purposes but have expanded to include more forms of care. Several years ago, a Hungarian man noticed that his ninety-one-year-old grandmother was depressed, so to revive her spirits he decided to turn her into a superhero. He staged photographs of her wearing superhero costumes and taking on heroic poses. People adored these pictures of a grandma superhero, but they also admired the attention the grandson gave her.[32] As the social structure shifts to where grandparents need less physical care or increasingly receive care from institutions, grandchildren can instead provide mental and emotional care when needed, assisting not only in physical survival but also providing a better quality of life.

SOCIOCULTURAL SHIFTS OF THE FAMILY

Shifts in economic, political, social, and cultural structures at various points change the amount of power grandparents wield. The first U.S. Census in 1790 indicated that the average American household was made up of just over five members, and grandparents were often a part of the household. The number of family members living together declined over the next two centuries.[33] Gratton and Haber argue that, even when grandparents lived with the family, many did not find the arrangement optimal: "grandparents in the home limited the happiness and prosperity of young and old alike."[34] Others concur that the image of the extended family as the norm in the United States was likely exaggerated.[35] While the ideal of intergenerational living may not be what has been imagined, kinship, and the integral role of grandparents within family structures, have always been present. Kornhaber and Woodward write, "The multigenerational household may indeed be a historical anomaly, but the extended family network is not. It has supported American immigrants in every century. It has nurtured neighborhoods in every city and flavored the life of every Faulknerian hamlet."[36] However, whether the family included grandparents living physically within the household or outside of it, the Industrial Revolution did impact the structure and purpose of families, influencing the roles grandparents would play.

The Industrial Revolution pushed many families from agrarian to urban life, and the conditions of city life changed the notion of the family. On the farm, all members of the family served different roles, and communities worked together toward common goals. Family was necessary to produce food and other goods for trade and survival, so loyalty to one's extended family was necessary.[37] In city life, social systems supplanted many of the tasks of the extended family, in part because of a necessity for mobility to wherever factories were located. Despite this, kin still retained its importance, and extended families whose members lived close to one another continued to play important roles.[38] Families, particularly immigrants, needed extended family networks to assist in finding jobs and shelter and to provide interim care.[39] Extended family still lived together in some households, and every member of the family, including young children, went to work to help ensure the survival of the family. In fact, Stephanie Coontz, in her book *The Way We Never Were: American Families and the Nostalgia Trap*, argues that one reason for the growth of the nuclear family was to protect women and children from grueling factory jobs by placing men into single-income provider roles. The nuclear family, reformers claimed, was the "true American" family.[40]

Increased mobility continued to upset these familial social networks. Children moved far from home, looking for better job prospects. In their research on the history of grandparenting, Ursula Adler Falk and Gerhard Falk declare mobility was the "final blow" to the extended family network.[41] As the Great Depression and World War II brought economic hardship and the need for able-bodied men to serve as soldiers abroad, extended kin networks rebounded.[42] After World War II, though, more white families sought out or were encouraged to begin nuclear families in suburban locations. Government services stepped in to assist the unemployed, disabled, and elderly, shifting obligations and responsibilities away from extended family.[43] Thanks to programs like Social Security, elderly people, including widows, had a new means to live independently.[44] In his book *Sapiens: A Brief History of Humankind*, Yuval Noah Harari recounts, "Over time, states and markets used their growing power to weaken the traditional bonds of family and community. The state sent its policemen to stop family vendettas and replace them with court decisions. The market sent its hawkers to wipe out longstanding local traditions and replace them with ever-changing commercial fashions." Most important, Harari argues that the creation of the concept of individualism at the expense of the needs of the family created major shifts in loyalty and familial bonds.[45] Coontz describes media images during this period as clashes of loyalties to marriage with allegiances to extended family: "Popular commentators urged young families to adopt a 'modern' stance and strike out on their own, and with the return of prosperity, most did."[46]

The development of suburbs supported the growth of nuclear families, but they largely excluded the elderly, with communities and services in the suburbs focused on activities related to youth and family.[47] The elderly would need to look elsewhere to find their own notions of community. Developers saw the market potential in creating housing exclusively for the elderly.[48] Youngtown in Arizona claims to be the first retirement community to restrict residents to adults only. Developers chose the name "Youngtown" to market themselves as young at heart, a place where retirees could spend their time surrounded by others of similar ages.[49] While different retirement communities vary in their age restrictions, many were drawn to communities with strict no-child rules.[50] Of course, the ability to "retire," particularly in a warm and comfortable location, is dependent on class, which may explain why grandparents of color and recent immigrants to the United States did not experience the same separation from their extended families. Ultimately, grandparents, children, and grandchildren no longer shared the interdependence that were once everyday conditions of the family, which changed how they saw their obligations and relationships.

RACE, ETHNICITY, CLASS, AND GRANDPARENTING POWER

While the figure of the grandparent as a regular presence was lost for some families, for others, the grandparent role followed the different trajectory of a constant support system. The role of grandmother for many African Americans evolved into a universal mother figure. Patricia Hill Collins describes the restricted access to motherhood women of color suffered during slavery: "By denying enslaved African women marriage, citizenship and even humanity, slavery provided no social context for issues of privatized motherhood as a stay-at-home occupation."[51] Instead, grandmothers were part of a network of women responsible for the care of all children. Herbert C. Covey and Paul T. Lockman, in their study of African American slave narratives, observe that despite the oppressive conditions and little protection for older slaves, "what is most amazing is that under these circumstances how often ex-slaves referred to grandparents and indicated that they had played a significant role in raising the children."[52] On the plantation, grandmothers were often in charge of nurseries housing children, and they distributed the food rations.[53] In addition, grandmothers were important storytellers in the community, serving not just a practical survival role but also to inspire and pass on their history to future generations.[54] Jillian Jimenez notes that the grandmother was a social, not biological, role: "For many African Americans, in fact, there was no constituted role of grandmother. Instead, the grandmother was another woman shouldering responsibility for the family's survival and community well-being. As this history suggests, grandmother is a protean role; the middle-class white ideal of the grandmother is socially constructed and depends not only on longevity but also more significantly on a measure of affluence."[55] While mothers worked in the fields, grandmothers assumed responsibility for all the children on the plantation. After the Civil War, grandparents would often take in children during the day so that parents could work, and grandchildren would help the grandparents, all working as a group to sustain the family.[56]

In his influential 1938 book *The Negro Family in the United States*, E. Franklin Frazier described African American grandmothers as "guardians of generations" because of their role not just in caring for the grandchildren but also helping to keep families together after Emancipation.[57] During Reconstruction, grandmothers played a significant role in preserving the structure of African American families. With little economic power, families relied on larger kinship. Jimenez writes, "Forced to work to help their families survive, they were the purveyors of domestic medicine and midwifery, preservers of family traditions, caretakers and educators of the community's children, and exemplars of pride in their African-American heritage."[58] During the Great Depression in the South, grandparents helped to care for their grandchildren even more than their grandchildren cared for them.[59] In the early twentieth century, because of systematic discrimination, it was easier for black women rather than black men to find work. As mothers worked in the homes of white families, grandmothers assisted with domestic tasks. They also filled a need that the child welfare system was woefully ill-equipped to serve, to care for children whose parents could not care for them.[60] As African Americans moved away from the rural South to urban areas for work during the twentieth century, grandparents would often care for their grandchildren for a period of time.[61] In addition, grandmothers were important for both their economic support and spiritual and religious guidance. Mildred A. Hill-Lubin observes in her study of autobiographies of African Americans, "While living in a racist, hostile world, grandmother is often depicted as mighty and powerful; she demands respect and obedience from her grandchildren."[62] After World War II, African American families retained their important kinship networks, with grandfathers and grandmothers playing key roles. In a recent article exploring grandmothers and their experiences of community in public housing, LaShawnDa Pittman and Deirdre Oakley found that grandmothers often provided caregiving for more than their own children in the community. Public housing "enabled grandmothers to live in close physical proximity to social support and neighborhood institutions, including food pantries, churches, afterschool programs, and vocational training."[63] Today, grandparents continue to be relied upon as integral players in the lives of African American families.

In addition to understanding how race may influence the role of grandparenting, it is also important to acknowledge the roles that social class and ethnicity play as well. Black and Latino families are more likely than white families to rely on kin, including grandparents, as support networks because of their relative lack of access to wealth. While they do provide financial assistance, grandparents offer other practical support roles as well, including childcare and errand-running.[64] Similarly, further research has shown minority groups often rely on grandparents for support in their family life. Because minority groups such as Latinos and African Americans are less likely to have economic advantages, the additional kinship help, as we saw in the history of African American grandmothers, helps with survival.[65] Immigrant groups migrating to the United States have, whenever possible, retained a grandparent figure to assist in caring for their children. One reason for this reliance was simply a pragmatic choice: as extended families often immigrated together, they stayed together to help each other navigate living in their new, unfamiliar land. Studies have shown that the elderly tend to maintain a stronger attachment than younger people to their country of origin, and thus are more likely to be dependent upon their children and grandchildren to mediate for them in a new country.[66] Another reason may be that some cultures value the elderly more, and they retain a prestigious role in the lives of younger people. For example, Chinese families traditionally set adult children and grandchildren as subordinate to their maternal and paternal parents, honoring a tradition of filial piety.[67] Like other groups, these families also are interdependent, but their younger generations feel obliged to serve their elders. In a more contemporary culture, the family still is bound together, but grandparents serve and prioritize the needs of their children and grandchildren.[68] One study found that "evidence from this research clearly testifies to the cohesiveness of linked lives and the adaptive intergenerational solidarity between grandparents and their children in contemporary China."[69] The history of grandparenting influence in China illustrates how cultures may adapt the grandparent role over time to best serve the family, but attitudes about the importance of grandparents are often deeply rooted in some cultures.

The idea of grandparenting as a unique stage of life with its own style of caregiving is not only a more modern idea; it is reserved for those with the economic power to allow grandparents to function in this way. In *Our Kids: The American Dream in Crisis*, Robert Putnam describes the influential role grandparents can play in modern society while explaining the inequities of poorer versus wealthier grandparents:

> Grandparents today are often more important in their grandchildren's lives than their counterparts were a half century ago, because grandparents are healthier and wealthier than they used to be. This trend plays out very differently in upper-tier and lower-tier families, however. Generally speaking, lower-tier grandparents mostly donate time, replacing parental resources, whereas upper-tier grandparents mostly donate money, supplementing parental resources.[70]

It also is important to note differences in assumptions and norms between cultures about the role of grandparents. The "norm of noninterference" is the idea that grandparents should avoid becoming too involved in the issues that come up within a nuclear family. Though this attitude may be assumed to be the default for grandparents, this actually is a European American cultural practice. As noted above and elsewhere, research has confirmed that African American families and other minority groups have a more fluid relationship than white families to blur boundaries of grandparenting and parenting.[71]

This multicultural history of grandparenting in the United States illustrates a larger phenomenon. Often, the function and role that grandparents take on is determined somewhat by the relative power they have in society. The re-emergence of active grandparenting in American life is not uniform; it is important to acknowledge that some cultural groups have never exchanged the extended family network in favor of a nuclear family structure, and that grandparents continuously have been an active presence in the family of these cultures for many generations.

REEMERGENCE OF GRANDPARENTING

Though some cultural groups always have maintained an active relationship between grandparents and their grandchildren, much of American society only recently has encouraged a reemergence of a more immersive grandparent experience, thanks to shifts in sociological, cultural, and political structures. This relatively new expectation of grandparenting evokes both earlier family structures and the fundamental relationship some cultures have preserved.

While kinship networks in general and grandparenting in particular suffered when families in the eighteenth and nineteenth centuries increasingly became mobile, more recently families have settled in one place for more than one generation. Since the 1980s, migration rates within the United States have been steadily decreasing.[72] Many Americans, particularly those with less education and lower income, stay close to their parents' homes.[73] The nature of the classic grandparent visit, which typically used to include holiday and summer travel in the 1960s and 1970s, now involves more frequent visits and sometimes even temporary co-residence.[74] Economic conditions often influence grandparenting relationships; as the Industrial Revolution increased mobility and decreased the proximity and power of grandparents, the Great Recession between 2007 and 2009 encouraged the increase of multigenerational living, described by some observers as "grand-families."[75] Though the segregation of the elderly into isolated communities in the mid-twentieth century promoted the ideal of the nuclear family, some lamented the loss of grandparents' involvement in the everyday life of their grandchildren.

Now, housing markets are taking into consideration the reintegration of the elderly, and grandparents in particular, with other age groups. Many people ready for retirement are choosing to forgo communities that ban children and instead decide to live among families in traditional homes outfitted for their needs.[76] In economic hard times, retirement communities with age restrictions often are not practical, especially when grandparents outlive their retirement savings or need to provide shelter for a child or grandchild. Some grandparents have entered into legal battles to be able to stay in their homes when they obtain custody of their grandchildren.[77] For grandparents with financial means who want to spend more time with their grandchildren, they can purchase luxury homes with grandchildren suites.[78] An article in the *Wall Street Journal* reveals that "in-law apartments" are becoming a new trend in real estate.[79] A photographic display in *Forbes* shows what are sometimes called "Granny Flats."[80] These types of living arrangements are a return, in many ways, to a time when grandparents were ever present with the family.

These trends are motivated also by a growing recognition of the challenges that grandparents relocating to a physically distant location from their children presents. Adult children have realized that isolating their aging parents leaves a vulnerable population without assistance. To address this problem, organizations and policy makers stepped in to create groups and activities that could re-create the experience of extended family life in the past, when older and younger people interacted on a regular basis. The first intergenerational program designed to increase connections between younger people and the elderly began in 1963 with an adopt-a-grandparent program in Florida.[81] Organizations and schools created additional intergenerational programs in the 1970s, but the 1980s brought a robust interest among scholars, social service agencies, and public policy makers in bridging the gap between the elderly and the rest of society. In 1981, the White House hosted a conference on the aging.[82] Schools began to introduce curriculum in classrooms about the elderly.[83] In the 1980s and continuing into the 1990s, many more organizations were formed that focused on bridging intergenerational gaps. While these efforts sometimes were framed as a way for young people to bond with and learn from an older generation, they often sought to provide assistance to the elderly, who were seen as a vulnerable population.[84] For these efforts, the term "grandparent" more generically referred to an older person in need of companionship.

These programs were popular enough to be featured in several television programs in the 1980s and 1990s. In these programs, the elderly were often depicted as lonely or in need of care. Some type of mischief would ensue in a sitcom as a result of a child spending time with a grandparent figure. Eventually a responsible adult (implying that the grandparent figure was not a responsible adult) would need to come in and fix the situation. On *Diff'rent Strokes*, the elderly man is grumpy, uninterested in participating in the program, and calls the child "a little brat," tainting the child's perception of the elderly. Mr. Drummond has to meet with the grumpy grandpa to sort out why he behaved this way, repair the relationship, and restore the child's faith in the elderly.[85] On *Full House*, teenager DJ volunteers at a nursing home and "adopts" a grandfather, who convinces her to take him home with her. Later, a nurse shows up at the house in search of the man, who left the home without permission. DJ's father explains to her that the man suffers from the early stages of Alzheimer's disease, for which there is no cure.[86]

In the twenty-first century, the adopt-a-grandparent movement has given way to new organizations that connect the elderly to families who are in search of a grandparent figure in their lives.[87] The perspective has reversed from the elderly being seen as the most vulnerable members in the social relationship and in need of charity from the younger people, to the younger members of society being dependent upon the wisdom and nurturing that older people can provide.

One factor that has played a role in the reemergence of the grandparent figure is the rise in divorce. Leslie Bennetts writes in *The Feminine Mistake*, "During the quarter century from 1970 to 1995, the number of families maintained by women with no husband present rose from 5.7 million to 12.2 million."[88] Divorced mothers, and others without a partner to help raise their children, would sometimes return to their own parents' homes, often with their own children in tow.[89]

Other grandparents sometimes must assume a parental role because parents have become unable to take care of their children. An epidemic of cocaine abuse among the upper middle class began in the mid-1970s. The crisis spread to lower-income communities with a crystallized version known as crack, which was cheaper to produce.[90] During the epidemic in the 1980s, grandparents, usually grandmothers, had to assume primary care of their grandchildren, as parents were either jailed or unable to care for their children because of their drug addiction. Scholars have documented the creation of "skipped generation" families, in which grandparents had to take over primary caregiving of their grandchildren.[91] Services and organizations formed that advocated for and provided assistance to grandparents, who were (and continue to be) largely unacknowledged and unsupported for their caregiving. In the twenty-first century, another drug epidemic has surfaced with the rising use of heroin. Just as the crack epidemic wreaked havoc in African American communities, the opioid crisis is affecting more whites in suburban and rural areas.[92] These addiction epidemics have shifted the nature of caregiving for those affected grandparents. Beginning to recognize that more and more grandparents are being thrust into full-time childcare, politicians and nonprofit organizations are scrambling to raise awareness and reorganize services. For example, in the spring of 2016, congressional representatives Danny Davis of Illinois and Todd Young of Indiana introduced a bill that would reduce interstate barriers to placing children with their grandparents instead of state institutions or foster care.[93]

The current political landscape is increasingly recognizing the power of grandparents. The movement of grandparents away from the physical proximity of their adult children and the rising incidence of divorce, which often weakens maternal or paternal ties, led to grandparents finding ways to assert their rights to spend time with their grandchildren. By the late 1960s, states began to adopt grandparent visitation statutes.[94] In 1979, President Jimmy Carter issued a proclamation declaring the first Sunday after Labor Day a holiday called National Grandparents Day. Included in his proclamation is the idea that grandparents are the connection between past events and the present: "Whether they are our own or surrogate grandparents who fill some of the gaps in our mobile society, our senior generation also provides our society a link to our national heritage and traditions."[95] Marian McQuade, a woman from West Virginia who worked to bring attention to the elderly in nursing homes, lobbied for the holiday.[96] The official flower for Grandparents Day is the forget-me-not, which positions the holiday as a day to remember the importance of grandparents in people's lives, implying that they are normally forgotten. The increasing presence of grandparenting activism during this period resulted in a congressional designation of 1995 as the Year of the Grandparent.[97]

Grandparents today are continuing to become a political force. In their research on Baby Boomers, Robert Hudson and Judith Gonyear found that the elderly are taking on a new political status, a group they call "Contenders." They write, "Just as Dependent and Advantaged positionings fundamentally shaped political and policy realities for the old historically, Contender status will do the same for the Boomers moving forward."[98] They argue that people will see the elderly less as a single group, but rather as people with diverse and competing interests. Like earlier historical periods, grandparents may need to align themselves with their children and grandchildren in order to leverage regulations and political power to their advantage. Grandmothers, for example, are beginning to see themselves as agents for disrupting social constructions of aging. Some grandmothers use the prevalent image society has of them as "frail" to surprise people as they engage in social movements.[99] Given that grandparents, with longer life spans than their ancestors, are developing closer and longer relationships with their grandchildren, it is possible that their identity as grandparents will influence how they advocate for themselves and how they teach their grandchildren to be future advocates. In these ways, grandparents can employ disarming techniques of playing to their gentle, loving, and frail stereotypes while becoming active sites of power.

GRANDPARENTING AS ITS OWN STAGE OF LIFE

The increasing life span of people living in the United States also has influenced the role of grandparents. Simply put, people in developed nations such as the United States are living longer. A report from the U.S. Census Bureau states, "In the United States, for example, life expectancy at age 65 has increased from 11.9 years in 1900–1902 to 19.1 years in 2009."[100] As people live longer, they have opportunities to be grandparents for a longer period in their lives. In the past, many experienced grandparenting while also being parents to small children, rather than as a third, separate life stage. Carole Haber writes, "The aging colonial couple might be both parents of infants and grandparents at the same time. Rarely was there a period when they were simply the third generation of an extended family network."[101] In addition, the age at which mothers give birth has risen over time, so it is more likely that one's children have become adults before parents become grandparents.[102] For many, grandparenting is no longer a practice performed during the middle years of one's life; it is a delineated third stage occurring in later years, with its own identity and traditions.[103] Today's grandparents also have more leisure time than in earlier periods of history. In farm life, most time for all members of the family was devoted to survival and chores, but now that grandparents often are finished raising their own children and have retirement income or social security, they can focus their attention on more pleasurable activities, including doting on their grandchildren.[104] Many senior citizens today likely have more spending money than in the past, and they use it on their grandchildren.[105] According to the Grandparents Cost Index, "There are 56 million Grandparents in the United States. On average $27.5 billion is spent nationwide on grandchildren per year."[106]

Concepts about aging are changing in other ways. Like the recent divisions of childhood, as people live longer, aging is dividing into several distinct stages. As researchers have studied the sociological effects of people living longer, they have paid more attention to these separate stages of aging.[107] People may identify as early elders, later elders, or whatever terminology they choose to embrace. This is not new, though. Historically, many cultures have conceptually divided their aged into separate categories. In the

Medieval period, up to twelve different ages defined human life, and early modern England referred to a "green" old age, when people were of old age but still could engage in many of the same activities as younger people.[108] In addition to retrieving some of these older categories, grandparenting is experiencing a set of implications not seen before.

Grandparenting in the future likely will exist in more than one stage. In research tracing the history of grandparenting through genealogy records, Gourdon found that it was unlikely before the nineteenth century that most people would ever reach the great-grandparent stage.[109] In earlier periods, the extended family ended with the grandparent. Grandparents either did not live long enough to become great-grandparents or were too feeble to meaningfully contribute to the family dynamic. But, now that great-grandparents live longer, they have become another family figure, often treated as someone to show off or be proud of. A YouTube search reveals thousands of videos of great-grandparents captured by their children and grandchildren. In these videos, they meet their great-grandchildren, sing, dance, and offer sage advice. They are almost universally adored, but simultaneously are relatively powerless. In 1979, the writer and philosopher Susan Sontag labeled "the double-standards of aging," bemoaning how society not only devalues the aged but also treats the aging of women more negatively than men. One reason she believes this occurs is because of our capitalist system: "This revaluation of the life cycle in favor of the young brilliantly serves a secular society whose idols are ever-increasing industrial productivity and the unlimited cannibalization of nature. Such a society must create a new sense of the rhythms of life in order to incite people to buy more, to consume and throw away faster."[110] Sontag's words are still relevant today, as conflicts appear in how emphasis on youthful engagement both worships grandparents at times but also keeps them distant and separate from the rest of society. Thus, an irony emerges that, as great-grandparents are celebrated as a new group to admire as old, wise, and something to watch, the grandparent stage of life also becomes another time to consume products and services as actors within the economy.

MEDIA ENVIRONMENTS AND CULTURE

A grandson in a YouTube video who is frustrated with his dating world decides to turn over his mate selection to his grandparents. Using the online dating site Bumble, and being instructed by their grandson to "swipe left and right," they ask questions like, "Do you like thongs?" and "Do you like fish?" They ultimately find for him three potential matches.[111] Part of the reason this video is funny is because the grandparents use new media like young people. But the video also reflects the tradition of grandparents playing the role of matchmaker for their family within a new media environment. The study of media as an environment posits that the dominant medium of a cultural age influences not only communication but also how people understand and place value in their world. In *Technopoly*, media scholar Neil Postman writes, "New technologies alter the structure of our interests: the things we think *about*. They alter the character of our symbols: the things we think *with*. And they alter the nature of community: the arena in which thoughts develop."[112] A dominant medium also influences who gains and loses power within a society. Digital and mobile media are doing just that for grandparents, influencing how society views and values it.

Without occupying as formalized a role as they do today, grandparents and the elderly served a clearly practical use, especially within a pre-literate society. Walter Ong, who studied the shift from oral to literate cultures, discussed the importance of the elderly in oral societies: "Knowledge is hard to come by and precious, and society regards highly those wise old men and women who specialize in conserving it, who know and can tell the stories of the days of old."[113] In earlier periods, grandparents held power through the material goods they could supply, such as their ownership of property, and through the wisdom that they imparted to others. They also were dependent on others to take care of them at times. In many ways, this symbiotic relationship was recognized by tribal cultures and is mirrored today in groups that retain some of these traditional rituals. In pre-literate societies, the elderly were valued for their longevity and ability to offer a continuity of advice. However, Bruce Rosenberg describes what happens when books replace people as a source of advice: "In an oral culture the aged are the repositories of a culture's wisdom; the elderly can be discounted somewhat in modern technological society, not so much because of rapid changes in successive waves of the 'future,' but because wisdom is available in books."[114] As knowledge could be purchased and stored whenever it was desired, free advice from one's own elders seemed less valuable and reliable.

Later, as families became more mobile and were no longer in close physical proximity to grandparents, others moved in to fill what can be labeled "the advice gap." In *No Sense of Place*, Joshua Meyrowitz writes, "An important issue to consider in predicting the effects of new media on group identities is how the new medium alters 'who shares social information with whom.'"[115] The advent of printing, and the later arrival of childhood experts providing advice, served to dismiss the wisdom of the grandparent figure. In *Raising America*, Ann Hulbert explores how experts, like the early twentieth-century child expert Dr. L. Emmett Holt, attacked advice provided by kin. Expert advice givers specifically warned mothers to ignore grandma's advice.[116] Unlike a grandmother who offers advice to her daughter about child rearing, published advice is a business. When a grandmother gives advice, one could assume she has the well-being of the family in mind, even though her idea may be different from the mother's. Outside experts, on the other hand, concern themselves with a generic family instead of the survival and needs of an individual family or community when giving advice. The business of advice also leads to confusion among its recipients, as advice constantly changes.[117] In fact, as much as Dr. Holt discouraged mothers from relying on their own mothers for parenting advice, in the 1950s Dr. Spock reversed Holt's recommendation. Instead, he encouraged parents to trust their own instincts and those of their parents before listening to any expert. Before Dr. Spock, Hulbert writes, experts believed "Grandmother had been the nemesis, and scientific progress had been the promise."[118]

Marshall McLuhan, writing about how electronic media reshape the world, prophetically imagined a future that abolished distinctions of time and space, and "when the creative process of knowing will be collectively and corporately extended to the whole of human society, much as we have already extended our senses and our nerves by the various media."[119] In this environment, grandparents become the property of a larger, often faceless, community. Returning to Papaw in the introduction of this book, he is a man who has been left by his grandchildren but adopted by viewers in cyberspace. They may not have a physically proximate, interpersonal relationship with him, but they can give him attention and affection, which is also real. Much like changes in our living patterns, evolutionary makeup, notions of family, and transportation and living arrangements have influenced the transformation of grandparenting, so has our technological environment.

As people spend more time in the grandparenting and even great-grandparenting stages of life, new challenges, concerns, and opportunities redefine these relationships. Advice columns have sprouted up to help grandparents negotiate these boundaries. Digital media offer the possibility of moving disagreements out of the family realm into the public. Countless websites, blogs, and advice columns are devoted to resolving disputes and negotiating the "rules" of grandparenting in the digital age.

Columns geared toward advice and counsel, such as one by AARP columnist Amy Goyer, focus on issues related to aging and grandparents. I conducted an interview with Paula Span, who writes a column for the *New York Times* called "The New Old Age." Her column focuses on ideas that would be of interest to grandparents, often incorporating her own personal experiences of becoming a grandparent. Span originally planned to call her column "Bubbe's Diaries" and pitched it to the *New York Times*, where she had previously written a column on aging. The newspaper liked the idea but suggested she broaden the name to be more inclusive and relatable to all grandparents. She finally decided on the name "Generation Grandparent."

Sometimes her columns focus on the practices and trends of grandparenting now. She describes the changes in parenting practices from when she was a parent, noting for instance the current culture's move away from sterilized environments to exposing babies to microbiomes.[120] When asked about aging and grandparenting, she observes, "One theory I have is that the pervasive, almost unquestioned ageism of our society, including older people ourselves, plays into the grandparent role." People becoming grandparents struggle between their desire to embrace this period and their anxiety over the recognition from others that they are aging. Span's column brings to the surface her own observations and those of others she talks to about the feelings and emotions people have in this stage of life.

Dr. Karen Rancourt, also known as "Dr. Gamma Karen," has been writing an advice column for an online mommy website for eight years geared specifically to helping the grandparent-grandchild relationship.[121] Dr. Gamma, trained in early childhood education and human behavior, is an expert on intergenerational relationships. When she was ready to retire from her career, she was thinking of what to do in the next stage of her life, and she was inspired by the "Dear Abby" columns she read as a child. She decided to start an advice column focusing on the dynamics between parents and grandchildren. Dr. Gamma takes advantage of new digital technology by frequently corresponding with her advice seekers to find out more information before she publishes her column. She tells me that one of the main areas of conflict grandparents have is over boundaries. She says, "Having used to be in the driving seat, it is difficult to realize they are backseat passengers and that they need to defer to the parents." She finds that parents also have issues with boundaries, and some want more advice from grandparents. "The grandparents are holding back," she says.

By positioning both grandparents and parents as target audiences for her column, she situates grandparents as both seekers of information and key contributors to family relationships. In one column about a mother seeking advice for her daughter's communication with her future mother-in-law, Dr. Gamma offers suggestions but also reminds the mother that she has her own advice and life experience to offer.[122] Dr. Gamma has had success in part because she recognizes the changing dynamics in the relationships of grandparents and parents. Her column, rather than treating grandparenting as an afterthought, raises the visibility of these potential conflicts.

Advice columns have a long history, with their roots set in the seventeenth-century "agony aunts" in newspapers. These were male or female figures who offered an opportunity for anonymous counsel from a supposedly wise source. These columns became popular with the rise of literacy and mass media in the mid-nineteenth century. Agony aunts often brought visibility to issues and topics not openly discussed in society, including sexuality and women's concerns.[123] These new grandparent columns, in a sense, are the latest iteration of the agony aunt, bringing to light concerns and conflicts that are not often discussed but that have emerged from shifting family relationships. Digital technology has made this advice more accessible. Dr. Gamma says about this technology, "It makes it easy for people almost impulsively, just on the spur of the moment, to say this issue is bothering me. I can take a short amount of time, get on the computer, zip this thing off." The digital age, with its abundance of information and availability of experts, has allowed for more specific types of advice to be disseminated. The grandparent generation can bring to light conflicts that may have been ignored in earlier periods.

SHIFTING VALUE OF CHILDREN

The changing understanding of childhood also has impacted our expectations of grandparenting. In *The Disappearance of Childhood*, Neil Postman identifies specific historical periods when the concept of childhood emerged. He links shifts in the information environment to changing understandings of what a child is. Postman argues that print and reading hid knowledge, excluding children from the adult world: "Eventually, knowledge of these cultural secrets became one of the distinguishing characteristics of adulthood, so that, until recent times, one of the important differences between the child and the adult has been that adults were in possession of information that was not considered suitable for children to know."[124] Postman's argument implies that the post-television world again shifts the separation of children and adults.

David Hackett Fischer, author of *Growing Old in America*, notes that in the mid-nineteenth century, parents acted less authoritarian toward their children. Grandparents went even further, becoming outright indulgent with their grandchildren:

> Another manifestation of the change in age relationships was the growth of that modern American institution, the indulgent grandparent, who showers upon the third generation presents which were denied to the second, smiles benevolently upon infractions of the strictest rules, and astonishes the righteous parent with an invincible determination to "spoil" the grandchildren at every chance.[125]

In *All Joy and No Fun: The Paradox of Modern Parenthood*, Jennifer Senior explores this changing understanding of childhood and parenthood. She claims our modern hyper-parenting is anxiety-ridden and a response to not having a clear understanding of what parents' larger goals are in raising children. She writes, "Today, we are far less clear about what 'parenting' entails. We know what it *doesn't* entail: teaching kids mathematics and geography and literature (schools do that); providing them with medical treatment (pediatricians); sewing them dresses and trousers (factories abroad, whose wares are then distributed by Old Navy). . . . What parenting *does* involve, however, is much harder to define."[126]

Today, intensive parenting, sometimes labeled "helicopter parenting," is on the rise. The inconsistent message to parents today encourages them to be active and engaged parents, though they are criticized when they are perceived to have crossed the line with their involvement. No clear roadmap exists for how to "turn off" parental engagement when parents become grandparents, especially as families increasingly remain codependent and entangled within complex relationships.

As the purposes and functions of parenting are changing, they also are changing with grandparenting. The role of grandparents today is a bit ambivalent. In the past, grandchildren were an important resource for practical labor, and they promised the future stability of the family. In addition, they provided insurance for the future caretaking needs of grandparents themselves. Reciprocally, grandchildren needed to endear themselves to their grandparents for their own future success. Yet, as power shifted in relationships between parents, grandparents, and children, emotional attachment and affection replaced duty.[127] Just as parent-child relationships moved beyond simple obligation and care to affection, grandparents experienced a similar realignment, and continue to do so today. It seems that the act of grandparenting begets more grandparenting. A study on relationships between grandparents and grandchildren by Valarie King and Glen H. Elder Jr. found:

> Consistent with the premise that family roles are learned through the culture and the interactions of family life, the degree to which grandparents are involved in playing their role and the type of involvement they have with their grandchildren are significantly related to having known one's own grandparents and to have learned about them through intergenerational history.[128]

As grandparenting becomes a deeper, longer, and more developed stage of life, it is likely that it will continue to strengthen our expectations of what grandparenting should look like.

FEMINISM, GRANDPARENTING, AND GENDER TODAY

Journalist Lesley Stahl has written a memoir exploring the joys and challenges that she and other grandparents of her generation are experiencing. She describes grandparenting as another phase of marriage: "Well, now we have a fourth phase, being a grandparent, and we're enchanted all over again. It's a whole new blossoming that comes with inexorable giddiness."[129] Stahl describes the conflicting emotions that some women feel as they begin grandparenting. One woman she meets worries her daughter resents her because she spends more time with her grandchildren than she did with her own children when she was focused on her career.

This woman's concern reflects the tension between caregiving and feminism. The question of where grandmothering fits within the feminist movement mirrors the situating of motherhood within feminism. Second wave feminism focused on giving women options to work outside the home and enter the public sphere. Third wave feminism explored intersections of race, ethnicity, and women. Within these movements, some have used motherhood as a way to enact power, while others have argued that the institution of motherhood is oppressive and not helpful in the pursuit of more rights.[130] At times, motherhood has been treated as an afterthought rather than as a central part of the challenge to ascribe more power to women. Politically, raising the issue of motherhood may have resulted in hindering the feminist movement, because the problem of how to balance family life and work for women was a problem not easily solved.[131] Some members of the current generation of grandparents have lived through second and third wave feminism. Older grandmothers may have been stay-at-home mothers themselves, and older grandfathers typically worked while their wives raised their children. Younger grandparents, though, have a different story. They spent their parenting years balancing work and family obligations. If society still has not quite figured out how to reframe motherhood as a feminist pursuit, then the power and rights of grandparents, while they assume more of the burden of childcare, falls even further behind in the queue to be addressed.

Many grandparents today understand the dilemma of the having-it-all paradox and the struggles to balance work and family life. Since they have experienced the challenge of it themselves as parents, they are working toward helping their children by assisting with their childcare needs. The early history of grandparents indicates that they also were likely helpful in propelling the survival of the family because of their assistance in childcare and other activities. Current research supports that grandparents still are highly valued for similar roles. A study of families in the Netherlands found that grandparents' help may lead to increasing their descendants: "Grandparents can enhance the reproductive success of their children by looking after the grandchildren, though only the children who actually receive childcare support, and not their siblings, have a higher fertility."[132] The helpful role of grandparents may be merely helpful to some, but it could be vital in places like Europe, where birth rates are declining.[133] Cuba is another example of a country facing a demographic problem similar to Europe's. The country issued a decree to expand parental leave to grandparents, hoping that offering this will be an incentive for more families to have children.[134] Grandparenting has the potential to bridge the gender gap often seen in debates about motherhood and fatherhood issues regarding family leave and workplace policies.

Arlie Hochschild identifies the additional work a mother performs at home after working outside the home.[135] Grandparents are playing more of a role in easing the burden of the second shift by taking on grandparenting shifts of their own. In many ways, they are retrieving an earlier evolutionary role that provided time for mothers to focus on reproduction. However, caregiving work often is invisible—expected and needed but not noticed. While reformers have raised awareness about the difficulty mothers and fathers face in balancing caregiving work, there is now an emergent group of caregivers who are eschewing leisure activities in retirement to provide unpaid labor for their children.

Grandparents may better address the gender gaps in childcare. Those studying modern grandparenting are finding less distinction between grandfathers and grandmothers; men and women are more likely to share domestic tasks at this age.[136] New research is revealing how grandfathers in the past have been understood only in their relation to grandmothers. In his review of portrayals of grandfatherhood in studies, Robin Mann concluded: "Findings from recent studies do indeed report 'new' norms of grandfatherhood focused on nurturing and mentoring."[137] Mann warns that it is not clear if actual evidence exists of changes in grandparent behavior, or if there are just new expectations of what grandfatherhood should look like. Either way, the role of grandfather is moving from patriarch and guardian to practical caretaker and nurturer. Grandparents may one day become a model for parents of how to more equitably balance family and work responsibilities. Once again, grandparents provide lessons to their children.

CONCLUSION

The history of grandparenting reflects the influence of evolution, changing cultural practices, the rise of experts, and shifting notions of childhood and race, class, and ethnicity. Grandparenting was invisible during its early history, most likely because it was evolutionarily necessary for the family. People took care of their grandparents as a family obligation. Sometimes they materially benefited from the promise of inheriting their grandparents' property or wealth, but most often they recognized the social contract of family caregiving, honoring the tradition of caring for their elders with the knowledge that their own children would care for them in their old age. As caregiving responsibility shifted from the family to the state, grandparents had to adjust to perform new roles for the family. They became valued for not only their practical resources but also for what they provided in terms of emotional support. Just as the role of children transformed from being an economic tool to a precious resource, grandparenting is following the same path. Now, grandparenting is becoming more visible as it becomes its own cultural practice. A new type of grandparenting is arising, serving both familiar roles and new ones as well. These new practices distinguish the activities, expectations, and responsibilities of grandparenting today from older periods.

NOTES

1. Dan Hurley, "Grandma's Experiences Leave a Mark on Your Genes," *Discover Magazine* (web page), June 25, 2015, http://discovermagazine.com/2013/may/13-grandmas-experiences-leave-epigenetic-mark-on-your-genes.
2. Arthur Kornhaber and Kenneth L. Woodward, *Grandparents/Grandchildren: The Vital Connection* (New Brunswick, NJ: Transaction Books, 1985), xxiii.
3. Kornhaber & Woodward, xxvi.
4. Kornhaber & Woodward, xxvii.
5. Pat Thane, "The History of Aging in the West," in *Handbook of the Humanities and Aging*, ed. Thomas R. Cole, Robert Kastenbaum, and Ruth E. Ray, 2nd ed. (New York: Springer Publishing Company, 2000), 21.
6. Rachel Caspari, "The Evolution of Grandparents," *Scientific American* (web page), December 7, 2012, https://www.scientificamerican.com/article/the-evolution-of-grandparents-2012-12-07/.
7. Vincent Gourdon, "Are Grandparents Really Absent from Family Tradition? Forbears in the Region of Vernon (France) around 1800," *The History of the Family* 4, no. 1 (1999): 89, https://doi.org/10.1016/S1081-602X(99)80266-8.
8. Gourdon, 82–83.
9. Brian Gratton and Carole Haber, "Three Phases in the History of American Grandparents: Authority, Burden, Companion," *Generations* 20, no. 1 (Spring 1996).
10. Ursula A. Falk and Gerhard Falk, *Grandparents: A New Look at the Supporting Generation* (Amherst, NY: Prometheus Books, 2002), 17.
11. Carole Haber, "Historians' Approach to Aging in America," in *Handbook of the Humanities and Aging*, ed. Thomas R. Cole, Robert Kastenbaum, and Ruth E. Ray, 2nd ed. (New York: Springer Publishing Company, 2000), 28.
12. Ron Lieber, "Parents, the Children Will Be Fine: Spend Their Inheritance Now," *New York Times*, September 19, 2014, https://www.nytimes.com/2014/09/20/your-money/estate-planning/parents-the-children-will-be-fine-spend-their-inheritance-now.html.
13. Cheryl L. Lampkin, "Insights and Spending Habits of Modern Grandparents" (Washington, DC: AARP Research, March 2012), 11, https://www.aarp.org/content/dam/aarp/research/surveys_statistics/general/2012/Insights-and-Spending-Habits-of-Modern-Grandparents-AARP.pdf.
14. Gratton and Haber, "Three Phases in the History."
15. Kornhaber and Woodward, *Grandparents/Grandchildren,* 25.
16. Margaret Mead, *Blackberry Winter: My Earlier Years* (New York: Kodansha America, 1995), 282.
17. Walter H. Sangree, "Grandparenthood and Modernization: The Changing Status of Male and Female Elders in Tiriki, Kenya, and Irigwe, Nigeria," *Journal of Cross-Cultural Gerontology* 7, no. 4 (October 1992): 339–340, https://doi.org/10.1007/BF01848698.
18. David F. Lancy, *The Anthropology of Childhood: Cherubs, Chattel, Changelings*, 2nd ed. (New York: Cambridge University Press, 2015), 82.
19. Aneri Pattani, "Living Another Day, Thanks to Grandparents Who Couldn't Sleep," *New York Times*, July 13, 2017, https://www.nytimes.com/2017/07/13/science/hadza-tanzania-sleep-grandparents-evolution.html?smid=nytcore-ipad-share&smprod=nytcore-ipad&_r=0.
20. Falk and Falk, *Grandparents: A New Look*, 17.
21. Lancy, *The Anthropology of Childhood*, 82.
22. Sarah Blaffer Hrdy, *Mothers and Others: The Evolutionary Origins of Mutual Understanding* (Cambridge: Harvard University Press, 2011), 31.
23. Kristen Hawkes, "Human Longevity: The Grandmother Effect," *Nature* 428, no. 6979 (March 2004): 128, https://doi.org/10.1038/428128a.

24. Hawkes, 129.

25. Judith Shulevitz, "Why Do Grandmothers Exist," *New Republic* (web page), January 29, 2013, https://newrepublic.com/article/112199/genetics-grandmothers-why-they-exist.

26. Chris Knight and Camilla Power, "Grandmothers, Politics, and Getting Back to Science," in *Grandmotherhood: The Evolutionary Significance of the Second Half of Female Life*, ed. Eckart Voland, Athanasios Chasiotis and Wulf Schiefenhövel (New Brunswick, NJ: Rutgers University Press, 2005), 88.

27. Lancy, *The Anthropology of Childhood*, 403.

28. Mhairi A. Gibson and Ruth Mace, "Helpful Grandmothers in Rural Ethiopia: A Study of the Effect of Kin on Child Survival and Growth," *Evolution and Human Behavior* 26, no. 6 (November 2005), 469–482, https://doi.org/10.1016/j.evolhumbehav.2005.03.004.

29. David A. Coall and Ralph Hertwig, "Grandparental Investment: Past, Present, and Future," *Behavioral and Brain Sciences* 33, no.1 (February 2010): 2.

30. Coall and Hertwig, 9, 2.

31. Hrdy, "Mothers and Others," 270.

32. Joey Paur, "Photographer Turns His 91-Year-Old Grandma into a Superhero to Cheer Her Up," *Geek Tyrant* (web page), accessed February 8, 2018, https://geektyrant.com/news/2010/11/18/photographer-turns-his-91-year-old-grandma-into-a-superhero.html.

33. Falk and Falk, *Grandparents: A New Look*, 27.

34. Gratton and Haber, "Three Phases in the History."

35. Stephanie Coontz, *The Way We Never Were: American Families and the Nostalgia Trap* (New York: Basic, 2005), 12.

36. Kornhaber and Woodward, *Grandparents/Grandchildren*, xxvii.

37. Shari Thurer, *The Myths of Motherhood* (New York: Penguin Books, 1995), 184–185.

38. Marvin B. Sussman, "Relationships of Adult Children with Their Parents in the United States," in *Social Structure and the Family Generational Relations*, ed. Ethel Shanas and Gordon F. Streib (Durham, NC: Duke University Press, 1963), 64–67.

39. Sussman, 73.

40. Coontz, *The Way We Never Were*, 12–13.

41. Falk and Falk, *Grandparents: A New Look*, 25.

42. Coontz, *The Way We Never Were*, 26.

43. Falk and Falk, *Grandparents: A New Look*, 25.

44. Gratton and Haber, "Three Phases in the History."

45. Yuval Noah Harari, *Sapiens: A Brief History of Humankind* (New York: Harper Collins, 2015), 359.

46. Coontz, *The Way We Never Were*, 26.

47. Susan Lucas, "From Levittown to Luther Village: Retirement Communities and the Changing Suburban Dream," *Canadian Journal of Urban Research* 11, no. 2: 327–328.

48. Michael E. Hunt, *Retirement Communities: An American Original* (New York: Haworth Press, 1984), 1.

49. James Brooke, "Young Unwelcome in Retirees' Haven," *New York Times*, February 16, 1997, http://www.nytimes.com/1997/02/16/us/young-unwelcome-in-retirees-haven.html.

50. Lancy, *The Anthropology of Childhood*, 144.

51. Patricia Hill Collins, *Black Feminist Thought: Knowledge, Consciousness and the Politics of Empowerment*, 2nd ed. (New York: Routledge, 2009), 56.

52. George P. Rawick, *The American Slave—A Composite Autobiography* (San Francisco: Greenwood Press, 1972), quoted in Herbert C. Covey and Paul T. Lockman Jr., "Narrative References to Older African Americans Living under Slavery," *Social Science Journal* 33, no. 1 (1996): 28.

53. Covey and Lockman Jr., "Narrative References," 29–30.

54. Mildred A. Hill-Lubin, "The African-American Grandmother in Autobiographical Works by Frederick Douglass, Langston Hughes, and Maya Angelou," *International Journal of Aging and Human Development* 33, no. 3 (October 1991): 177.

55. Jillian Jimenez, "The History of Grandmothers in the African-American Community," *Social Service Review* 76, no. 4 (December 2002): 525.

56. Jimenez, 526–528.

57. E. Franklin Frazier, *The Negro Family in the United States* (Chicago: University of Chicago Press, 1939), 148.
58. Jimenez, "The History of Grandmothers," 528.
59. Jimenez, "The History of Grandmothers,"531.
60. Elizabeth M. Bertera and Sandra Edmonds Crewe, "Parenthood in the Twenty-First Century: African American Grandparents as Surrogate Parents," *Journal of Human Behavior in the Social Environment* 23, no. 2 (February 2013): 180.
61. Sandra Edmonds Crewe, "Guardians of Generations: African American Grandparent Caregivers for Children of HIV/AIDS Infected Parents," *Journal of Family Strengths* 12, no.1 (2012): 6, http://digitalcommons.library.tmc.edu/jfs/vol12/iss1/4/.
62. Hill-Lubin, "The African-American Grandmother," 182.
63. LaShawnDa Pittman and Deirdre Oakley, "'It Was Love in All the Building They Tore Down': How Caregiving Grandmothers Create and Experience a Sense of Community in Chicago Public Housing," *City & Community* 17, no. 2 (June 2018): 473, doi: 10.1111/cico.12280.
64. Naomi Gerstel, "Rethinking Families and Community: The Color, Class, and Centrality of Extended Kin Ties," *Sociological Forum* 26, no. 1 (March 2011): 4.
65. Gerstel, 5
66. Judith Treas, "Transnational Older Adults and Their Families," *Family Relations* 57, no. 4 (October 2008): 469.
67. Hao-Min Chen and Denise C. Lewis, "A Changing Relationship: Visiting Chinese Grandparents and Their Adult Children in the United States," *Journal of Ethnographic & Qualitative Research* 11, no. 2 (2016): 89.
68. Feinian Chen, Guangya Liu, and Christine A. Mair, "Intergenerational Ties in Context: Grandparents Caring for Grandchildren in China," *Social Forces* 90, no. 2 (December 1, 2011): 575.
69. Chen, Liu, and Mair, " 588.
70. Robert Putnam, *Our Kids: The American Dream in Crisis* (New York: Simon & Schuster, 2015), 132.
71. Andrew J. Cherlin and Frank F. Furstenberg Jr. *The New American Grandparent: A Place in the Family, a Life Apart* (Cambridge: Harvard University Press, 1992), 120; Andrew J. Cherlin, "On Single Mothers 'Doing' Family," *Journal of Marriage and Family* 68, no. 4 (2006): 800–801.
72. Raven Molloy, Christopher L. Smith, and Abigail Wozniak, "Internal Migration in the United States" (working paper 17307, National Bureau of Economic Research, Washington, DC, August 2011), 13, http://www.nber.org/papers/w17307.
73. Quoctrung Bui and Claire Cain Miller, "The Typical American Lives Only 18 Miles From Mom," *New York Times*, December 23, 2015, https://www.nytimes.com/interactive/2015/12/24/upshot/24up-family.html.
74. Renee R. Ellis and Tavia Simmons, *Coresident Grandparents and Their Grandchildren: 2012* (Washington, DC: The United States Census Bureau, 2014), 3, https://www.census.gov/content/dam/Census/library/publications/2014/demo/p20-576.pdf.
75. Steve Inskeep and Jennifer Ludden, "When Grandma's House Is Home: The Rise of Grandfamilies," *Morning Edition NPR Radio* (web page), December 15, 2014, https://www.npr.org/2014/12/15/369366596/when-grandmas-house-is-home-the-rise-of-grandfamilies.
76. Ann Carrns, "Boomers near Retirement Changing Housing Trends," *The Seattle Times*, March 11, 2015, http://www.seattletimes.com/business/real-estate/boomers-near-retirement-changing-housing-trends/.
77. Stefanos Chen, "More Over 55 Communities Evict Kids as Families Double Up in Downturn," *Huffington Post*, January 6, 2012, http://www.huffingtonpost.com/2012/01/06/over-55-communities-evict-children_n_1189029.html.
78. "Retirement Homes Get the Luxe Treatment," *Realtor Magazine* (web page), September 15, 2016, http://realtormag.realtor.org/daily-news/2016/09/16/retirement-homes-get-luxe-treatment.

79. Katy McLaughlin, "The Hottest Home Amenity: In-Law Apartments," *Wall Street Journal*, November 6, 2014, https://www.wsj.com/articles/the-hottest-home-amenity-in-law-apartments-1415288579.

80. Ashlea Ebeling, "Whimsical Garage Addition—10 Chic Granny Flats," *Forbes*, accessed February 3, 2018, https://www.forbes.com/pictures/mjh45eehil/10-chic-granny-flats-2/#7e01
505930a3.

81. Sally Newman, ed., *Intergenerational Programs: Past, Present, and Future* (Washington, DC: Taylor and Francis, 1997), 63.

82. Newman, 68.

83. Newman, 68–69.

84. Newman, 79.

85. *Diff'rent Strokes*, "Sam Adopts a Grandparent," Season 7, Episode 15, NBC, January 19, 1985, directed by Gerren Keith, written by Susan H. Lee and Sylvia Alan.

86. *Full House*, "The Volunteer," Season 5, Episode 7, NBC, October 29, 1991, directed by Joel Zwick, written by Jeff Franklin and Marc Warren.

87. Matthew Cattin, "Surrogate Grandparents Startup Gives the Gift of Generations," *Stuff* (web page), November 3, 2016, https://www.stuff.co.nz/life-style/parenting/85989924/surrogate-grandparents-startup-gives-the-gift-of-generations.

88. Leslie Bennetts, *The Feminine Mistake: Are We Giving Up Too Much?* (New York: Hyperion Books, 2007), 108.

89. Rosalyn Baxandall and Elizabeth Ewen, *Picture Windows: How the Suburbs Happened* (New York: Basic Books, 2000), 220.

90. Meredith Minkler and Kathleen M. Roe, *Grandmothers as Caregivers: Raising Children of the Crack Cocaine Epidemic* (Newbury Park, CA: Sage Publications, 1993), 6.

91. Minkler and Roe, 3.

92. Katherine Q. Seelye, "Children of Heroin Crisis Find Refuge in Grandparents' Arms," *New York Times*, May 21, 2016, https://www.nytimes.com/interactive/2016/05/05/us/grandparents-heroin-impact-kids.html.

93. Danny K. Davis, *Modernizing the Interstate Placement of Children in Foster Care Act*, Floor Statement, Official Website for U.S. Representative Danny K. Davis, 7th Congressional District of Illinois, Democratic Party, March 22, 2016, https://davis.house.gov/floor-statements/modernizing-the-interstate-placement-of-children-in-foster-care-act/.

94. Tammy L. Henderson and Patricia B. Moran, "Grandparent Visitation Rights: Testing the Parameters of Parental Rights," *Journal of Family Issues* 22, no. 5 (July 1, 2001): 621.

95. Jimmy Carter Proclamation 4679—National Grandparents Day, Issued September 6, 1979, The American Presidency Project (web page), http://www.presidency.ucsb.edu/ws/?pid=32826.

96. National Grandparents Day, 2009, National Grandparents Day Council (web page), accessed April 5, 2017, http://www.grandparents-day.com/y2009/history_new/chronicles.html#.WLcLfpK0agT.

97. Kornhaber and Woodward, *Grandparents/Grandchildren*, 9.

98. Robert B. Hudson and Judith G. Gonyear, "Baby Boomers and the Shifting Political Construction of Old Age," *The Gerontologist* 52, no. 2 (April 1, 2012): 279.

99. Amanda Grenier and Jill Hanley, "Older Women and 'Frailty': Aged, Gendered and Embodied Resistance," *Current Sociology* 55, no. 2 (March 2007): 211–228.

100. Wan He, Daniel Goodkind, and Paul Kowal, "An Aging World: 2015" (Washington, DC, U.S. Census Bureau, International Population Reports, March 2016), 35.

101. Carole Haber, *Beyond Sixty-Five: The Dilemma of Old Age in America's Past* (New York: Cambridge University Press, 1983), 10.

102. Rae Ekken Bichell, "Average Age of First-Time Moms Keeps Climbing in the U.S.," *NPR* (web page), January 14, 2016, https://www.npr.org/sections/health-shots/2016/01/14/462816458/average-age-of-first-time-moms-keeps-climbing-in-the-u-s.

103. Cherlin and Furstenberg, *The New American Grandparent*, 27.

104. Cherlin and Furstenberg, 28.

105. Dionne Searcey and Robert Gebeloff, "America's Seniors Find Middle-Class 'Sweet Spot,'" *New York Times*, June 14, 2015.
106. Grandboomers.com, http://www.grandboomers.com/page/grandparents-spend-275-billion.
107. Susan Dominus, "Life in the Age of Old, Old Age," *New York Times Magazine*, February 22, 2004, http://www.nytimes.com/2004/02/22/magazine/life-in-the-age-of-old-old-age.html.
108. Pat Thane, "The History of Aging in the West," in *Handbook of the Humanities and Aging*, ed. Thomas R. Cole, Robert Kastenbaum, and Ruth Ray, 2nd ed. (New York: Springer Publications, 2000), 10.
109. Gourdon, "Are Grandparents Really Absent," 81.
110. Susan Sontag, "The Double Standard of Aging," *The Saturday Review*, September 23 1972, 31.
111. Jukin Media, "Grandparents Try Dating App for Grandson," YouTube, May 25, 2016. https://www.youtube.com/watch?v=MTaY5QeirhU.
112. Neil Postman. *Technopoly: The Surrender of Culture to Technology* (New York: Vintage Books, 1993), 20.
113. Walter J. Ong, *Orality and Literacy: The Technologizing of the Word* (New York: Routledge, 1991), 41.
114. Bruce A. Rosenberg, "The Complexity of Oral Tradition," *Oral Tradition* 2, no. 1 (1987): 76.
115. Joshua Meyrowitz, *No Sense of Place: The Impact of Electronic Media on Social Behavior* (New York: Oxford University Press, 1986), 55.
116. Ann Hulbert, *Raising America: Experts, Parents and a Century of Advice about Children* (New York: Alfred A. Knopf, 2003), 70.
117. Laura Tropp, *A Womb with a View: America's Growing Public Interest in Pregnancy* (Santa Barbara, CA: Praeger, 2013), 39.
118. Hulbert, *Raising America*, 254.
119. Marshall McLuhan, *Understanding Media: The Extensions of Man* (Cambridge, MA: MIT Press, 1994), 3.
120. Paula Span, "Fear the Blanket, Not the Germs," *New York Times*, October 9, 2017, https://www.nytimes.com/2017/10/09/well/family/parenting-grandparents-babies.html?rref=collection/byline/paula-span&action=click&contentCollection=undefined&region=stream&module=stream_unit&version=latest&contentPlacement=10&pgtype=collection.
121. Mommybites—Support Education Resources Connections for Moms (blog), accessed January 19, 2018, https://mommybites.com/.
122. Karen Rancourt, "Mom Foresees Problems with Her Daughter's Relationship with Future MIL," Mommybites.com, November 14, 2017, https://mommybites.com/col2/grandparents/mom-forsees-problems-with-her-daughters-relationship-with-future-mil/.
123. Lucy Mangan, "A Brief History of Agony Aunts," *The Guardian* (web page), November 12, 2009, https://www.theguardian.com/lifeandstyle/2009/nov/13/agony-aunts.
124. Neil Postman, *The Disappearance of Childhood* (New York: Random House, 1982), 49.
125. David Hackett Fischer, *Growing Old in America* (Oxford: Oxford University Press, 1978), 155.
126. Jennifer Senior, *All Joy and No Fun: The Paradox of Modern Parenthood* (New York: HarperCollins, 2014), 130.
127. Cherlin and Furstenberg, *The New American Grandparent*, 45.
128. Valarie King and Glen H. Elder Jr., "The Legacy of Grandparenting: Childhood Experiences with Grandparents and Current Involvement with Grandchildren," *Journal of Marriage and Family* 59, no. 4 (November 1997): 856.
129. Lesley Stahl, *Becoming Grandma: The Joys and Science of the New Grandparenting* (New York: Blue Rider Press, 2016), 36.
130. Amber E. Kinser, *Motherhood and Feminism* (Berkeley: Perseus Books, 2010), 7.
131. Joan Williams, *Unbending Gender: Why Family and Work Conflict and What to Do about It* (New York: Oxford University Press, 2000), 44.

132. Ralf Kaptijn et al., "How Grandparents Matter: Support for the Cooperative Breeding Hypothesis in a Contemporary Dutch Population," *Human Nature* 21, no. 4 (December 2010): 402.

133. Ashifa Kassam et al., "Europe Needs Many More Babies to Avert a Population Disaster," *The Guardian*, August 22, 2015, https://www.theguardian.com/world/2015/aug/23/baby-crisis-europe-brink-depopulation-disaster.

134. Nick Miroff, "Cuba Wants More Babies, so It's Giving Parental Leave to Grandparents, Too," *Washington Post*, February 10, 2017, https://www.washingtonpost.com/news/worldviews/wp/2017/02/10/cuba-wants-more-babies-so-its-giving-parental-leave-to-grandparents-too/?utm_term=.30e74cfe5992.

135. Arlie Russell Hochschild and Anne Machung, *The Second Shift* (New York: Penguin Books, 2003).

136. Kaptijn et al., "How Grandparents Matter," 402.

137. Robin Mann, "Out of the Shadows?: Grandfatherhood, Age and Masculinities," *Journal of Aging Studies* 21, no. 4 (December 2007): 289.

Chapter Two

Grandparenting as a Life Stage

When I was young, a popular playground song children sang to tease each other went something like this: "First comes love/ then comes marriage/ then comes [name] with a baby carriage." To future children, however, it's likely that this order of stages might not be so recognizable. Baby Boomers, the generation that makes up many grandparents today, are redefining their life stages. Boomers initiated new types of intensive parenting and planted the seeds of present-day conversations about the struggle of work-life balance. Throughout their lives, cultural, political, and social events influenced them, but in turn they shaped the world themselves. They taught the world to rethink the definitions of and expectations of marriage, relationships, and work. As they become older, they are redefining and disrupting aging. This chapter examines the emergence of grandparenting as a life stage through media coverage of this period, studies and reports on grandparenting, and the voices of grandparents describing what grandparenting means to them.

My mother describes this period of her life, with a substantial investment in the lives of her grandchildren, as her "third act." She often jokes that her grandchildren are her hobby. She spends a considerable amount of time with them, planning activities that they might like, keeping up with their interests, and developing ongoing relationships with them that mature as they mature. Her experience is not unusual. Just as Baby Boomers created new life stages for themselves throughout their lives, they are reinventing what it means to be a grandparent. For some, it means an active and engaging relationship with their grandchildren, but for others it involves rethinking their own relationships and boundaries with their children and considering how grandparenting fits in with their active lifestyles. Through interviews with grandparents around the country and research on the changing life stages of grandparents, this chapter sheds light on the rich and meaningful relationships they are developing with their grandchildren.

OLD IS THE NEW BLACK

The shifting definition of grandparenting follows a transformation in the way we age. The editors of *Baby Boomers and Popular Culture* argue that Baby Boomers are a "Revolutionary Generation." According to them, Boomers are "literally changing the landscape of social, political, and mediated life in the United States in ways that led to radical shifts from the practices and ways of life in the decades of the 20th century preceding their arrival and ascendancy."[1] Baby Boomers cover a wide range of ages, encompassing individuals born between 1946 and 1964, with some groups experiencing different historical events.

The first half experienced the end of World War II and aged into the social upheaval of the 1960s and 1970s with feminist and sexual revolutions, and major technological disruptions influenced the latter half of this population.[2] Both groups, in contrast to their predecessors living under the weight of World War I and World War II and economic insecurity, were now able to live more comfortably, and their parents offered them indulgences.[3] This influenced how they saw themselves as consumers, parents, and their goals and lives. Lori Bitter, a strategic consultant specializing in mature consumers, describes it this way:

> Post-war optimism and high fertility rates created a huge generation of young people, and a corresponding marketplace of products and services to meet their needs. The suburbs grew to house them, school districts expanded to educate them, companies exploded to meet their "modern" needs: baby food, disposable diapers, baby furniture.[4]

As industries rose to meet these new consumer demands, the Baby Boomers became adept at influencing not only how they were seen as a new consumer market, but also how aging in general could be transformed.

As the Baby Boomers age, people are living longer and healthier lives. In wealthy countries such as the United States, people are living longer due in large part to a combination of better living habits and advances in medicine. The National Institute on Aging stated, "In 2010, an estimated 524 million people were aged 65 or older—8 percent of the world's population. By 2050, this number is expected to nearly triple to about 1.5 billion, representing 16 percent of the world's population."[5] While many worry about the toll this will take on the resources to manage an aging population, Boomers themselves see an opportunity to redefine their aging lifestyles. In *A Fresh Map of Life: The Emergence of the Third Age*, Peter Laslett argues that older adults, who have looked to their own parents and grandparents as models for aging, are no longer finding those traditions in retirement as relatable.

Laslett defines a new period of "the Third Age" emerging because of changes within the reality and practice of aging:

> All of our ageing expressions have become inaccurate, and many of them obsolete. They provide us with the misleading images of children, adults, those in the prime of life, a phrase to be noted because we are going to shift the prime of life a long way towards the later years, as well as those in middle age, late middle life and those already in retirement. For the age constitution of our society has been transformed, quite suddenly and without our realizing what has happened.[6]

Baby Boomers are differentiating between their chronological age and their "subjective" age. An age that the public may have labeled "old" no longer feels that way. Just as society now segments childhood into different stages from toddlers to tweens, new categories are beginning to emerge to define the elderly as well. In health care, some gerontologists are advocating that society needs to differentiate the ages between the 70s and the 90s, as they have different medical needs.[7] The varying expectations and needs of these age groups extend socially as well and influence how they participate in and are defining grandparenting.

Grandparenting presents a challenge to people's conceptions of age. Becoming a grandparent is in itself a signifier of aging. Many reaching the grandparent stage experience a cognitive dissonance, feeling young but saddled with the connotation of being old. The older Americans I interviewed often challenged this contrast. Instead, they talked about engaging in active lifestyles and taking their grandchildren along for the ride. In addition to other aspects of our culture, Baby Boomers have the potential to revolutionize grandparenting as a new life stage. A grandmother from the West Coast, Anna, discussed with me her perspective on how grandparenting is changing. "The word 'grandparent' today is totally different than when I was growing up," she said. "Grandparents today don't sit in a rocking chair." She told me that one of her young granddaughters said to her, "You are so much younger than my other grandmother. You do things like ski, bike ride, and camping." She and the other grandmother were the exact same age at the time. She explained to her granddaughter that people have different lifestyles. Her granddaughter thought for a minute and said, "I'm going to do the same things you do when I'm going to become a grandmother."

That's likely to be true. More studies are not only suggesting the importance of healthy active daily life in adults but also that active physical lifestyles in childhood are likely to continue through adulthood.[8] The grandparents I spoke to often expressed their desire to do activities with their grandchildren while teaching them about the importance of physical activity. One woman,

Jan, talks of convincing her grandson to hike a mountain with her. While it was a challenge for him, she said that, by the end, "It turned out to be a really nice thing, and he was pretty awed by being up in the fire tower and seeing as far as he could see." The current younger generation will likely grow up instilled with the importance of a healthy, active lifestyle, with new sports and leisure activities that could enforce habits for a lifetime.

Not only does becoming a grandparent offer new opportunities to remain active, but it may inspire the feeling of being youthful. One recent study suggests that grandparents over seventy who provide childcare report feeling younger.[9] For many people, grandparenting becomes yet another lifestyle in which to become an active participant. A MetLife Study finds that "more than half of grandparents are active outdoors with grandchildren (55%), going to the zoo, having picnics, going to playgrounds or beaches, and such."[10] Another grandmother, Alice, compares the difference between her actual age and her own vision of her stamina: "My health is good and I don't feel tired, and I'm more likely to go out hiking and canoeing and I'm pulling them along. . . . I'm more likely the one to put on a backpack and suggest we go camping." More programs and opportunities for aging grandparents to be seen in public have appeared. In Phoenix, Arizona, older people can try out to become a member of the Golden Grannies, who perform dance routines for the Phoenix Suns NBA team.[11]

While those in the past saw retirement as a well-deserved break from work, aging adults today, particularly those who are financially comfortable, are looking for an alternative way to approach this period of their life.[12] Many Baby Boomers are not retiring as quickly, or they are doing it in phases. Some don't even call what they are doing retiring but rather "a lifestyle shift."[13] Some enjoy their job and do not want to stop working, and others have concerns about having enough income in retirement.[14] In fact, many people choose to "un-retire" by shifting to a new profession or to what some label "encore careers" after retiring from their first job. This may stem from a variety of circumstances, including the need to continue working for financial reasons. Some retirees were used to leading active and busy lives and do not want to face what they may perceive as the idleness of retiring. For many women who didn't have a chance to focus on their careers when facing the earlier demands of child-rearing, an encore career may be their first entry into the workforce.[15] For some, devoting time to providing childcare for their grandchildren becomes their second career.

THE RISE OF INTENSIVE GRANDPARENTING

In the United States, a significant portion of the population is engaged in the act of grandparenting. Early in 2017, the *New York Times* reported: "The number of grandparents in the United States rose to 69.5 million in 2014, up from 65.1 million in 2009. . . . The youngest baby boomers turned 50 in 2014, and the country's 75.4 million boomers make up an exceptionally large pool of potential grandparents."[16] Not only is the sheer volume of grandparents increasing; the culture of grandparenting is changing as well. More are participating in the lives of their children as influential figures and caregivers. We can speculate on a variety of reasons for this growth in attention and caregiving, including increased longevity and active lifestyles. Other factors, including economic influences and shifts in the culture and expectations of parenting, have contributed to these changes.

While Baby Boomers themselves were granted a respite from economic burdens as they aged, many of their children entered the labor market during the Great Recession. The economic crisis between 2007 and 2009 involved a collapse of financial firms and the housing market, leading to widespread foreclosures and layoffs. Though the recession officially ended in 2009, the effects of it have continued.[17] For example, the employment rate of Millennial men dropped to 68 percent, compared with an average of 78 percent for previous generations.[18] Many grown children, unable to fully support themselves, have had to return to their parents' homes. So many have done this that they now have a name all their own: "Boomerang Kids."

These children have returned, often after completing a college degree, to live for an indeterminate period of time under their parents' roofs.[19] This movement is not restricted to those in the nascent stage of adulthood. Because of increased economic uncertainty, adult children are sometimes moving in with their parents, with their own children in tow. The Pew Research Center reports, "Without public debate or fanfare, large numbers of Americans enacted their own anti-poverty program in the depths of the Great Recession: They moved in with relatives. This helped fuel the largest increase in the number of Americans living in multi-generational households in modern history."[20]

A cultural shift in parenting during the lifetime of Baby Boomers influenced how many saw the purpose of childhood and responsibility of caretakers. Many of those labeled as Baby Boomers were raised with more relaxed styles of parenting, popularized by baby experts like Dr. Spock.[21] This has not only shaped their development into adults but also how they chose to parent, and now grandparent. Boomers, adapting these parenting styles—like a focus on more cooperative parenting—see themselves as working with their children to guide them through life decisions and make constructive choices.[22] They were more involved in the care and everyday experiences of their children. This resulted in more intensive parenting, leading some to criticize this style today as helicopter parenting.

Extended life and new possibilities within reproductive science allow for women to start raising their children later and the period of child-rearing to last longer. Christine Overall, a scholar who researches feminism and aging, writes:

> The ideas of, and the length of time committed to, parenthood and child rearing could change as the relationship of parent to child becomes ever longer. We would live to see our great-grandchildren and even our great-great-grandchildren grow to adulthood, and larger multigenerational extended families, not necessarily all living in the same place or even the same country, would be possible.[23]

The extended involvement of parents in the lives of their children has ushered in a type of endless parenting. Studies indicate that within the United States, Baby Boomers are more engaged with their adult children than when they were in similar relationships with their own parents.[24]

Perhaps as a result of the symbiotic relationships that have developed between grandparents, parents, and grandchildren during times of economic pressure, as well as the additional time grandparents and grandchildren are spending together, fewer generational gaps have appeared between age groups in recent periods of time. In the 1960s, when a key cohort of Baby Boomers were entering adulthood, they experienced conflicts with their parents and authority figures. In contrast, younger people today define their conflict points with adults in their lives as less serious, mainly regarding technological differences.[25] A major life goal seems to mirror those of older generations: family.[26] In fact, studies demonstrate that they possess a high degree of respect for their elders. A Pew Research Center study reports: "A majority say that the older generation is superior to the younger generation when it comes to moral values and work ethic. Also, more than six-in-ten say that families have a responsibility to have an elderly parent come live with them if that parent wants to. By contrast, fewer than four-in-ten adults age 60 and older agree that this is a family responsibility."[27]

In addition to having more respect and less conflict between generations, those in intergenerational relationships also are increasingly likely to engage in activities together. National attention greeted a young rapper and an elderly woman who bonded after being randomly assigned as partners to play the puzzle game Words with Friends on their mobile phones. They started playing as strangers but ended up developing a friendship by using the chat feature.[28] A cooking school in New Jersey reports that a frequent request from their young students is to be allowed to bring their grandparents with them to a class.[29] A high school student in Alabama wanted to take his granny to his prom because she had never attended one, causing an ensuing protest after the school refused to allow it.[30] One teenager in San Antonio, Texas, began attending college while her grandfather was enrolled in classes there. Though they are at different life stages, the two bonded over their desire to pursue a higher education.[31] Surely, grandparents and their grandchildren have always engaged in activities with each other, but there is now a more formal recognition of their involvement and an opportunity to encourage—or even capitalize on—it. Baby Boomers, who had been used to having an active presence as parents, and Generation X and Millennials, who are used to having parents more intensively involved in their lives, are setting up the same expectation when it comes to grandparenting.

Madonna Harrington Meyer, a scholar who studies the caregiving of grandmothers, argues, "It appears that just as motherhood has intensified in the United States, becoming very centered on the strategic development or purposeful cultivation of children, so has grandmotherhood."[32] In earlier periods, grandparenting would often begin while people were still in an active stage of parenting. Now, grandparenting often begins after their own children are grown, with no young children of their own to rear.[33]

We are witnessing new activities grandparents embark upon to engage with their grandchildren. While grandparenting may once have been something entered into without much thought or deliberation, grandparenting today is filled with much more intention and attention. Hospitals now offer grandparenting classes in addition to the typical parenting classes to help grandparents catch up with the latest professional advice.[34] These classes serve dual roles: the children, used to relying on experts for advice, can now have their parents take these classes to make sure they are all on the same page. The classes also help to recognize grandparents and reposition their role. While grandparents themselves had been the source of advice, now both grandparents and their children are deferring to experts for guidance, leaving them to enjoy each other's company in new and engaging ways.

Another factor influencing the shifting roles of grandparenting coincides with a blurring of the distinct ages that separate adults and children. This obfuscation allows children and adults to share activities without being thought of as acting above or below their age. In *The Disappearance of Childhood*, Neil Postman explores how new media environments blur the line between children and adults. More recently, in *The Vanishing American Adult*, Ben Sasse has lamented what he sees as young people not being encouraged or guided to grow up: "denying meaningful rites of passage and obscuring the distinction between childhood and adulthood cheats the generation coming of age of something vital."[35] While Postman sees this problem developing as a result of the adoption of electronic media, Sasse argues that over-coddling children and age segregation contribute to a struggling society. Sasse concludes that the separation of young and old in society fails to instill wisdom in the young, including an appreciation for work and resilience.

The merging of adult and child entertainment, though, presents an opportunity for grandparents to indulge in activities, experiences, and lifestyles that allow them to remain connected to young people. For example, they increasingly engage in activities that might earlier have been labeled "too young" for them. Those between 55 and 64 years old have doubled their usage of online dating.[36] Described as "the Golden Girls effect" after the 1980s television show of elderly female roommates, more women are sharing housing with others of the same sex, a trend that had once been limited to young women and men before they married. Women seek out these arrangements both out of financial necessity and for the social companionship they provide.[37]

Conversely, activities previously limited to the elderly are now becoming popular with a younger generation. Knitting, a hobby that was once the domain of elderly women, is spreading among young people as a hip, "new" hobby.[38] Instead of the exception, this is becoming the trend. Millennials seem to enjoy a fascination with the hobbies and pastimes of their grandparents. Vintage toys are popular enough that game companies release new versions fashioned to look like older ones. Young people are drawn to typewriters and turntables, raiding their grandparents' storage boxes for vintage records to play.

They like to spend time together, often enjoy the same things, and the age barriers that might have typically divided them seem to be disappearing. For example, coloring books have become a new trend to help older adults ease anxiety and stress. At the same time, it becomes an opportunity for grandparents and grandchildren to bond over this mutual activity. On her blog, one grandmother recommends purchasing matching coloring books for the grandparent and grandchild to work on together.[39] Video games are another popular activity for grandparents and grandchildren to share. Retirement columns mention online gaming platforms like Minecraft as potential spaces to bond with grandchildren.[40] The Entertainment Software Association reports that, other than their spouses, older Americans are most likely to play with their grandchildren when playing video games in person.[41] In a world with a fast learning curve for new technologies, grandparents and their grandchildren bond in their reliance on helping them master these technologies.

Grandkids often share and remark upon the hipness of their grandparents, expressing both shock and appreciation. Countless videos on the Internet show young people teaching their grandparents a new game or trend. These trends also seem to influence the changing activities of grandparents. One study indicates that grandparents were more likely—even more so than their children—to pursue similar online activities as their grandchildren, including their use of the Web to surf and engage in instant messaging.[42] One might conjecture that both grandchildren and their grandparents have similar amounts of leisure time in which to engage in these hobbies and new technologies. As older people reinvent the activities involved in their daily lives as they age, grandparenting itself is being reinvented among those with the time and means to invest in this phase of life.

GRANDPARENT INTUITION

Recent studies are demonstrating the value of grandparenting for the physical and mental well-being of the aging. Dr. George E. Vaillant, who has spent his career chronicling aging, notes that it was only during the twentieth century that scientists and doctors developed theories on stages of childhood development. While this has allowed an ability to predict children's behavior and milestones, he laments that less research explores older adult development.[43] Building on the work of developmental psychologist Eric Erikson, Vaillant examines the importance of "generativity," which involves building a connection with and guiding the next generation.[44] In his study, those that seemed most happy and satisfied as adults were those who fostered a sense of connection to the next generation, often through involvement as a grandparent.[45]

Some identify a type of "grandmotherly instinct." One grandmother I interviewed, Bernadette, describes it this way: "It was just this complete love for this child. I went into the room where he was born, and it was just like, he's mine, everybody go away." She describes the feeling as a stronger love than she had even for her own children: "I think it's because my grandchild loves me back unconditionally—there's no baggage. I can devote myself completely to him. I don't have to do anything else but play. It must be a release of some kind of hormone."

Hillary Clinton, in one of her early speeches prior to running for president, frequently referred to herself as having a grandma glow. Likewise, an environmental activist wrote in the *New York Times* of her personal experience of hormonal surges as she became a grandmother: "But then I became a grandmother. Nothing compares to the experience of holding six pounds of newborn boy against an older, wiser, pounding heart, a heart burnished with the patina of age, a heart that bears the traces of fractures, the patchwork or plaster lathed over bad breaks. That heart suddenly, unexpectedly, floods with . . . hormones."[46]

Some of the women I spoke to compared their desire for grandchildren as a type of biological urge. Perhaps one could consider it the second biological clock ticking. Arleen is a grandmother to her granddaughter who lives in Florida. She talks about the difficulty in having that distance and describes her feelings about wanting to be with her grandchild as akin to a biological need. She also differentiates her feelings from her husband's: "He's thrilled to be a grandfather, yes he'd like to see more of her, but I don't think he has the need. I feel like it's a need. Like oxygen, air, to be a grandmother to my grandchild."

Arleen had a strong connection with her own grandmother, living with her for a portion of her childhood. Even after she moved out of their home, they stayed in close touch, and she fondly recalls regular Sunday dinners with four generations sitting around the table. She longs to replicate that relationship with her own grandchild, telling me a story about planning for a grandchild long before she ever found out she was going to be one. She was browsing through a bookstore and saw a children's book about mittens. She thought about her own grandmother, who always made her mittens, and thought that she could buy this book, make mittens, and read the book with her granddaughter. So, she bought the book, hoping for that opportunity one day. Ironically, now that she finally has a grandchild, she lives in Florida, so the last thing she needs is mittens.

Like the studies that examine changes in male and female hormones upon the birth of children, newer studies are questioning whether these same changes occur in the bodies of grandparents.[47] Recognizing grandparenting as a unique life stage, some researchers are studying how social work can help with coping and personal growth adjustment for grandparents.[48] Other scholars research how grandmothers and their daughters have shared and different understandings of the meaning of life after the birth of a child.[49] Studies now explore how grandparents deal with the loss of a grandchild, acknowledging that grandparents experience their own bereavement that merits attention.[50]

GRANDPARENT INFLUENCE

Adding to the numerous studies on the effects of parental choices in the health of babies, scientists now are going even further back to the choices made by other relatives, including grandparents. Researchers explore the potential intergenerational effects of lifestyles, such as diet, on successive generations, including grandchildren.[51] There is new research that suggests your feelings about trust may be influenced by where your grandparents immigrated from. Eric Uslaner has studied levels of trust over generations. He writes, "Overall, there is evidence for both culture and context. Where you live shapes your level of trust. But the evidence is far stronger that where your grandparents came from shapes your values. Who you are seems to matter more than who your neighbors are."[52] Other studies indicate that grandparents can be influential in spreading religion among families.[53] Using grandparents to make connections to familiar roots is particularly important for ethnic communities. Studies find that minority grandparents are more likely than nonminorities to see their role in instilling religion and spirituality as important.[54]

Other studies examine how grandparenting provides benefits to both grandparents and their grandchildren. Research is studying how grandparents, in particular grandmothers, may be better than parents at identifying early signs of autism.[55] Another group of researchers is now recruiting grandparents to participate in future research to explore this area.[56] The grandparents I spoke with sometimes mentioned how they could recognize challenges their grandchildren faced and offered advice to help. For example, one grandfather talked about identifying with a granddaughter who has a learning disorder, and he offered to arrange for tutoring. He said, "I go to bat for her a lot."

More people are finding out the value grandparents can provide. Contrary to the image of the grumpy elderly person, newer studies are revealing that, as people age, they actually may develop more empathy and be able to sympathize in a constructive and useful way.[57] Grandparents may be better able to evaluate the feelings of others while remaining detached from the emotional pain that a child or grandchild is experiencing.[58] One study of college athletes had them recall the support they received after they played competitive sports. It found that grandparents were the ones they wanted to be with the most. While parents placed pressure on their children to do well and would often critique aspects of their performance, grandparents were happy to just watch them play.[59]

Popular news media use these studies to create headlines about the budding influence of grandparents. Universities send out press releases to media outlets about their faculty's latest research. As grandparents live in this stage longer and consider what their roles should be, one can see why media would report stories that tout their influence, which would be well received by older audiences and shared with others via social media. But what happens when complex research studies are summarized with headlines like "Your Diet Affects Your Grandchildren's DNA, Scientists Say," or "What Grandmothers Can Teach Science about Autism?"[60] On the one hand, these stories offer recognition and help to acknowledge the potential influence of grandparents. However, these stories sometimes exaggerate the influence of what researchers actually have found. As their power and influence are promoted, grandparents may develop similar feelings of guilt and anxiety that many parents currently experience. This also raises boundary concerns, as grandparents wrestle with messages claiming their role is significant and then try to put that into practice within their everyday activities with their grandchildren.

BOUNDARIES

When Australian model and television host Rachael Finch and her husband were interviewed for a magazine, they didn't think much about their pronouncement that they send their two-year-old daughter to her grandmother's every weekend so that they can enjoy couple time. They certainly were not expecting the media tirade that greeted this revelation. They were described in the media as "selfish" and taking advantage of the grandmother.[61] The couple, of course, saw it in a completely different light. They thought it was important for their family; preserving their couple time helped their marriage, and they wanted their daughter to develop her own relationship with her grandmother. This story illustrates the complicated boundaries being negotiated between grandparents and parents today, and how they sometimes run counter to American expectations of family duties. Some people see parental responsibility as so central that it is considered problematic when they sacrifice some of this autonomy to other members outside of their "nuclear" (immediate) family. Grandparents also are taxed with the conflict of needing to be involved but not interfering. These are lines that are not always clearly drawn.

Richard Settersten writes about the disappearance of traditional life stages and transitions. Age longevity gives new meaning to life and death for people but also can disrupt family relations. He writes, "Family life and social life are infused with new forms and levels of risk, disruption, complexity, ambiguity, and uncertainty than ever before."[62] One possible benefit but also disruption to past life patterns is that more people are taking an active role in grandparenting. Earlier research had argued how age and biology itself prevented people from being too active or even interfering as grandparents. A journal article written in 1954 describes expectations that grandparents should not interfere in the lives of their grandchildren. It found that, if grandparents had excessive love for their grandchildren, it remained well hidden, arguing: "Nature may have a way of avoiding extremes in later maturity by reducing available energy."[63] As people engage in active lifestyles longer, though, grandparents are not only more involved but also have more influence in the lives of their grandchildren. In many ways this is a positive shift, as everyone can benefit from an active and healthy lifestyle. However, beyond being devoted to the physical care of their grandchildren, grandparents also are spending mental energy worrying about them. This can lead to stress for the grandparent and boundary issues as well.

Most of the grandparents I spoke with are mindful of avoiding boundary confusion, and they pay attention to how they can avoid conflict with their children. At the request of her son and daughter-in-law, Alice moved in to help watch their newborn twins. Later, when she moved out and changed to weekly visits, she would frequently tell herself, "These are not my kids. These are my kids' kids. I had to remind myself that I'm the grandparent, not the parent. I had bonded with them for three months, and then I had to leave. I had to literally say the words to myself and remind myself of that." Another woman, Jan, made sure to avoid interfering: "I have such a deep unconditional love for them, and I have it for my kids. Sometimes I've really had a hard time with kind of feeling like when I was speaking too directly to my daughter and maybe judging. . . . I had to step back and say this is her family and her life and give my input and support, but I have to let go. I can't control."

Others, though, seem determined to rewrite the rules for interference. Marty, for example, who regularly leaves work early to provide babysitting care, describes himself as an "interventionist grandfather." "I really serve as a sounding board, and an advice seeker and advice giver," he said. He gives this speech to his children when he begins to help caring for his grandchildren: "Here's the deal. I'm going to step up on behalf of my grandchildren whether you like it or not. Sometimes, I'm going to ruffle your feathers, and you are going to get pissed at me. I'm going to be my grandchildren's advocate. You need to tell me that's okay."

Negotiating expectations of caregiving was a main issue that came up for grandparents. Some grandmothers worry about saying no, fearing the result might be losing more opportunities to be with their grandchildren. One grandmother described it as: "You're afraid to say no because if you say no, they might stop asking." She finds herself agreeing to babysit all the time, even at times where she's feeling a bit overwhelmed. Alice, the grandmother of twins and now an additional grandchild, mentioned friends who suffer from a type of "grandparent abuse," where the parents do not respect the time of the grandparent. She decided to establish with her son and daughter-in-law a policy they call the "right to first refusal." She doesn't want her children to be afraid to ask her to babysit because they imagine she's too tired. Instead, she always prefers to be asked first and be given the opportunity to say no if she does not feel up to it. One study suggests that Alice is wise to be mindful of doing too much. Research suggests that babysitting regularly for a grandchild can lower the risk of Alzheimer's and lead to a smarter brain; however, too much babysitting, defined as five days per week, actually lowers cognitive performance.[64]

Some grandparents see their role as not only building a relationship with their grandchildren, but also protecting the family. One grandmother I spoke with, Kathy, described her goals in her grandparenting: "Part of the reason I do what I do, I have been in bad marriages with children, and I think those marriages may have had a better chance if I'd had more support." She encourages her children to go out for dinner dates and overnight trips while she watches their children. She thinks her plan is working, too: "I think it's being rewarded. My oldest daughter has been married 15 years."

JUST ENOUGH RESPONSIBILITY

Grandparents are providing support and caregiving that can be a precious resource for families. Some grandparents have noticed the differences between parenting and grandparenting and see grandparenting as a more rewarding life stage. Many of the grandparents I spoke with described this period of their life as gratifying because of the intense care and attention they can provide for their grandchildren. This is borne out in research by the Zero to Three Organization, which indicates why this may be the case: "First, the grandparent role is different—less discipline and more love. Second, grandparents said that they, themselves, are different than they were as parents—more patient, more experienced, and less anxious."[65] Their focus groups and my own interviews with grandparents offer an explanation for the joy grandparents experience: they are able to be a part of the lives of children they love without bearing a larger responsibility for them.

A common theme that emerged when I spoke with grandparents is that this role includes enough tasks to feel useful but not so much as to feel responsible. One woman I spoke to, Vivian, describes it this way: "You have none of the responsibility or very little responsibility of ultimately who these people are going to be. You are much less invested." At the same time, she describes feeling an unconditional love.

Grandparents often contrast experiences with their grandchildren with their own parenting history. One grandfather, Marty, found parenting while working as a professional challenging. He depicts grandparenting as "more liberating, less stressful." He continues by observing that parenting for him was "more impactful, or at least it seems to be, because when you are raising little kids and you are both working, you don't have much time to sit around and think about the impact. So much of life with little kids is putting one foot in front of another until they grow up. I wish I had done certain things differently." Marty describes his "Poppy Days" as a great joy of his life now. Vivian echoes this sentiment: "I have zero chores to do. I can just focus on them. I'm not in my life at that moment. I can give 150% attention. When I was raising my own kids, I was in a relationship, with friends, and politically involved, and had a job. There were other things going on."

In an age when mindfulness activities increasingly are more popular, grandparenting becomes another opportunity to be present-centered and reflective. One grandmother, Alice, describes her own realization of how she thinks differently as a grandparent: "I'm aware of being less busy, and I think that makes me think differently. I see parents racing out, and I always felt like I was pulling at least one kid behind me. . . . That definitely feels different. If they want to walk slowly, I walk slowly. If they want to stop and look at something, I can stop and look. If in a practical way, it's different."

In fact, studies on grandparent caregiving reflect this difference. One study concludes: "One clear generational difference for both genders was the much lower proportion of grandparents' care that was multi-tasked. Compared to both mothers and fathers, a higher proportion of grandparents' childcare time was spent doing only child care, suggesting they focus more directly on children during the time they are together."[66] Grandparents are able to spend more of their energy directly focused on their grandchildren, rather than distracted by other aspects of parenting.

Grandparenting allows these people the opportunity to be reflective and mindful, something most of them didn't feel able to do while parenting. These grandparents also seem to recognize the importance of having these experiences and recording them so that their grandchildren can remember them. Grandmothers talk of making photo books so that the children can one day see them and remember their time together. Kathy makes photo books in five-year time spans. She said her grandchildren were so excited the moment they received their first book. As the children have grown, they have taken a more active role in the construction of these books. Grandparents both appreciate the importance of the everyday moments that they are experiencing with their grandchildren and recognize the limits of time and the importance of preserving those memories.

FINANCIAL SUPPORT

Increasingly, grandparents are providing financial support for their children and grandchildren. In a study by the AARP, 96 percent of grandparents surveyed indicated that they spend money on their grandchildren.[67] Some grandparents, in contrast to their own grandparents, more likely enjoyed economic security in their youth, so they were able to invest or simply feel comfortable with the idea of not saving everything they earned. Today, grandparents are likely to give smaller gifts over a lifetime than wait until their death to grant an inheritance.[68] Simultaneously, because many children and grandchildren face financial instability today, many grandparents are stepping in to provide assistance.

The grandparents I spoke with frequently discussed the ways they help to support their grandchildren. Often, the grandchildren were not even aware of their financial support. One grandmother described how she helped her grandchildren: "We were able to provide them with things their parents could not afford financially. If there was a major object they wanted, we were often the people who could buy it. If they needed a new computer, we would treat them to it for Christmas." Another related the joy of treating their grandchildren to experiences they otherwise might not have had, including visits to museums and shows.

Sometimes grandparents pay for care traditionally handled by parents, such as music lessons, sports activities, or even orthodontics. More grandparents are willing to pitch in with college costs. According to one study, 53 percent expected or are willing to help pay for college, with an anticipated median amount of $25,000 as a contribution.[69] Grandparents are even beginning to help their grandchildren buy homes.[70] In fact, these kinds of support occur with such regularity that financial advisors have taken notice and are tailoring advice particularly for these groups.

The grandparents I spoke with describe the joy they receive in watching their grandchildren enjoy a present. Parents are grateful for the extra support and for the way their children benefit from the gift. Yet sometimes conflict ensues. Some parents I spoke with said that they have refused gifts from grandparents because of the strings they felt were attached. One woman lamented that her mother would only pay for classes for her granddaughter if the child took specialized music lessons. Another described her child's grandfather as interested in buying presents but judgmental of her recommendations for them. Sometimes the expectations attached to gifts become even more extreme. The *New York Times* reports that parents-to-be have felt pressured to name their baby with their parents' preference in mind in order to receive financial support.[71] As grandparents today are more likely to spend their money during their lifetimes, these conflicts will continue to arise.

Financial planners and those seeking charitable contributions are rethinking methods for appealing to grandparents in consideration of new financial relationships between grandparents, parents, and grandchildren. For example, now that many grandparents want to contribute money toward college, they need to consider how their gifts may prevent their grandchildren from receiving larger financial aid packages from schools or the government.[72] There is also concern about the impact that gift giving may have on grandparents' own retirement. A Pew Research study comparing Italy, Germany, and the United States finds that "financial help is more likely to flow down to adult children than up to aging parents" in all three countries.[73] Though people who were surveyed agree that providing support to their aging parents is a responsibility, the study indicates that children and grandchildren provide support in the form of time and physical assistance rather than money. It is important to note, as Robert Putnam explores in *Our Kids: The American Dream in Crisis*, the type of support that someone provides as a grandparent is linked to their income status.[74] Those with more money are able to provide luxury services, while those with less can afford only to help with a little money or basic resources for survival. A study of African American grandparents found that the type of spending they did often was connected to necessities rather than requests from parents: "African American grandparents are more like [*sic*] to say they spend money on their grandchildren to *help with everyday living expenses,* and *because grandchildren ask for things*" (emphasis in original).[75] The grandparent-giving world, then, mimics the rest of the world in continuing to show an economic divide in how people live.

GRANDPARENTING AS DÉJÀ VU

In the 2016 Olympics, the family of gold-medalist gymnast Simone Biles was thrust into the international spotlight. Adopted and raised by her maternal grandfather, Ron Biles, and his wife, Nellie Biles, Simone referred to them as her parents. When an NBC sports commentator refused to identify them as her parents, calling them her grandparents, social media exploded with anger. People complained that the decision reflected struggles adoptive parents have with a family's right to choose its own identity and labels. While many picture grandparenting as a part-time, voluntary relationship, for some, the grandparent experience is not so narrowly defined. Many grandparents, sometimes reluctantly, take on a parental role for their grandchildren, working as full-time caregivers.

Grandparents sometimes suddenly have to take care of grandchildren full time when their grandchildren's primary family suffers a crisis. In these cases, grandparents are enlisted to preserve and sustain the family, often for an unforeseeable length of time, and become what are sometimes referred to as "skipped generation" households. The United States Census reports, "In 2012, 2.7 million grandparents in the U.S. were raising their grandchildren."[76] The need to assume primary care of grandchildren is a problem that crosses race and ethnicity, though the issue is more prevalent among ethnic and racial minorities: "While 4 percent of all people aged 30 and over lived with their grandchildren, 3 percent of White, non-Hispanics did so. Higher proportions were found among other racial and ethnic groups: 6 percent of Blacks and Asians, 7 percent of Hispanics, 8 percent of American Indians and Alaska Natives, and 11 percent of Native Hawaiians and other Pacific Islanders."[77]

I spoke with Paige, the program director of *Grandparents Raising Grandchildren* in Georgia. She says that year after year, most children end up in the care of their grandparents due to substance abuse, incarceration, or the death of a parent. Sometimes, military enlistment by a single-parent family may result in grandparents needing to assume care. These grandparents struggle with everyday care, and they find it harder to gain access to government support funds when their role as permanent caretakers or adoptive parents is not clearly defined.

A major issue for these families is that the current social services model is not set up to help support them. Often, those grandparents with the least economic resources themselves are required to provide grandparental care. LaShawnDa Pittman, in her study of survival strategies among African American grandmother caregivers found "inadequate and punitive welfare policies that engender competition over scarce resources."[78] For example, a study on Native American grandparents engaged in custodial care found:

> Grandparent care is especially common in nonmetropolitan areas of so-called Indian states. . . . Our findings that grandparents living in these settings are more likely to be responsible for a grandchild may reflect high need for care as a result of poverty, unemployment, and other social conditions.[79]

Sometimes, grandparents are immigrants or undocumented workers and are not able to apply for social service support.[80] Many immigrants, including those coming from China to the United States, leave their children behind with their grandparents because of their lack of access to childcare.[81] Unlike foster parents, who are strangers to the children, these grandparents often face a balancing act of trying to retain relationships with their children while assuming the care of the grandchildren and working within government bureaucracies that do not officially acknowledge or support their caregiving. Paige says the grandmothers who often retain primary responsibility for the caregiving feel a sense of responsibility to their families. One woman told Paige, "'I've just been raising kids my whole life. Even when I was younger, I was raising my younger brothers and sisters.' It's the culture they were brought up in."

For those with privilege, grandparenting can provide opportunities to remain and engage in healthy lifestyles, but research documents the unique health risks facing grandparents and grandchildren when they are forced to partake in full-time childcare.[82] Grandparents raising children experience changes in their daily living, including strain on their finances and emotional and physical stress.[83] Grandparents who are involved in primary care of their grandchildren will at times sacrifice their health to focus on the needs of their grandchildren.[84] Also, when grandchildren had difficulties (health, learning, or psychological), it would add to the stress of the grandparent.[85]

Studies of Mexican American grandparents found that, though they did experience joy in establishing a family life for their grandchildren, living in over-crowded situations under the pressure of caring for their grandchildren was stressful.[86] Other investigations are showing that grandparents and grandchildren may suffer from a lack of medical and psychological attention. One study explores the strain and stress they feel from being "second time parents," as they are disconnected from social networks and peer groups.[87] Part of the problem is that grandparents are going through a life stage outside the norm, preventing them from having access to friends and social resources that they had when they were parents. Organizations like the one Paige heads and government programs are finding more ways to recognize these problems and respond to these pressing needs. In New York City, for example, Housing Authority worked with advocacy groups to create the building project development GrandParentFamily Apartments, which is the first public development in the United States created specifically for grandparents who are raising grandchildren.[88] Organizations such as the AARP are offering online communities, information, and research for people to access legal networks and support from others in these situations.[89] Despite these efforts, the grandparent experience these people have is not the same lifestyle that others have the opportunity to cultivate.

THE GRANDPA SHIFT

A plethora of research already has explored the difference between fathers and mothers in terms of parenting. Newer studies, though, examine the differences between grandfathers and grandmothers in caregiving. Society has shifted to promote more egalitarian distribution of parenting and housework and encouraging fathers to spend more time with their children. According to a Pew Research Study, "In 2015, fathers reported spending, on average, seven hours a week on child care—almost triple the time they provided back in 1965."[90] Consequently, more men are finding it challenging to meet the increased expectations of family participation and work demands, creating additional work-family conflicts for fathers. Baby Boomers, for the most part finished with the daily care demands of their children, have observed this shift in the expectation of fathers to spend more time with their children. For many, it's a chance to try their hand at more intensive parenting. Becoming a grandfather, then, presents a new life phase in which men can balance the needs of personal and professional life differently.

Newer studies are finding that gender differences, while still present, are less pronounced between grandfathers and grandmothers than between fathers and mothers. Grandfathers did not necessarily provide more care by themselves, but they were more likely to offer assistance with childcare duties.[91] The grandparent stage sometimes requires grandparents to adjust their relationships when providing childcare. When I spoke with Jan, she was still wrestling with feelings of resentment that she sometimes felt toward her husband's newfound participation in the lives of their grandchildren: "I've been pleased, but also at times having a hard time with the fact that my husband, who was not a super-present dad because of his work, is now as a granddad. When they were growing up, I was a single parent because of his intense work schedule, but now he as a grandfather is totally in love with them, and it's quite wonderful to see him stepping up to it." Jan understood the demands on his time while they raised their children, but couldn't help but be wistful for the imagined caregiving relationship they could have had together.

Others recognize grandparenting as a second opportunity to parent in a new way. Grandmother Eileen discusses the difference between her husband Tom's experiences as a father and his time as a grandfather:

> Tom was a loving, wonderful father who was often frustrated by the fact that work kept him from attending more of the girls' games and activities. He never knew his grandparents and worried that he wouldn't know how to do the job. He was wrong. He is an outstanding, selfless grandfather who always makes time for his grandchildren. The four children adore him. I love watching this interaction. The joy they share is a beautiful thing.

Marty reflects:

> As it happens with most older people, I'm smarter and wiser than I was when my kids were born. I'm retired now, and I don't have to have the pressures and anxieties that come along when you are raising two children. There have been times when I have sort of stepped up for my kids to make sure what I did wrong didn't happen again. That's the way I did it as a father, I'm not going to repeat that mistake if I have the opportunity to change it.

While some may experience resentment or longing for the new fatherly caregiving style that was not accessible to their generation, others have realized that grandparenting becomes a real opportunity to experience new aspects of fatherhood. For some blended families, becoming a grandparent presents a chance to connect with their family in a way they may never have before. Divorce rates rose in the United States when the Baby Boomers were young adults.[92] This caused many families to have more than one father or mother figure and often led to confusion, conflict, and stress among families. Some grandfathers described to me their excitement at fitting in with their families without feeling like the odd person out. One grandfather, David, saw grandparenting as a first chance at parenting, not a second one. He married his wife and took on a fatherly relationship with her two young daughters, yet he said that in some ways he was still the "stepfather," and his daughters often introduced him that way. To his delight, the moment he became a grandparent, they identified him just as "Grandpa." He commented, "There's no such thing as a step-grandpa. It doesn't matter how many grandparents you have. To the children, I'm just another grandpa." He was even more thrilled that the children called him "Grandpa," while they qualified their other grandfather with his first name attached, "Grandpa John." Another grandmother, Kathy, said her husband, who is not the biological father of her children, became a grandfather and was completely accepted in that role. "He's an awesome grandfather," she said. "There's never been any question of who he is. He's Pop to everybody. They have a strong bond with him."

Being part of a generation that has redefined the composition of families, Baby Boomers have had to work through labels applied to people, both related and not, who had entered into their lives. Debates about what makes a parent have been ever present during their youth and adulthood, including discussions about divorce and remarriage, single-parent households, adoption, foster care, and, more recently, LGBTQ families. Many reasons may contribute to why people do not apply the prefix "step" to grandparent figures. Grandparents are genetically more distant than parents from children, providing less distinction between biological and socially constructed relationships. Often, children have two sets of grandparents, as opposed to one mother and father, making it less likely a singular grandparent fills that role. In addition, the greater acceptance of blended families today may reduce the need for feeling a biological connection to a grandparent. Whatever the reason, many grandparents are pleasantly surprised to find that their role is one in which it is relatively easy to find acceptance.

THE GRANDMA TRACK

Grandparenting has provided for many men the opportunity to experience childcare. For women, though, grandparenting brings with it many of the same conflicts, feelings, and challenges they faced with parenting. Many women, either by choice or necessity, take on a major role in caring for their grandchildren, changing their lifestyle to do so.

We already have labels for women who decide to "opt out" of the workforce or choose the "mommy track" when they leave the workforce for a period of time or take on a less ambitious career path. Now, some grandmothers are choosing again to leave the workforce or reduce their work in order to help support their children with childcare. For some women, like my own mother, becoming a grandmother leads them to replace their own paid work with new, unpaid family labor. My mother announced her retirement from teaching shortly after I announced I was expecting our first child, and she became instrumental in assisting my husband and I with caregiving. Studies have found that "for women, the arrival of a new grandchild is associated with more than an 8% increase in the chances of retiring."[93] It should also be acknowledged, though, that the burden of retirement often falls on the matriarch as opposed to the patriarch, and that some women likely are retiring less out of a desire to do so than out of an obligation to help with childcare. Some studies indicate that grandmothers who can do so often choose to reduce their work hours rather than retire completely, and many indicate a preference to remain, at least partly, in the workforce.[94] In the United States, the pressure to turn to family members, especially grandparents, is greater, as this country has little support for paid family leave. However, the trend is definitely a global one. In Shanghai, for example, 90 percent of the city's grandchildren are being watched by grandparents.[95] Describing the challenges of working and raising children in Europe, Gaby Hinsliff writes, "A generation of older women, many of whom put themselves second in order to raise a family, are doing so all over again so that daughters can pursue career opportunities that were sadly not open to their mothers."[96] In Spain, where half of all grandparents take care of their grandchildren during the day, the UGT general workers' union organized a grandparent strike. The strike was meant to raise awareness of the crisis in childcare they would have if not for the assistance of grandparents.[97] It has become so prevalent that grandmotherhood, then, becomes yet another time when many women must decide how to balance their work and professional lives, often sacrificing one, the other, or both.

For some, the opportunity to grandparent fulfills an emotional caregiving need they sacrificed while they were engaged in parenting. A few observers have connected this to the feminist push for women to enter the workplace. Madonna Harrington Meyer has examined grandparenting as a chance for women to enjoy children more thoroughly than at previous times in their lives: "Some were focused on education and career advancements, including promotions, partnerships, and tenure."[98] In her book *Becoming Grandma*, journalist Lesley Stahl echoes these views with interviews of people using grandparenting to resolve struggles from their own attempts to balance work and family life. She concludes, "We're more like the men who were so involved in building their careers that they were all but absent from their children's lives. They end up lamenting their rationed fatherhood, so they go all in with the grandkids."[99] Grandparenting provides another opportunity for many of these people to focus attention on children.

As family relationships continue to evolve, grandparents are relied upon in new ways. In *All the Single Ladies*, Rebecca Traister argues that more women are considering "separating the question of partnership from the question of parenthood."[100] Jane Mattes is a psychotherapist and founder and director of Single Mothers by Choice, an organization that supports single women seeking to become parents. Mattes noticed that when many of these women decided to become single mothers, they had to "grieve the dream" by accepting they would not achieve parenthood the way that they had imagined. Mattes also found that the parents of these women sometimes had to grieve their imagined grandparent life as well. However, some parents encourage their adult daughters to contact the organization because they do not want them to delay having children. Grandparents can be a factor in women deciding whether to become a single mother. Mattes tells me, "Because there is no second parent, a lot of single mothers by choice consider or do move to be closer to their parents so their child has a little more of their extended family nearby. They seek another person to lend their child practical and emotional help."

In fact, studies demonstrate that having a grandparent involved in one's life can provide important emotional support for children in single-parent families because they have another adult to rely on.[101] In interviews I conducted with moms who have chosen to be single, they spoke of the important role of their own parents in the lives of their children. Many of the tasks and activities grandparents contributed to were similar to what I've found with other grandparents, such as helping to care for the children before or after school or taking their grandchildren on outings to give moms a break. However, moms also spoke about their parents as the ones to consult for a second opinion in making important life decisions. One single mom of young children, Julie, described her reliance on her own mother: "I probably bounce more ideas off of her and questions. Whether if I had a partner, I'd be doing that at home." Another single mom, Susan, thought about her parents before becoming pregnant: "I definitely considered their age and that if I waited a bit longer, it would get harder for them to help me." Susan also described the importance of her father to her children: "My father is the biggest male role model for my son, both kids actually. He's the closest male figure in his life." These grandparents become additional adults that single moms can choose to rely on when they need it. As families become more broadly defined, a grandparent can step in and serve in activities formerly performed by more traditional roles. This applies to not only single moms, but also to other newer family compositions. Eileen and Tom are grandparents to the children of a lesbian couple. Tom, as a grandfather, often fills in at "dad" events at their grandchildren's school. Tom's experience conforms with a research study that shows that grandfathers often step in to serve as a male figure for children of lesbian mothers.[102]

While some grandparents are quick to embrace these new roles and their children's requests for their involvement, other grandparents struggle to balance the expectations that they will help with their own needs. One woman, Lillian, talked about her mother's limits on her interactions with her grandchildren: "My mother always says, 'I had my children. I love my children, and they've given me a certain amount of fulfillment, but. . . .'" Lillian continues, "It's the 'but' I can't compete with." Ultimately, her mother's true fulfillment, she believes, comes from the career she started after her youngest child reached primary school. Her grandparenting "comes more out of resources and less out of emotional connection." She describes her mother as a product of the feminist movement of the 1960s and '70s and recognizes her mother's joy of establishing herself in a professional career. From that moment forward, that was her main focus. In contrast, her father became a very present-centered dad and grandfather.

Another woman I interviewed, Amanda, said she was surprised about how she felt about her mother's involvement in the daily lives of her grandchildren. When her first child was born, she asked her mother to help her one day per week by watching the baby for an hour and a half so she could work. Her mother replied, "I can't. I have too many things. I have my card game, my exercise class, and I can't be committed to a day." Amanda had expected her mother to become so involved with her grandchildren, and she sees friends that have that type of everyday relationship with their parents, so she was shocked at her mother's unwillingness to accommodate what Amanda perceived as such a minimal time commitment.

More grandmothers, however, are beginning to express uncertainty about the expectation that they babysit. Some feel that they already did their job raising children, while others like to have flexibility in their schedule and not be tied down by a regular babysitting commitment.[103] One woman I spoke with discussed the ambivalence she feels as a grandparent who provides a significant amount of care: "One thing that surprises me is that occasionally I get these feelings in my own self as a sixty-nine-year-old woman; wow, maybe I'm missing out on what people who retire have. My free time is grandparenting, and I do love it, but sometimes I'm surprised and think I could be traveling."

The divide that appears in the financial resources of grandparenting also is present in regard to grandparents providing childcare. Some see it as an opportunity to invest free time, when desired, in providing additional assistance to their children. For others, it is a chance to engage focused attention on their grandchildren, an experience they may have missed with their own children because of work demands. Yet for many grandparents, the requests, or even demands, from their children to provide childcare conflict with their desire to enjoy retirement or need to devote time to their own work or other obligations.

CONCLUSION

Grandparenting is becoming a new phase of life. The Baby Boomer generation is responsible for redefining grandparenting, just as they changed how we see parenting, feminism, politics, activism, and other cultural shifts within the United States. Grandparenting provides a new stage in which they can create new rituals and engage in intensified experiences with children. Grandparenting is becoming more intensified for a number of reasons. For some, it is a natural extension of the more expansive parenting they practiced, which differentiated them from their parents. For others, it is a chance to resolve long-fraught work-life conflicts they encountered while raising their own children. It also provides an opportunity to enjoy a new identity while defying the age expectations traditionally associated with grandparents. While they often label this stage as different—the second or third act—many seem to recognize it as an opportunity to be able to enjoy aspects of life in a different way than they had in the past. While grandparenting roles are shifting for many in the middle class, for others, grandparents have always been essential. The experience of grandparenting and retiring is different for those with low socioeconomic status. Non-white Americans and immigrants are also more likely to be poorer than white Americans, and those who have less education are more likely to have family instability, which weakens family ties and changes how the grandparent relationship may develop.[104] It is important to acknowledge that the experiences people have with grandparenting are different and often dependent on access to resources. For some grandparents, it is a chance to be a fun person in the life of their grandchild, but for others, the role becomes one that ensures the survival of the family. Grandparenting care can be seen as a burden and full-time experience, but for those with comfortable incomes the grandparenting experience becomes a matter of choice.

NOTES

1. Brian Cogan and Thom Gencarelli, eds., *Baby Boomers and Popular Culture: An Inquiry into America's Most Powerful Generation*, (Santa Barbara, CA: Praeger, 2015), x.
2. Karen Fingerman and Megan Dolbin-MacNab, "The Baby Boomers and Their Parents: Cohort Influences and Intergenerational Ties," in *The Baby Boomers Grow Up: Contemporary Perspectives on Midlife*, ed. Susan Krauss Whitbourne and Sherry L. Willis (Mahwah, NJ: Lawrence Erlbaum, 2006), 238.
3. Michael L. Hilt and Jeremy H. Lipschultz, *Mass Media, an Aging Population, and the Baby Boomers* (New York: Routledge, 2013), 17.
4. Lori K. Bitter, *The Grandparent Economy: How Baby Boomers Are Bridging the Generation Gap* (Ithaca, NY: Paramount Marketing Publishing, 2015), 4.
5. Richard Suzman and John Beard, "Global Health and Aging" (Washington, DC: National Institute on Aging, National Institutes of Health and World Health Organization, October 2011), 4, https://www.nia.nih.gov/sites/default/files/2017-06/global_health_aging.pdf.
6. Peter Laslett, *A Fresh Map of Life: The Emergence of the Third Age* (Cambridge, MA: Harvard University Press, 1991), 2.
7. Louise Aronson, "Stop Treating 70- and 90-Year-Olds the Same," *New York Times*, August 11, 2017, https://www.nytimes.com/2017/08/11/opinion/sunday/vaccinations-elderly.html?_r=0.
8. Katherine Brookfield et al., "The Home as Enabler of More Active Lifestyles among Older People," *Building Research & Information* 43, no. 5 (2015): 616–630, https://doi.org/10.1080/09613218.2015.1045702; Simone Dohle and Brian Wansink, "Fit in 50 Years: Participation in High School Sports Best Predicts One's Physical Activity after Age 70," *BMC Public Health* 13 (December 2013): 1–6, https://doi.org/10.1186/1471-2458-13-1100.
9. Valeria Bordone and Bruno Arpino, "Do Grandchildren Influence How Old You Feel?," *Journal of Aging and Health* 28, no. 6 (September 2016): 1068, https://doi.org/10.1177/0898264315618920.
10. "Grandparents Investing in Grandchildren: The MetLife Study on How Grandparents Share Their Time, Values, and Money" (New York: MetLife Mature Market Institute and Generations United, September 2012), https://www.metlife.com/assets/cao/mmi/publications/studies/2012/studies/MMIGrandparentsStudy_web.pdf.
11. Golden Grannies, the Official Site of the Phoenix Suns (web page), http://www.nba.com/suns/fans/goldengrannies0809.html.
12. Laslett, *A Fresh Map of Life*, 71.
13. Fred Brock, "Baby Boomers' Second Act," *New York Times* (web page), accessed January 17, 2017, http://www.nytimes.com/ref/realestate/greathomes/GH-Retire.html.
14. "Health and Retirement Study: A Longitudinal Study of Health, Retirement, and Aging," Institute for Social Research, University of Michigan, National Institute on Aging, January 2017, 24.

15. Carolyn Rosenblatt, "Bored with Retirement? Then Un-Retire and Go Back to Work," *Forbes,* December 4, 2013, https://www.forbes.com/sites/carolynrosenblatt/2013/12/04/bored-with-retirement-then-un-retire-and-go-back-to-work/#681639153cc1.

16. Sharon Jayson, "More Grandparents Than Ever," *New York Times*, March 20, 2017, https://www.nytimes.com/2017/03/20/health/grandparents-population-census.html?smid=nytcore-ipad-share&smprod=nytcore-ipad.

17. John Weinberg, "The Great Recession and Its Aftermath," Federal Reserve History, (Washington, DC: Federal Reserve Board, November 22, 2013), https://www.federalreservehistory.org/essays/great_recession_and_its_aftermath.

18. Eileen Patten and Richard Fry, "How Millennials Today Compare with Their Grandparents 50 Years Ago" (Washington, DC: Pew Research Center, March 19, 2015), http://www.pewresearch.org/fact-tank/2015/03/19/how-millennials-compare-with-their-grandparents/.

19. Adam Davidson, "It's Official: The Boomerang Kids Won't Leave," *New York Times*, June 22, 2014, https://www.nytimes.com/2014/06/22/magazine/its-official-the-boomerang-kids-wont-leave.html.

20. Rakesh Kochhar and D'Vera Cohn, "Fighting Poverty in a Bad Economy, Americans Move in with Relatives" (Washington, DC: Pew Research Center, October 3, 2011), http://www.pewsocialtrends.org/2011/10/03/fighting-poverty-in-a-bad-economy-americans-move-in-with-relatives/?src-prc-headline.

21. Becky Ebenkamp, "Think Granny Don't Surf?" *Brandweek* 45, no. 34 (September 27, 2004): 20.

22. Judith Hunt, "Make Room for Daddy. . . . And Mommy: Helicopter Parents Are Here!" *The Journal of Academic Administration in Higher Education* 3, no. 1 (Spring 2008): 10.

23. Christine Overall, "Longevity, Identity, and Moral Character: A Feminist Approach," in *The Fountain of Youth: Cultural, Scientific, and Ethical Perspectives on a Biomedical Goal*, ed. Stephen G. Post and Robert H. Binstock (Oxford: Oxford University Press, 2004), 291.

24. Karen L. Fingerman et al., "The Baby Boomers' Intergenerational Relationships," *Gerontologist* 52, no. 2 (April 1, 2012): 203. doi:10.1093/geront/gnr139.

25. Paul Taylor and Scott Keeter, eds. *Millennials: Confident. Connected. Open to Change* (Washington, DC: Pew Research Center, February 24, 2010): 7, http://www.pewsocialtrends.org/2010/02/24/millennials-confident-connected-open-to-change/.

26. Taylor and Keeter, "*Millennials: Confident*", 17.

27. Taylor and Keeter, 3.

28. Daniel Victor, "He's 22. She's 81. Their Friendship Is Melting Hearts," *New York Times*, December 6, 2017, https://www.nytimes.com/2017/12/06/us/words-with-friends-meeting.html.

29. Nora Sherman, "An Academy for Chefs Both Young and Old," *Grandparents.com* (web page), accessed February 3, 2018, http://www.grandparents.com/grandkids/you-and-your-grandkids/academy-for-chefs.

30. Andy Gray, "Alabama High School Bans Grandma from Prom" (web page), *Sports Illustrated*, accessed October 5, 2017, https://www.si.com/extra-mustard/2017/03/31/alabama-high-school-bans-grandma-from-prom-hot-clicks.

31. Jennifer Earl, "This Teen Girl and Her 82-Year-Old Grandpa Are Going to College Together" (web page), *CBS News*, August 30, 2016, http://www.cbsnews.com/news/melanie-salazar-and-her-82-year-old-grandpa-rene-neira-going-to-college-together/.

32. Madonna Harrington Meyer, *Grandmothers at Work: Juggling Families and Jobs* (New York: New York University Press, 2014), 3.

33. Gunhild O. Hagestad and Mary E. Lang, "The Transition to Grandparenthood: Unexplored Issues," *The Journal of Family Issues* 7, no. 2 (June 1986): 117.

34. K. C. Summers, "Grandparenting 101 for Baby Boomers," *Washington Post*, May 7, 2015, https://www.washingtonpost.com/opinions/grandparenting-the-baby-boomer-way/2015/05/07/c8b95094-f350-11e4-bcc4-e8141e5eb0c9_story.html?utm_term=.d8b016aeffb2.

35. Ben Sasse, *The Vanishing American Adult: Our Coming-of-Age Crisis—and How to Rebuild a Culture of Self-Reliance* (New York: St. Martin's Press, 2017), 55.

36. Aaron Smith, "15% of American Adults Have Used Online Dating Sites or Mobile Dating Apps" (Washington, DC: Pew Research Center, February 11, 2016), http://www.pewinternet.org/2016/02/11/15-percent-of-american-adults-have-used-online-dating-sites-or-mobile-dating-apps/.

37. Lori Bitter, "Sharing Your Home: It's the Golden Girls for Real," *Grand Lifestyle Magazine* (web page), February 28, 2017, posted by Christine Crosby in *GRAND Voices*, http://www.grandmagazine.com/2017/02/sharing-your-home-golden-girls-style/.

38. Carole E. Lee, "A Pastime of Grandma and the 'Golden Girls' Evolves into a Hip Hobby," *New York Times,* March 30, 2005, http://www.nytimes.com/2005/03/30/opinion/a-pastime-of-grandma-and-the-golden-girls-evolves-into-a-hip-hobby.html?_r=0.

39. "Coloring Books Have Graduated to a Way for Grandparent and Grandchild to Feel Better Together," in *Grandma Lessons: A Grandmother's Blog on Life*, June 26, 2015, http://grandmother-blog.com/blog/2015/06/26/coloring-books-have-graduated-to-a-way-for-grand-parent-and-grandchild-to-feel-better-together/.

40. Alexandra Samuel, "How to Use Online Games and Activities to Connect to Grandchildren," *Wall Street Journal*, November 27, 2016, https://www.wsj.com/articles/how-to-use-online-games-and-activities-to-connect-to-grandchildren-1480302541.

41. Oscar G. Anderson, "Video Games: Attitudes and Habits of Adults Age 50-Plus" (Washington, DC: AARP Research, June 2016): 29, https://doi.org/10.26419/res.00125.001.

42. Ebenkamp, "Think Granny."

43. George E. Vaillant, *Aging Well: Surprising Guideposts to a Happier Life from the Landmark Harvard Study of Adult Development* (New York: Little, Brown, and Company, 2003), 40.

44. Vaillant, *Aging Well*, 44–47.

45. Vaillant, *Aging Well,* 130–133.

46. Dominique Browning, "The Bliss of Grandmother Hormones," *New York Times*, May 7 2016, https://www.nytimes.com/2016/05/08/fashion/grandmother-hormones-love-grandchild.html?_r=0.

47. M. Samms-Vaughan and P. B. Gray, "Investigating Potential Hormonal Associations of Grandmaternal Care in Jamaica," *The Internet Journal of Biological Anthropology* 4, no. 1 (January 2010), http://doi.org/10.5580/104c .

48. Orit Taubman-Ben-Ari and Shirley Ben Shlomo, "Measuring Personal Growth of New Grandparents: A Practical Tool for Social Workers," *Research on Social Work Practice* 26, no. 6 (October 1, 2016): 704–711, https://doi.org/10.1177/1049731514564165.

49. Orit Taubman-Ben-Ari, Shirley Ben Shlomo, and Liora Findler, "Personal Growth and Meaning in Life among First-Time Mothers and Grandmothers," *Journal of Happiness Studies* 13, no. 5 (October 1, 2012): 1–20, https://doi.org /10.1007/s10902-011-9291-5.

50. Kobi Tourjeman, Israel Doron, and Miri Cohen,"Losing a Grandchild: The Mourning Experience of Grandparents in Israel," *Death Studies* 39, no. 8 (September 2015): 491–499, http//doi.org 10.1080/07481187.2014.970298.

51. See, for example Marcus Pembrey, Lars Olov Bygren, Gunnar Kaati, Sören Edvinsson, et al., "Sex-Specific, Male-Line Transgenerational Responses in Humans," *European Journal of Human Genetics* 14, no. 2 (February 2006): 159–166. doi: 10.1038/sj.ejhg.5201538; Lars Olov Bygren, Petter Tinghög, John Carstensen, Sören Edvinsson, et al., "Change in Paternal Grandmothers' Early Food Supply Influenced Cardiovascular Mortality of the Female Grandchildren," *BMC Genetics* 15, no. 12 (February 2014), https://doi.org/10.1186/1471-2156-15-12.

52. Eric M. Uslaner, "Where You Stand Depends upon Where Your Grandparents Sat: The Inheritability of Generalized Trust," *Public Opinion Quarterly* 72, no. 4 (January 2008): 739, https://doi.org/10.1093/poq/nfn058.

53. Casey Copen and Merril Silverstein, "Transmission of Religious Beliefs across Generations: Do Grandparents Matter?" *Journal of Comparative Family Studies* 38, no. 4 (Autumn 2007): 497–510, http://www.jstor.org/stable/41604175.

54. Jane C. Bittner, "Insights and Spending Habits of Modern Grandparents: A Look at African American and Hispanic/Latino Grandparents" (Washington, DC: AARP, August 2012), 19, https://www.aarp.org/content/dam/aarp/research/surveys_statistics/general/2012/In-

sights-and-Spending-Habits-of-Modern-Grandparents-A-Look-at-African-American-and-Hispanic-Latino-Grandparents-AARP.pdf.

55. Nachum Sicherman, George Loewenstein, Teresa Tavassoli, et al., "Grandma Knows Best: Family Structure and Age of Diagnosis of Autism Spectrum Disorder," *Autism* 22, no. 3 (February 2018): 368–376, doi: 10.1177/1362361316679632.

56. Jim Dryden, "Study of Grandmothers Seeks Clues about Genetics of Autism," Washington University School of Medicine in St. Louis, News Release, August 25, 2016. https://medicine.wustl.edu/news/study-grandmothers-seeks-clues-genetics-autism/.

57. Jocelyn A. Sze et al., "Greater Emotional Empathy and Prosocial Behavior in Late Life," *Emotion* 12, no. 5 (October 2012): 1129–1140, https://www.ncbi.nlm.nih.gov/pmc/articles/PMC3766763/.

58. Gillian Ragsdale, "Empathy in Old-Age: Less Heat and More Light," *Psychology Today*, April, 24, 2014, https://www.psychologytoday.com/blog/empathy/201404/empathy-in-old-age-less-heat-and-more-light; see the original study: Yao-Chu Chen et al., "Aging Is Associated with Changes in the Neural Circuits Underlying Empathy," *Neurobiology of Aging* 35, no. 4 (April 1, 2014): 827–836.

59. Steve Henson, "What Makes a Nightmare Sports Parent—And What Makes a Great One," *The PostGame* (web page), February 15, 2012, http://www.thepostgame.com/blog/more-family-fun/201202/what-makes-nightmare-sports-parent.

60. Christopher Wanjek, "Your Diet Affects Your Grandchildren's DNA, Scientists Say," *LiveScience* (web page), July 27, 2012, http://www.livescience.com/21902-diet-epigenetics-grandchildren.html; and Nicholette Zeliadt, "What Grandmothers Can Teach Science about Autism," *The Atlantic*, (November 14, 2016), https://www.theatlantic.com/health/archive/2016/11/grandmas-and-autism/507446/.

61. Isabelle Khoo, "Rachael Finch Child: Model Criticized for Kid-Free Weekends," *Huffington Post* (blog), May 12, 2016, https://www.huffingtonpost.ca/2016/05/12/rachael-finch-child_n_9932110.html.

62. Richard A. Settersten Jr., "The New Landscape of Adult Life: Road Maps, Signposts, and Speed Lines," *Research in Human Development* 4, no. 3–4 (July 2007): 245, https://doi.org/10.1080/15427600701663098.

63. Ruth Albrecht, "The Parental Responsibilities of Grandparents," *Marriage and Family Living* 16, no. 3 (August 1954): 203–204, https://doi.org/10.2307/348486.

64. Katherine F. Burn et al., "Role of Grandparenting in Postmenopausal Women's Cognitive Health: Results from the Women's Healthy Aging Project," *Menopause* 21, no. 10 (October 2014): 1069–1074, https://doi.org/10.1097GME.0000000000000236.

65. Kathy Kinser and Rebecca Parlakian, "Executive Summary: 7 Things You Should Know about Grandparents," Zero to Three Organization (web page), September 7, 2017, https://www.zerotothree.org/resources/1998-executive-summary-7-things-you-should-know-about-grandparents.

66. Lyn Craig and Bridget Jenkins, "The Composition of Parents' and Grandparents' Child-Care Time: Gender and Generational Patterns in Activity, Multi-Tasking and Co-Presence," *Ageing & Society* 36, no.4 (April 2016): 785–810, 804, http//doi.org 10.1017/S0144686X14001548.

67. Cheryl L. Lampkin, "Insights and Spending Habits of Modern Grandparents," (Washington, DC: AARP, March 2012), 11, https://www.aarp.org/content/dam/aarp/research/surveys_statistics/general/2012/Insights-and-Spending-Habits-of-Modern-Grandparents-AARP.pdf.

68. "Grandparents Investing in Grandchildren: The MetLife Study on How Grandparents Share Their Time, Values, and Money" (New York: MetLife Mature Market Institute and Generations United, September 2012), 6, https://www.metlife.com/assets/cao/mmi/publications/studies/2012/studies/MMIGrandparentsStudy_Web.pdf.

69. Fidelity Study cited in Kelley Holland, "Grandparents Are Paying for College—Again," *CNBC* (web page), June 5, 2014, http://www.cnbc.com/2014/06/05/s-are-paying-for-college—again.html.

70. Bill Spink, "Boomer Grandparents Give Back—Redefining Generation 'Me' (Pt. 2)," *DMW Direct*, March 9, 2012, http://www.dmwdirect.com/2012/03/the-grandparents-give-back-redefining-generation-me-pt-2/.

71. Alyson Krueger, "The New Tug of War over Baby Names," *New York Times*, October 3, 2015, https://www.nytimes.com/2015/10/04/fashion/your-choice-or-theirs-the-new-tug-of-war-over-baby-names.html.

72. Jean Chatzky, "Is Grandma Too Generous for Your Own Good?" *Money* 34, no. 10 (October 2005): 30–32, http://connection.ebscohost.com/c/articles/18245128/grandma-too-generous-your-own-good.

73. Kim Parker and Juliana Menasce Horowitz, *Family Support in Graying Societies: How Americans, Germans and Italians Are Coping with an Aging Population* (Washington, DC: Pew Research Center, May 21, 2015), 6, http://assets.pewresearch.org/wp-content/uploads/sites/3/2015/05/2015-05-21_family-support-relations_FINAL.pdf.

74. Robert D. Putnam, *Our Kids: The American Dream in Crisis* (New York: Simon & Schuster, 2015), 132.

75. Bittner, *Insights and Spending Habits*, 2.

76. U.S. Census Bureau, "10 Percent of Grandparents Live with a Grandchild," news release no. CB14-194, October 22, 2014, https://www.census.gov/newsroom/press-releases/2014/cb14-194.html.

77. Renee R. Ellis and Tavia Simmons, "Coresident Grandparents and Their Grandchildren: 2012," (Washington, DC: United States Census Bureau, October 2014): 16.

78. LaShawnDa Pittman, "How Well Does the 'Safety Net' Work for Family Safety Nets? Economic Survival Strategies among Grandmother Caregivers in Severe Deprivation," *The Russell Sage Foundation Journal of the Social Sciences* 1, no. 1 (November 2015): 93. http://www.jstor.org/stable/10.7758/rsf.2015.1.1.05

79. Jan. E. Mutchler, Lindsey A. Baker, and SeungAh Lee, "Grandparents Responsible for Grandchildren in Native-American Families," *Social Science Quarterly* 88, no. 4 (December 1, 2007): 1006, https://doi.org/10.1111 /j.1540-6237.2007.00514.x.

80. Esme Fuller-Thomson and Meredith Minkler, "Central American Grandparents Raising Grandchildren," *Hispanic Journal of Behavioral Sciences* 29, no. 1 (February 1, 2007): 14, https://doi.org/10.1177/0739986306293680.

81. "China's 'Left Behind' Kids Raised by Grandparents While Parents Earn in U.S." *PBS News Hour*, transcript, May 21, 2015, https://www.pbs.org/newshour/show/chinas-left-behind-children-will-join-parents-u-s.

82. William Ge and Andrew Adesman, "Grandparents Raising Grandchildren: A Primer for Pediatricians," *Current Opinion in Pediatrics* 29, no. 3 (June 2017): 379–384, https://doi.org/10.1097/MOP.0000000000000501.

83. Melanie R. Goodman and Satya P. Rao, "Grandparents Raising Grandchildren in a US-Mexico Border Community," *Qualitative Health Research* 17, no. 8 (October 2007): 1128, https://doi.org/10.1177/1049732307308457.

84. Bert Hayslip, Heidemarie Blumenthal, and Ashley Garner, "Health and Grandparent-Grandchild Well-Being: One-Year Longitudinal Findings for Custodial Grandfamilies," *Journal of Aging and Health* 26 (2014): 4, 561-562, doi: 10.1177/0898264314525664

85. Hayslip, Blumenthal, and Garner 575.

86. Goodman and Rao, "Grandparents Raising Grandchildren," 1134.

87. Eunju Lee, Michael Clarkson-Hendrix, and Yeonggeul Lee, "Parenting Stress of Grandparents and Other Kin as Informal Kinship Caregivers: A Mixed Methods Study," *Children and Youth Services Review* 69 (October 2016): 36, https://doi.org/10.1016/j.childyouth.2016.07.013.

88. Timothy Williams, "A Place for Grandparents Who Are Parents Again," *New York Times*, May 21, 2005, http://www.nytimes.com/2005/05/21/nyregion/a-place-for-grandparents-who-are-parents-again.html?_r=1.

89. Michael Winerip, "Grandpa Does More Than Baby-Sit," *New York Times*, December 10, 2009, http://www.nytimes.com/2009/12/13/fashion/13genb.html.

90. Kim Parker and Gretchen Livingston, "6 Facts about American Fathers" (Washington, DC: Pew Research Center, June 15, 2017), http://www.pewresearch.org/fact-tank/2017/06/15/fathers-day-facts/.

91. Craig and Jenkins, "The Composition of Parents and Grandparents' Child Care," 804.

92. Renee Stepler, "Led by Baby Boomers, Divorce Rates Climb for America's 50+ Population" (Washington, DC: Pew Research Center, March 9, 2017), http://www.pewresearch.org/fact-tank/2017/03/09/led-by-baby-boomers-divorce-rates-climb-for-americas-50-population/. In fact, the Baby Boomers are still divorcing at higher levels than their contemporaries at the same stage of life. "Grey" divorces, for those fifty and older, are on the rise.

93. David Weir, ed., *The Health and Retirement Study: Aging in the 21st Century: Challenges and Opportunities for Americans* (University of Michigan: Institute for Social Research, Survey Research Center, 2006), 22, http://hrsonline.isr.umich.edu/sitedocs/databook/inc/pdf/HRS-Aging-in-the-21St-Century.pdf.

94. Robin L. Lumsdaine and Stephanie J. C. Vermeer, "Retirement Timing of Women and the Role of Care Responsibilities for Grandchildren," *Demography* 52, no. 2 (April 2015): 452, https://doi.org/10.1007/s13524-015-0382-5.

95. Kelly Yang, "In China, It's the Grandparents Who 'Lean In,'" *The Atlantic*, September 30, 2013, https://www.theatlantic.com/china/archive/2013/09/in-china-its-the-grandparents-who-lean-in/280097/.

96. Gaby Hinsliff, "We Lumber Grandparents with the Care of Our Children—but It Has a Price," *The Guardian*, April 16, 2015, https://www.theguardian.com/commentisfree/2015/apr/16/crucial-role-grandparents-working-lives-older-women.

97. Giles Tremlett, "Spain's Burnt Out 'Babysitter Grandparents' Urged to Strike," *The Guardian*, September 24, 2010, https://www.theguardian.com/world/2010/sep/24/spain-grandparents-childcare-strike-union.

98. Meyer, *Grandmothers at Work*, 48.

99. Lesley Stahl, *Becoming Grandma: The Joys and Science of the New Grandparenting* (New York: Blue Rider Press, 2016), 44.

100. Rebecca Traister, *All the Single Ladies: Unmarried Women and the Rise of an Independent Nation* (New York: Simon & Schuster, 2016), 284.

101. Sarah A. Ruiz and Merril Silverstein, "Relationships with Grandparents and the Emotional Well-Being of Late Adolescent and Young Adult Grandchildren," *Journal of Social Issues* 63, no. 4 (December 1, 2007): 793–808, https://doi.org/10.1111/j.1540-4560.2007.00537.x.

102. Charlotte J. Patterson, Susan Hurt, and Chandra D. Mason, "Families of the Lesbian Baby Boom: Children's Contact with Grandparents and Other Adults," *American Journal of Orthopscyhiatry* 68, no. 3 (July 1998): 398, https://doi.org/10.1037/h0080348.

103. Sharon Jayson, "Need a Babysitter? Don't Count on Grandma," *Well* (blog), *New York Times*, August 9, 2016, https://well.blogs.nytimes.com/2016/08/09/need-a-babysitter-dont-count-on-grandma/?_r=0.

104. Judith A. Seltzer and Jenjira J. Yahirun, "Diversity in Old Age: The Elderly in Changing Economic and Family Contexts" (New York: Russell Sage Foundation, American Communities Project of Brown University, November 6, 2013), 43–44, http://www.s4.brown.edu/us2010/Data/Report/report11062013.pdf.

Chapter Three

Chasing Visibility

LeBron James is probably the last image that comes to mind when thinking of grandmas. After attending enough of his games in the Cleveland area, though, what becomes hard to miss is a group of elderly ladies who refer to themselves as "The LeBron James Grandmothers' Fan Club." Founded in 2006, the club has over 100 members and is featured in media stories and social media celebrating his wins.[1] Though their main connection is their devotion to and fandom for LeBron James, they also meet regularly to plan volunteer activities and bond as a group.[2]

The LeBron Grannies represent a group bonding through the commonality of being grandmothers. They use their grandmotherly image both to subvert public expectations and to do good works. Many other grandparents, though, remain invisible because they cannot serve in the grandparent role that many in our society envision as ideal. This chapter explores what happens after the emergence of a new type of grandparent lifestyle, which not all grandparents can achieve. The visibility of grandparents ranges from people who have been denied the ability to grandparent to those who use the image of the grandparent to advocate for other causes.

INVISIBILITY

Some grandparents, because they do not conform to the stereotypical image of grandparents, are often shut out from the cultural celebration of grandparenting, and they sometimes are barred from developing a relationship with their own grandchildren.

Caitlyn Jenner, an Olympic-winning athlete and part of the Kardashian family made famous by reality television, received much international attention when she announced in 2015 that she was transitioning from a man to a woman. In a more recent episode of the show *Keeping Up with the Kardashians*, Caitlyn's daughter (by marriage to Kris Jenner) Kourtney was talking to her own daughter Penelope about a story. Kourtney was surprised when Penelope said a story character reminded her of her grandma, referring to Caitlyn. Kourtney confesses on the show that she never thought of Caitlyn as a grandmother.[3] When grandparents do not conform to dominant gender norms in society, they often face struggles to identify and situate their roles within family structures.

Researchers are studying the challenges that grandparents of non-normative families face with interviews of grandparents in these roles. Nancy Orel writes:

> This invisibility of the nonbiological grandmother's role caused conflicts for the lesbian couples with grandchildren. Often the biological grandmothers were jealous of the co-grandmother's freedom from the assumed responsibilities of being a grandparent, but at other times, biological grandparents were angry at their partner's lack of interest in the grandchildren.[4]

Within a culture that currently is trying to understand how to handle people and families that do not conform to stereotypical gender roles, those that do not fit into these norms face either challenges or invisibility. Another study explored LGBTQ families' frustration with the lack of public language to describe their family relationships:

> The participants in our study "do family" in rich and diverse ways; yet the traditional dominant discourse about family—that families involve two heterosexual parents with children—continued to influence the way many of the children and grandparents understood family and presented their family to the outside world.[5]

Still, grandparents, who often came from heteronormative backgrounds themselves and had initial confusion about the role structures in the families, worked hard to develop strong and key identities within their families.[6] Some people are trying to combat these obstacles. A museum exhibit at the Boston Children's Museum works to make transgender grandparenting more visible. In a display titled "Mimi's Family," Mimi is both a grandmother and a transgender woman, and children are encouraged to notice ways in which their lives are similar to and different from her grandchildren's.[7]

Unfortunately, society is still far from acceptance, as indicated in part by the lack of legal protections for these grandparents. One grandparent couple I interviewed discussed how all their experiences with their grandchildren were similar, whether they were from a heteronormative home or a same-sex family. They did express the worry that their daughter, who does not have a biological connection to her children, should begin formal legal adoption proceedings to protect the whole family, given the fraught political times. They even offered their daughter and her wife financial support for the legal fees because of how important they thought this was. Grandparents of LGBTQ families worry that, if a legal connection to children is threatened, they will lose all rights to their grandchildren as well. While for some, access to grandchildren and being identified as a grandparent is taken for granted, for others, it is a role that must be negotiated. Grandparenting is likely to adapt as our cultural expectations on gender and sex shift.

ALIENATED GRANDPARENTS

Some grandparents experience the grandparent lifestyle in which they have a choice as to how involved they are in their grandchildren's lives, while others have had to take on the responsibility of full-time caregiving. However, some grandparents are denied a chance to participate in the experience of grandparenting. These alienated grandparents have no control over their relationship with their grandchildren. Dr. Amy Baker, an expert in parental alienation and parent-child relationships, explored with me the effect of alienation on grandparents. She says that how they are impacted depends often on the type of alienation that they experience:

> In addition to not having contact with their grandchildren, they've either lost a child which is very painful, or they are cut off from their child which is very painful, or they have to witness their child being cut off from their child, which is also very painful. It's not just the loss of their grandchild but these other losses that have to get figured in.

Since the experience of the alienated grandparent is not universal, it is challenging to find ways to intercede or understand the sense of loss.

Sometimes grandparents who have had a strong relationship with their grandchildren lose that relationship at some point. I interviewed Joyce, who was surprised to become a grandparent. She learned that the mother of her son's child, whom she did not know, was going to jail. She and her son, who was still living at home at the time, took responsibility for her grandson, and later a granddaughter as well. She provided much of the care on and off for the coming years, until her son abruptly cut her off from them after he had remarried and taken over primary care of the children. Despite legal efforts to gain grandparental rights, which were eventually granted to her but not enforced, she has a strained and limited relationship with her grandchildren. Joyce expressed her frustration with her son, who won't let her into the lives of her grandchildren, and the legal system, which acknowledges the rights grandparents have for visitation but has no real system to enforce those rights, particularly when the children are estranged.

The grandmothers I interviewed often look for answers either within themselves, from their families, or from some larger force as to why they were cut off. Most cannot find a single moment that offers insight as to why they were cut off, despite many hours of examining. They go through cycles of blaming themselves, their own children, or the spouses of their children. One woman, Bernadette, ultimately faults her daughter-in-law for the estrangement. Bernadette describes her excitement at finding out that she was going to be a grandmother. She saw a difference, though, in her daughter-in-law's own mother: "She didn't have the same grandmotherly instinct. I would go up and visit, iron for her, let her take care of the baby. As the baby got older, I got more comfortable to him, bought my own stroller and higher chair. We fell in love with each other. We just bonded completely."

She ended up as a regular additional caregiver in his life, picking him up from daycare and watching him when he was sick. She noticed moments when the baby's mother would see how bonded they were: "Because I was fun, he wanted to hang out with me." She describes the difference between being a grandmother and a mother as partly contributing to the problem: "As a mother, I was always worried about the house, and the groceries. The grandmothers are the ones who get to have fun with the kids." Ultimately, Bernadette says her daughter-in-law felt that the bond went too far, and the relationship between the two deteriorated: "She has yelled at me, screamed at me." Though she now has a second grandchild, she describes her daughter-in-law as purposely keeping the child away from her and her husband. She feels helpless: "I go between accepting it, not liking it, but accepting it, or wanting to call them up and scream at them, which I would never do." She has become extremely depressed, and she does not see a solution in the immediate future.

Research on grandparent ties supports the idea that grandparents are more likely to have the strongest ties with the children of their daughters.[8] One study on offspring and in-law relationships indicates, "In particular, given the potentially tenuous link grandparents may have to the children of their son, their ties to the daughter-in-law may influence relationships with these grandchildren."[9] When Bernadette's relationship with her daughter-in-law suffered, she lost the link to her grandchildren. Like other grandmothers in similar positions, Bernadette finds herself wistful when hearing about the relationship her friends have with their grandchildren:

> I had some friends over Sunday night and they said they would die if we had that situation. They can just go whenever they want. I would be happy if we got to see them every two weeks. My friends take them to museums, to the park, to the library. They stop in and have lunch. It's hard for me to have my friends over, and that's basically what they talk about. I had to take my pictures down. I couldn't keep thinking about them.

Another woman, Alisa, was able to spend time with her granddaughter the first six months of her life. She and her husband took care of their granddaughter every weekend and had so much fun with her, until she was abruptly removed from their lives. She says her friends do not really understand what she's going through, and she describes how it "hurts to talk to them about it. They got the bond and you don't." She has found others who are in similar situations and who can relate to her. She also has tried to use a surrogate grandparent website to find another child to spend time with. So far, though, nothing has worked out, mostly because of her geographic location in the Pacific Northwest.

To help herself and other grandparents in similar circumstances, Joyce started an Alienated Grandparents group. "We meet once a month for two hours and we have new people every time," she said. "We started out being a grandparent alienation group, but it's grown to become a family support group (with a mix of people). It is a helpful group because a lot of the people still thought they were the only ones who were in the situation." Joyce describes the shock that many in the group feel from the contrast between how they saw family when they were raising their children and today. Joyce says, "It's not something I would have ever thought of doing when I had my kids, keeping them away from family. Something in society has definitely happened." One exercise the group has done involves looking over family trees and noting their estranged relatives. Joyce thinks a new trend is emerging: "It's happened before, but it didn't have a name and it didn't happen often. I don't know if the 30- or 40-year-old kids were entitled when they were growing up and they had no respect for the parents. Unfortunately, it's going to be the norm for my grandchildren as well. They are being groomed to know that family doesn't matter." In fact, it is unclear whether the phenomenon of the alienated grandparent is a new trend or is just being reported more now.

This group of grandparents does not receive much attention in culture. One reason may be because it does not conform to expectations of the grandparenting experience. The stories from this group are not happy or satisfying, and they often are relegated to the background. There are few places in which they can share these experiences, and many feel ashamed about their inability to conform to the social expectations of the grandparent experience. Another reason may be that many people have ambiguous feelings about what rights and responsibilities grandparents should have within a family; the issue often is relegated to being merely a family problem, rather than recognizing a disenfranchised group of people. Yet the psychological issues that affect these groups can be profound.[10] Many of the grandparents I spoke with feel an experience similar to grieving over a familial loss.

Organizations are working to raise awareness and provide support for these types of groups. I spoke with Amanda, who is the founder of the

Florida-based Alienated Grandparents Anonymous (AGA). Her organization lends support and resources to those who have been cut off from their grandchildren. She says their mission is "to help people know that they are not the only people going through this." She compares this alienation to a cancer, mainly for the lack of visibility this group has received. Amanda says that when she talks with new members, they often describe the feeling of being relieved that they are no longer isolated in their experience. Amanda sees grandparent alienation becoming a global phenomenon. The AGA has members within the United States and has expanded to twenty-one other countries outside the United States.

Amanda has collected many stories of toxic relationships that have alienated grandparents from their children, but she also cites foster and adoption systems that ignore and isolate grandparents from families as a problem. Through advice and counsel, her organization has successfully helped grandparents develop relationships with their grandchildren. Amanda thinks that alienated grandparents are a growing trend; she speculates that an entitled generation, unresolved childhood issues, and shifts in family structures as people move outside small towns or the country have contributed to this problem. Whatever the causes, the AGA is working to make these grandparents more visible.

LEGAL WORLD

American courts are deliberating over which rights and privileges should be extended to grandparents. Estrangements between grandparents and grandchildren have resulted in court challenges, where the law has had to determine what constitutes a family and what types of familial obligations are inherent rights. This leads to questions about what is a grandparent and how their role and privileges should be defined.

Some states are passing legislation that guarantees grandparents certain visitation rights for their grandchildren. As parents have challenged these statutes, interesting cases have appeared before the courts. For example, a Florida law allowed for grandparent visitation rights in certain cases, including when the marriage of a child's parents ended or when a parent died. Despite a legal challenge, grandparent visitation in these cases was upheld in 1990.[11] In another case, *Beagle v. Beagle*, a grandparent sued when parents denied a request for visitation, but the courts ruled against the case because they found that the request invaded the parents' right to privacy.[12] In *Troxel v. Granville*, grandparents in Washington State sued to increase their visitation rights with the children of their deceased son, but courts denied their request because it violated the parents' privacy rights.[13] In a later case, *Butler v. Harris*, the California Supreme Court ruled that if a father supported grandparent visitation, even though the mother opposed it, the grandparent had a right to visit, and the grandparent visitation statute in California was upheld.[14]

Despite this decision, it is apparent in the dissents, discussions, and court hearings that questions about grandparents' fundamental rights to see a child remain. The state of Tennessee provided an early model for grandparent visitation as early as the 1960s. Yet since the late 1990s, court battles have questioned at what point a grandparent deserves these rights, including whether a child and grandparent have a significant relationship in the first place.[15] In one case, *Carr v. McMillan*, the courts found that since the grandmother had served as a mother figure and provided daily care when the child lost his mother, visitation would be beneficial to the child.[16] In July 2017, a Michigan court of appeals ruled that grandparents' rights interfered with parents' rights to raise their children as they saw fit. It determined that, if both parents were deemed to be "fit parents," then it was up to them to decide whether or not the grandparents could see their children.[17]

Many of these cases rest on whether visitation is in the best interest of the child, without evaluating whether the grandparent would benefit from visitation rights and developing a relationship as well. The grandparent relationship is relegated not as a guarantee but as one that is largely granted by parents. While in the past, the primacy and finality of parental decisions might have made sense, now that grandparents are living longer, providing financial and emotional assistance to the family, and as grandparenting itself has become a more sharply defined phase of life, there may be more pressure to resolve the disconnect between those who are allowed to experience grandparenting and those who are not.

FILLING THE GRANDCHILD DEFICIT

While the law has struggled to negotiate boundaries of what the formal role of grandparents should be in the lives of parents and children, the consumer marketplace has offered a more flexible way to solve grandparenting problems. Consumer products and services can offer interesting alternatives for those who desire but have been unable to serve a grandparent role.

Some people miss out on being grandparents because they have not had children themselves. While people are living longer, giving them the potential to be a grandparent for a longer period, some worry that declining birth rates both globally and in the United States will create a shortage of children, and grandchildren, creating a "grandparent gap." Susanna Schrosbdorff, an editorial manager at *Time* magazine, worries about a "grandparent deficit." She writes that delaying having children could cause problems not only for becoming a parent, but also for being an effective grandparent: "We knew that three or four years could make a huge difference in our fertility, but it turned out that three or four years could also mean the difference between a grandmother who can take a toddler to the beach and one who can't lift her newest grandbaby out of a kiddie pool because of arthritis."[18]

The concept of a biological clock received much attention as women entered the workforce and were forced to negotiate their job demands with the limits of fertility. More recently, studies have shown that the biological clock applies to men as well, as children conceived from older sperm may have health problems. Now, studies showing the positive impact grandparents have on the lives of their grandchildren have stoked the idea of a "grandparent clock," or the need to become a grandparent before it is too late.

Because of the powerful and positive role of grandparents, more people are seeking out a grandparental relationship. Some potential grandparents are taking matters into their own hands, offering to pay for their daughters to freeze their eggs.[19] Some people find and build their own relationships. One woman I interviewed, Connie, told me about meeting her neighbors and developing such a warm relationship with them that they became like family. Connie said, "She invited me into the delivery room to see the first baby being born and then the second." She became their "nana," a name they decided on that reflects their closeness and the grandmother role Connie plays in their relationship. As the girls grow, she babysits for them, lets them sleep overnight in her home, and has even volunteered at their pre-schools. She says she plays "the Nana role. I let them take over the house. We are always doing something for them because they are ours." Connie joins many other families before her who, over time, develop relationships organically out of familiarity and need. More recently, though, more formal grandparent relationships are being created. The grandparent deficit has inspired organizations to fill this need in society.

Outside the United States, some organizations connect couples who have no grandparent in their lives with those who want to be grandparents. When Cate moved from Germany to Australia, she created the "Find a Grandparent" Organization. She explained to me what had given her the idea for this: "We don't have any family here. When our children were little, I had a feeling that they were missing out on an important experience growing up without grandparents. I spent a lot of time with my grandma and really benefited from it, so I wanted our children to have the same experience." Modeling surrogate grandparents that are found within local councils in Germany, she created a website to help match older Australians with families seeking a grandparental figure. She has noticed a pattern in that people often seek to replace a missing relationship in their life. "Many families know exactly what they are looking for," she said. "So a single mum might look for a surrogate granddad to give the children a male role model, and another mum might be looking for a surrogate grandma after she lost her own mother."

In the United States, the Facebook group "Surrogate Grandparents USA" helps connect potential surrogate grandparents with grandchildren. Donna, the creator of the Facebook group, had personal reasons for creating the site: "My husband and I are alienated grandparents. I was looking for something to help fill a void in our lives." Though she looked into foster grandparenting, she found the rules too formalized for her taste, requiring a commitment of forty hours per week minimum and mentoring children in classrooms. Instead, she wanted to mimic the more casual relationships grandparents often have, where they can decide with parents their level of involvement. After researching models she had seen in other countries, she created the Facebook group, which now has over two thousand members enrolled. "It's a mixture of everybody," she said. "Alienated grandparents, adult children who have alienated themselves from their parents, families seeking grandparents because they have lost them from death or are too far away." Like the Australian group, Donna found that some parents seeking grandparents wanted to re-create the positive experience they remembered having grown up with their own grandparents. For the grandparents-to-be, it might be their only opportunity to experience grandparenting. Donna now has about an equal number of families seeking grandparents and grandparents seeking grandchildren. In the spirit of the casual and voluntary nature of the group, she lets families work out their own arrangements.

Arleen was a visitor to the surrogate grandparent group but found that she couldn't find a family through it that was local enough and wanted her level of engagement. Instead, she has found some solace from missing her granddaughter, who lives across the country, by forming a relationship with a young boy of an international couple who had just moved to the United States for work. She realized that she could help the family by being an extra person to babysit, and the child could share her everyday experiences since she could not share these with her own grandchild. "I don't want to be his nanny," Arleen says. "I want to have a relationship with him where I'm more of a grandparent type. I'm there for him. I show him how to do things."

The concept of borrowing a grandparent represents a key shift in the understanding of grandparenting. Instead of being part of an evolutionary process that works toward the goal of extending the family, the shift separates the practice of grandparenting from that process. Grandparenting itself becomes a distinguishable and unique stage rather than merely a part of aging. However, a market-generated service is not the same as a natural, organic one. In *The Outsourced Self*, Arlie Russell Hochschild describes a world where the outsourcing of practices originally relegated to the family is shifting how we see American society. She writes, "In the face of the market's depersonalization of our bonds with others, we do what we can, consciously or not, to repersonalize them, to make the market feel less like a market."[20] Grandparenting moves from something for which there was no choice in its selection, to a consumer model where grandparents can be selected for the purposes they may serve, such as providing a father figure or childcare. No longer bound by the grandparents someone inherits, people can design their own grandparent to fill their specific needs. The practice of offering a surrogate grandparent to those who have lost their grandparent or live too far away from them can help fill a void in people's lives. At the same time, the reforming of the grandparent experience creates an entirely new environment. One can imagine parents rejecting their own parents to act as grandparents in favor of a surrogate that better serves their needs. Taken to its extreme, the roles and purposes of grandparenting itself may also shift. When one's own grandparents aren't fulfilling one's needs, will it generate anxiety that they could be replaced at any moment? Will this drive the desire to be the perfect grandparent? This commodified experience envisions an ideal grandparent relationship, keeping invisible or labeled as deviant those grandparents who are unable to or do not want to conform to that ideal.

MEDIATING GRANDPARENTING

An online viral video in the spring of 2017 involved a professor struggling to continue a live interview with the BBC from his home office while his young children rushed into the room and interrupted. Though many viewers commented on the professor's attempt (and failure) to manage his work-life balance, less discussed was the reaction from the professor's own parents. As the children's grandparents live far away, they feared they were to blame for the disastrous interview since they had become used to live chats with them on a regular basis. While the father was being interviewed, the children thought he was talking with their grandparents.[21] While this family's sudden attention may not be the norm, it is becoming pretty standard for grandparents to build and maintain relationships with their grandchildren through social media and other technologies. For many, it's a chance to enhance their relationship often hampered by distance. Technology can be empowering for those seeking to achieve the grandparent lifestyle, but it also presents new challenges in understanding the social and unwritten rules of these new media.

Globalization is changing how families exist, and in turn, the concept of grandparenting is changing. To be sure, this is not the first time in history that grandparents and grandchildren have been separated due to migration patterns. Yet in this period of time, with access to modern technology and travel possibilities, a new type of grandparent has emerged: the transnational grandparent. Grandparents play an important role in families, connecting grandchildren to extended kin and instilling a sense of obligation to familial ties.[22] For some, mediated technology offers new ways to connect to grandchildren. A Johnson & Johnson campaign targets Middle Eastern grandparents unable to stay in touch regularly with their grandchildren because of a lack of access to or knowledge of social media. Included in the ad are grandparents lamenting that they cannot regularly see their grandchildren. A statement appears on the screen: "Knowing the vast majority of grandparents in the Middle East are not familiar with technology and therefore aren't engaged in any social platform." In response, the company announces they have created a "Grandparent Frame." The app is joined with a digital picture frame, allows parents to regularly load pictures remotely. When the grandparents see the photos of their grandchildren in the frame, they smile, laugh, and cry, and the grandmother picks up the frame and kisses it.

Technology, though, brings with it a double-edged sword, instilling both a sense of connection and feelings of longing for a deeper, more physical connection. In a study on Israeli-American grandparents and grandchildren, grandparents explored their feelings of "cultural alienation" because they can see aspects of their grandchildren's life that they are not able to participate in directly.[23] Simultaneously, they are proud of their ability to extend their grandchildren's global worldliness by exposing them to other cultures and places: "The grandparents also provide the transnational sojourns that expose the children to the experience of a culture different from their Israeli home, an experience that is also crucial to their future success as global citizens."[24]

Some mediated technologies allow grandparents to find creative ways to be virtually present in the lives of their grandchildren. Mihaela Nedelcu's study of Romanian migrants in Switzerland and Canada found that conferencing software devices, such as Skype, that are left on continuously allow them to be continually present in the family during everyday activities. They even can provide a form of long-distance babysitting: "Many of the interviewed grandparents highlight that ICT mediated communication routines brings a transnational dimension in their everyday life, replacing absence and separation by a feeling of usefulness and ongoing solidarity that give sense to their life, especially after retirement."[25] At the same time, the technology can produce anxiety in that grandparents can help only so much without being physically present. Technology, while having the potential to forge a new type of relationship, also creates another level of grandparenting in which these grandparents have a virtual, less physical presence with their grandchildren. The grandparents themselves, though, extend their matriarch and patriarch roles into not just being the cultural historians of the families but also cultural tourists and tour guides as well, working to bridge physical space by creating an emotional attachment to places and families that are now distantly connected.

With the Trump administration pushing for more immigration restrictions, transnational grandparenting within the United States is becoming even more challenging. Grandparents and grandchildren, however, are rising to the challenge of making their relationships and needs more visible. One Iranian American journalist, Mona Khalifeh, wrote about how the initial Trump administration travel ban would affect her ability to see her grandmother: "She's the matriarch of our family, a touchstone that we look to for sound advice and the reassurance that everything will be alright. She's our family's feminist role model, a woman who raised three children on her own." In a different version of the travel ban, the Supreme Court agreed to allow a scaled-back version, only allowing people with a "bona fide relationship" to come into the country. Immediately, the administration ordered that grandparents did not fit into that relationship. Later, an appeals court in Hawaii decided that grandparents "are the epitome of close family relationships. The government's definition excludes them. That simply cannot be."[26] The hashtag #GrandparentsAreNotTerrorists accompanied pictures people posted of themselves in loving relationships with grandparents or photos of their grandparents with captions such as "Is this the face of terror?" The campaign was a way to counter the policy and raise awareness of how the ban seems ridiculous when paired with images of elderly, innocent grandparents.[27]

In addition to allowing new access to grandparents, new media also serve to heighten the roles of grandparents. Valerie Frissen's research on information and communication technologies (ICTs), including devices like mobile phones, demonstrates that they play an important role in a new stage of life, the "rush hour of life," when partners must balance their work and home life activities.[28] Once they are connected to mobile devices, grandparents, intentionally and sometimes reluctantly, become a part of this rush hour. A grandparent is another family member to rely on to balance domestic tasks.[29] Many families I spoke with told me how they can text, call, or email their parents to assist with caregiving. Grandparents participate with other parents (and grandparents) in carpools, exchanging texts, directions, and drop-off and pick-up schedules. A changing media environment allows for new possibilities for communication and integration of the grandparent in the daily life of the family, but it also disrupts what had once been their solitary time. As children grow older, grandparents and grandchildren are able to use new technologies to bypass parents and develop their own private form of communication. Connie told me that after her granddaughter received her own email account, they were able to make plans directly on their own. She says that now they sometimes communicate in advance to decide what they want to do and then they separately go about convincing the child's mother. Another grandmother, Louise, described the moment when her granddaughter started emailing her on her own: "It is changing now with my older granddaughter, who is eight now, using the technology independently. She can write the messages independently, without her mother's knowledge, and read my messages. It is just the beginning of what may be frequent technology use." Louise, though, describes having to learn the new rules for these technologies. At one point her granddaughter asked her when she was next visiting. Louise answered:

> In a couple of days. She responded with one word: cool. And then I didn't reply to that because with an adult you wouldn't be bothered to make a response. She became very anxious having not heard a response. What I should have done was respond in a cute way—double cool or super cool. She might have chosen to drop it or not, and I think what the grandparent has to do is let the child decide when the thread has ended. In the future, I will respond even if there is no response needed.

The technology not only allows grandparents unfiltered communication with their grandchildren, it also enables parents to avoid having to mediate the relationship between their children and parents. One mother I spoke to, Ann, describes how her daughters' emergent use of their mobile phones eased her in-law relationship: "It made things so much less tense with my in-laws because the children could now text their grandparents and make arrangements to meet for dinner, and I never had to interact with them anymore." On the other hand, Ann also found that her daughter would sometimes screen her calls but never those of her maternal grandmother: "My daughter wasn't answering my texts, but I know she never screens her grandmother, so I asked her to text her and sure enough, she texts her right back." The technology allows for deeper and more personal connections but also can be a challenge for parents who previously were the gatekeepers for these relationships.

Sometimes the rules of new technologies needed to be clarified. A mother I spoke with was particularly frustrated when she found her mother-in-law posting pictures of the grandchildren's adventures on her social media account. The mother felt her mother-in-law was inferring she was the one who took the children on these adventures instead of the mother and was resentful that the grandmother implied a type of relationship that her daughter-in-law felt she had not earned. Some grandparents feel a pressure to compete with their friends and push boundaries, and others may not even be aware boundaries exist in their quest to create a digital representation of grandparenting and conform to the idealized grandparent experience.

THE GRANNY CARD

The consumer market and the widespread use of social media to promote grandparenting relationships and images makes the grandparenting stage of life noticeable, valuable, and more easily attained. It is no surprise then that it would become a tool of persuasion in the political world. When Senator Jeff Flake wanted to denounce the Trump administration, he did so in a speech on the Senate floor in which he referred to his obligation as a grandparent to preserve the country for the next generation. He said, "I have children and grandchildren to answer to, and so, Mr. President, I will not be complicit or silent."[30] The grandparent duty has become a technique to soften an image or a weapon to push for a political agenda, and this strategy has been used particularly among female politicians of late.

In the political realm, the grandmother politician is emerging as a recurring figure. Whether it's Hillary Clinton deliberately using her grandma status to soften her image, House Minority Leader Nancy Pelosi talking about her role as a grandmother for rhetorical purposes, or Sarah Palin reluctantly adapting the grandmother image, grandmothers are now plentiful in politics. Some see the emergence of grandmotherhood in politics as a response to women's challenges in the workforce. Liza Mundy writes that older women, post-children, have a different experience than women of child-bearing age: "women, often held back in midlife by domestic responsibilities, are in many ways suited to shift into high gear at a later age than men—to have it all, as the saying goes, by having it at different times."[31] Older women can take on high-power jobs in the workforce without the demands of childcare, allowing them to progress professionally at this later stage in life. Earlier, a maternal wall prevented them from advancing, whether due to the demands of motherhood or the unfounded patriarchal perception that they were distracted with family obligation. In fact, political careers may be ideally suited for older women because running for office does not necessarily require a specific type of training or experience that other professions might.[32] These women can use grandmotherhood in a way that they haven't been able to use motherhood.

In the 2008 U.S. presidential campaign, one reason Sarah Palin, then governor of Alaska, was selected to be John McCain's running mate was to use her "momness" to appeal to voters across America. Indeed, much of the initial media coverage focused on her being a mom to five children, including a child with Down syndrome. Media coverage embraced her maternal nature but questioned whether she would be able to do the job of vice president while raising young children.[33] Once she became a grandmother, politicians and media continued to critique Palin. Unlike Nancy Pelosi or Hillary Clinton, who were able to use their grandmother image to help soften their public persona, Palin became a grandmother unexpectedly, due to the pregnancy of her teenage daughter.

News media did not publicly embrace the role. In fact, during the 2008 campaign, Sarah Palin herself and the news media rarely portrayed Palin as a grandmother-to-be. Instead, they focused on her role as mother of a pregnant teenager, and she used the opportunity to reinforce her own views against abortion. It was only more recently, after she became a grandmother for the third time, that media coverage began to embrace her grandmother role. A *New York Post* article titled "Nobody Does the 'Cool Grandma' Look Like Sarah Palin" discussed a recent visit to the White House where she appeared, "looking oh-so-trendy in an off-the-shoulder white lace top."[34] Palin is now more public about her connection to the grandmother role and politics. When Hillary Clinton announced that she was going to be a grandmother, Palin used it as an opportunity to inform Clinton, and the public, that she would change her mind on abortion once she became a grandmother. In an interview with *Extra*, Palin said:

> Her daughter Chelsea is pregnant with the baby. It's a real baby, you know, it's not some disposable somethin' and I know that's gonna be controversial, but those who perhaps get in the position now as a parent or a grandparent, they realize that sanctity of life, how innocent, how precious it is. And of all places, it should be in the womb that these babies are protected. So maybe even on a social issue like that she'll open her eyes.[35]

Palin also made the statement that "anyone who is a grandparent really starts looking further down the road. We start thinking about things like 17 trillion dollar debt that our nation is under and what we're going to hand that to our grandkids for them to pay off."[36] In this way, Palin is challenging Hillary Clinton to live up to what she claims is the responsibility of a grandparent. Palin also promotes the idea that being a grandmother naturally moves one to become more conservative. Some have found that the grandmother image can imply a conservative viewpoint, no matter what the actual perspectives of the candidate may be.[37] Simply being older presents to people the image of a settled-in conservative rather than someone open to change.

For Hillary Clinton, becoming a grandmother represented a chance to transform her image. Clinton was widely criticized throughout the campaign as anti-feminine and anti-maternal.[38] As a result of sexism in our culture and within media coverage of her campaign, Clinton constantly had to soften her image to appear more palatable to the public. Becoming a grandmother presented a new opportunity for rebranding her image. Even prior to her run in the 2016 campaign, Clinton began to embrace her grandmother role in public. Media coverage questioned whether Clinton becoming a grandmother might make her choose not to run for president.[39] For many women, moving past the childbearing stage to the grandmother stage might put to rest the question of having to choose work over family. News media and political opponents, however, positioned Clinton yet again as having to choose between two options—being a grandmother or being president—when there is no rational reason why she couldn't be both. This is not a question that is asked of men running for president who are also becoming grandparents.

Despite these questions from critics, Clinton continued to use her granddaughter Charlotte's birth as a chance to relish this new role publicly. In interviews, she reiterated how spending time with her granddaughter makes her want to make the world better.[40] During her run for the 2016 presidency, Hillary Clinton explained in an interview for Quora, a community website, how being a grandmother would make her a better politician: "Being a grandmother also makes you think about the future, and I'm constantly thinking to myself, 'How can I make sure this precious little girl has every opportunity in the world?' More than anything, I want to make sure she grows up in a country that is peaceful and prosperous—one that gives everyone an opportunity to live up to his or her potential."[41] Clinton used the hashtag #GrandmothersKnowBest in a post about vaccines: "The science is clear: The earth is round, the sky is blue, and #vaccineswork. Let's protect all our kids." During the campaign, Clinton appealed directly to Latina grandmothers with a post on her campaign website titled "7 Things Hillary Clinton Has in Common with Your Abuela." The influence of grandmothers within Hispanic and Latina culture was noticed by Clinton and the Democratic Party, who saw this group as a key force for turnout. Jeremy Peters reported that their goal was "leveraging the unique influence and respect that older women command among Hispanics."[42] Yet not all found her appeals to be authentic enough. She was accused of "Hispandering," and people responded with the hashtag #NotMyAbuela.[43] Some critics even mocked her for planning to enforce a "Granny State."[44]

Nancy Pelosi has used the grandmother image to help support a political career in which she can be seen as caring and nurturing. An article on *Grandparents.com* describes Pelosi as a "Power Nana," telling readers: "Building a better future for our children and grandchildren is what drives me to do the work I do each day. I believe that my work in Congress is a continuation of my work as a mother and grandmother."[45] Pelosi used the image of the grandmother to make political appeals in the 2017 health-care debate. In one speech she warned, "If you're a senior, you know almost half of Medicaid is about long-term healthcare. Do you want grandma living in the guest room?"[46] Of course, even cultivating the grandmother image cannot inoculate Pelosi from attacks. Herman Cain criticized her for not wanting grandma in the guest room: "Nancy Pelosi knows how you feel about your Grandma. You think she's old and annoying. At this point, she's just a big ol' pain in the rump. You don't want Grandma living in your guest room, do you? Of course you don't. Grandma is awful."[47] Another conservative author threatened to expose "the Pelosi-as-children-loving-grandmother deception."[48]

In the political world, grandmotherhood can be seen as both a tool and a weapon. It becomes a tool in promoting the type of maternal thinking posed by feminist scholars such as Sara Ruddick, who writes about feminist motherhood. She argues that, because of women's constant involvement in the lives of children, they learn practices that make them think differently about the world:

> I speak about a mother's thought—the intellectual capacities she develops, the judgments she makes, the metaphysical attitudes she assumes, the values she affirms. A mother engages in a discipline. That is, she asks certain questions rather than others; she establishes criteria for the truth, adequacy, and relevance of proposed answers; and she cares about the findings she makes and can act on.[49]

It follows, then, that a world run by grandmothers would take maternal thinking even further. In this way, Pelosi can use her role as a grandmother to articulate what others may perceive as a nurturing agenda. For Clinton, embracing the grandmother role becomes a type of second chance, where she can replace her image of being too masculine with one of a grandmother who is a leader that knows best. Being a grandma is a chance for politicians to assure the public that, just by the very nature of that status, they will have the best interests of the population in mind. At the same time, others can use the grandmotherly image to attack opponents. Sometimes they claim the grandmother image opponents generate is inauthentic, such as Clinton's appeal to the Abuelitas or Pelosi's use of her image. At other times, they are criticized for not being grandmotherly enough, such as when Palin challenged Clinton to become more grandmotherly in her political views. Once this image is used for these purposes, it can become difficult to reclaim. Politicians, capitalizing on grandmotherly maternal thinking that the public assumes applies to them, turn being a grandmother into a political act.

Maternal thinking is also used by many with an activist agenda. In 2008, comedian Sarah Silverman produced a campaign designed to mobilize the elderly to vote for Barack Obama. The hook of the campaign targeted young people to persuade their grandparents who live in Florida to vote. Titled "The Great Schlep," it was produced in conjunction with the Jewish Council for Education and Research. The announcement started with the question "If you knew that visiting your grandparents could change the world, would you do it?"[50] The ads even suggested that grandchildren use their visits as collateral: "You don't have to use facts, use threats. There's nobody more important or influential over your grandparents than their grandkids—you. If they vote for Barack Obama, they're going to get another visit this year. If not, let's just hope they are still healthy until next year."[51]

In a nod to the Silverman video, another PAC in 2016, Bend the Arc Jewish Action, created a video to support Hillary Clinton. In a reversal of the Silverman video, grandparents tried to persuade their grandchildren to vote for Clinton. The video featured Jewish grandparents stressing how important it was to make sure Trump would not be elected: "I have tremendous fears for this country and for you, my grandchildren," and "If you don't vote, I'll haunt you when I die." The accompanying social media campaign used the theme "We've seen this before." Implying a connection between Trump and Nazism, the campaign attempted to use seniors to warn young people about what was at stake for the future of the country.[52] These two campaigns, situated eight years apart, illustrate shifts in the power dynamics of grandparents. The 2008 campaign is about young people influencing older folks, while the 2016 campaign has grandparents persuading their grandkids to vote. Both political mobilizations see grandparents as a potentially strong voting bloc, but the newer campaign recognizes the power, connection, and influence that grandparents have over youth in our society. The power of grandparents comes not just from their family relationship, but from the historical wisdom they possess. The hashtag "#weveseenthisbefore" positions grandparents as authority figures by nature of their age. Social media's ability to spread messages quickly to larger audiences opens grandparents to giving advice beyond their own family. With a tweet or YouTube video that goes viral, a grandparent can become a public sage or worldwide advisor. In some ways, this mimics a tribal world in which a patriarchal or maternal figure is the leader. This resembles the global village initiated by modern electronic technology envisioned by media scholar Marshall McLuhan, as he wrote, "But certainly the electro-magnetic discoveries have recreated the simultaneous 'field' in all human affairs so that the human family now exists under conditions of a 'global village.'"[53] Now, the grandparent figure can return as a new leader in control of a global, anonymous tribe.

GRANDPARENT ACTIVISM

Grandparents, more often grandmothers, have become noticeable as a part of social movements across the world. Hawaiian grandmother Teresa Shook helped inspire the worldwide Women's March after the inauguration of President Trump. After the 2016 election, she encouraged women on Facebook to mount a protest march.[54] In fact, the march became a place not only for protesting the new administration in the United States but also for grandmothers to introduce their granddaughters to protesting on behalf of women's rights. Women marched with family members and dedicated their marching to their grandmothers and granddaughters.[55] Grandmothers can be a powerful force in political action and protests because of the way they can represent their knowledge of history, serve as warnings to future generations, and promote the importance of sacrifice for the next generation.

Photojournalist Paola Gianturco documents the role of grandmothers globally in activism, ranging from promoting social justice, to contributing to environmental causes, to becoming active in health initiatives. Gianturco offers a variety of reasons for what seems to be a trend of grandmothers becoming more publicly involved in activism (including a tradition of activism among the Baby Boomer generation), troubled political times, and a large demographic of grandmothers around the world. She says, "Now, at least in the developed world, grandmothers are healthier, better off, and younger than ever before."[56]

Ruddick's notion of maternal thinking is also apparent in organizations that use the image of the grandmother to promote social activism. Ruddick makes an analogy between mothering and peace: "Peace, like mothering, is sentimentally honored and often secretly despised. Like mothers, peacemakers are scorned as powerless appeasers who are innocent of the real world."[57] Ruddick goes on to explore how mothering and maternal action are nonviolent and can help to reconceptualize peace. The mobilization efforts using the image of the grandmother combine Ruddick's image of the peaceful maternal figure with that of the aging. The grandmother figure, just by nature of her position, becomes a new archetype for social activism.

Raging Grannies started as a Canadian peace movement and spread to the United States. They use their role as grandparents as a motivation for their protests, arguing that they are making the world better for their grandchildren. On their website, they promote a "starter kit" that tells visitors, "All it takes to start a gaggle of Raging Grannies in your own home town is to gather around you a few good women 'of that certain age' who share your commitment to peace, social justice, and environmental sustainability." They explain the success of Raging Grannies: "One of the things that makes the Raging Grannies so beloved—in addition to our commitment to the issues we rage about—is the startling nature of hearing such strong lyrics coming from such 'sweet little old ladies.'"[58] They encourage protesters to wear stereotypical "granny garb" in order for people to notice them.

I spoke with Granny Anita, a member of the Raging Grannies in Ontario, Canada. She described the group to me as a community rather than an organization because of the lack of hierarchies and titles. They use online technology, including the "Raging Grannies E-Vine," to discuss and vote on choices and approaches. Granny Anita describes their use of the granny image: "We'll present the image of Granny as wanting the best for everyone, wise and experienced and knowing, but feisty. We always challenge the stereotype of the sweet, little old lady." For their activism, they often use songs, and Granny Anita explains why:

> Songs have a strong granny association, from lullabies and nursery songs, to old timey folk songs, and of course the old standards. We are well aware this is comfort music, and we use it. But our lyrics are not comfort music. We use wit and humor to get people's attention, rather than stridency, because nobody likes to be scolded; but our lyrics are often sharp when we want to make a point.

Granny Anita also elaborates on their granny outfits:

> We have a very recognizable brand now, colorful and cheerful and fun, but spiced with resolve. Actually, my own grandmother was like that—tough, bossy, took no nonsense from anyone—and she wasn't even an activist. The old-fashioned granny outfits have another effect; they remind us of the past, bringing a sense of continuity. This is even more obvious when not everyone in the group is in granny gear. Some Grans opt for a more modern gran look, in jeans and tees and baseball caps.

The goal of this organization is to capitalize on the cognitive dissonance for their audience; these seemingly innocent and aged women have powerful messages. In the United States, ninety-two-year-old raging grandmother Shirley Morrison was arrested while protesting a controversial oil rig in Seattle. Morrison and four other raging grannies brought rocking chairs and knitting needles, drank tea, and shared pictures of their grandchildren while simultaneously protesting the serious issue of dangerous environmental effects from drilling in the Arctic. Those watching the protest shouted, "Rock on, grannies."[59]

The crowd's appreciation of the grannies illustrates the way these grandmothers counter aging stereotypes while promoting specific causes. Dana Sawchuk studies Raging Grannies, and she found that the grandmother identity became a source of empowerment for many of these women, especially as they were able to role-play the grandmother figure rather than focus on themselves as individuals. Sawchuk writes, "A common theme among the women was also the notion that, since they were of a certain age, they could act with much less fear of reprisal."[60]

Others question aspects of movements like these. May Chazan and Stephanie Kittmer examined a grandmothers campaign that organized older women to confront the HIV/AIDs crisis in Saharan Africa. They asked whether grandmother mobilization campaigns create a problem by universalizing the grandmother experience around narrow conceptions. They write, "This raises questions about whether such a strategy normalizes images of 'grandmotherhood' according to certain White, middle-class, North American perspectives, thereby 'othering' those whose experience or perspectives of what it means to be a 'grandmother' differ."[61] Using the grandmother image can allow for a certain advantage in advocating for a cause, but it often leaves out people as it attempts to generate a universal image.

Other movements are concerned less with advocating for a specific cause. Instead, some promote using one's free time during this life stage to promote generosity and advocacy for others. The website of Global Grandmothers encourages people to "Be a grandmother to the world's children."[62] The organization makes connections between the personal and the political with the notion of linked giving, encouraging grandparents to use their organization to donate to a child in need at the same time that they give presents to their own grandchildren. Diana McDonough, founder and president of Global Grandmothers, described to me the birth of her own granddaughter as the moment when she started thinking about this. "I was increasingly shocked and concerned with how many kids lived in such poor conditions," she said, "and the contrast I saw to her [McDonough's grandchild]." A lawyer by career, she began thinking of what she could do next that would allow her to be positively engaged. "I just thought if we could get people into the habit of regularly giving to kids in need in the same way that they regularly gave to their grandchildren, if they got into that habit, I felt it would be good for everyone." McDonough knew that some grandparents liked to give gifts but preferred buying something for their grandchildren instead of simply giving to a faceless cause. She thought that, if given the opportunity to give to those in need at the same time as they gave to their grandchildren, grandparents might take advantage of the opportunity. What's particularly important to her is modeling the donations as a gift for the next generation: "We are trying to expand the world of our grandkids," she said. Her organization positions the grandmother as someone who considers the needs of the global community. In some ways, this mimics earlier tribal societies, with matriarchs that protect the larger community in addition to their own family. In "The Prolonged Old, the Long-Lived Society, and the Politics of Age," Robert H. Binstock speculates that this model is possible as long as there is a large demographic of older people so that they may group together to form social and political movements.[63] With these grandmother movements, the identity of the aged is being used to articulate social movements. However, the charge of these movements seeks to improve conditions for the next generation rather than to articulate a particular need specific to their own population. In other words, the Baby Boomers, once referred to as the "Me Generation," have now moved on to advocate for the next generation.

CONCLUSION

Grandparenting is a unique stage of life in that not everyone is allowed to reach this stage, and there is no real control over one's ability to participate in it. Your children, if you have them, are the ones who decide whether to make you a grandparent, and as the legal system has affirmed, they are the ones who hold the power to grant grandparents access to participate in the lives of their children. While many people take for granted their ability to become grandparents and to choose when and how they participate in it, the stories in this chapter illustrate that grandparenting sometimes functions as a privilege. Grandparents do not always have a choice in how, when, or even whether they participate in the lives of their grandchildren. Unfortunately, these stories often remain invisible. As grandparenting continues to become a distinct and prevalent phase of life for many, those who do not get to experience it at all or to the level they desire often feel left out and unfulfilled, mourning the missed opportunities. Services, advice, and legal counsel are emerging to deal with these conflicts and longings. Technology has moved in to shift grandparent relationships, but there are new rules that need to be negotiated for both the parents and the grandparents. The new lifestyle of grandparenting that is being created, consumed, and idealized is an opportunity for some to join a new and engaging way of life, but for others, it is a missed experience. At the same time, others have seen the opportunity to make the grandparenting image more visible, and they have embraced this image to engage in political action, to protest, and to promote movements and causes.

NOTES

1. Ben Cohen, "LeBron James's Biggest Fans: A Gang of Rowdy Grannies," *Wall Street Journal*, June 8, 2015, https://www.wsj.com/articles/lebron-jamess-biggest-fans-a-gang-of-rowdy-grannies-1433779319.
2. Alex Wong, "LeBron James's Wildest Fan Club Is Made up of Grannies—and They're Ready for a Repeat," *GQ*, October 25, 2016, http://www.gq.com/story/lebron-james-grandmothers-fan-club.
3. Kaitlin Kimont, "Why Penelope Disick Calling Caitlyn Jenner 'Grandma' Is so Significant," *Romper* (web page), May 23, 2016, https://www.romper.com/p/why-penelope-disick-calling-caitlyn-jenner-grandma-is-so-significant-11122.
4. Nancy Orel, "Lesbian and Bisexual Women as Grandparents: The Centrality of Sexual Orientation in the Grandparent-Grandchild Relationship," in *Lesbian, Gay, Bisexual, Transgender Aging: Research and Clinical Perspectives*, ed. Douglas Kimmel, Tara Rose, and Steven David (New York: Columbia University Press, 2006), 187, http://psycnet.apa.org/doi/10.7312/kimm13618-010.
5. Amaryll Perlesz et al., "Family in Transition: Parents, Children and Grandparents in Lesbian Families Give Meaning to 'Doing Family,'" *Journal of Family Therapy* 28, no. 2 (May 2006): 196, https://doi.org/10.1111 /j.1467-6427.2006.00345.x.
6. Perlesz,195.
7. Britni de la Cretaz, "What's Life Like with a Transgender Grandmother?" *Washington Post*, December 11, 2015, https://www.washingtonpost.com/news/inspired-life/wp/2015/12/11/whats-life-like-with-a-transgender-grandmother-this-boston-museum-exhibit-gives-visitors-an-idea/?utm_term=.064a94c594d1.
8. Karen L. Fingerman, "The Role of Offspring and In-Laws in Grandparents' Ties to Their Grandchildren," *Journal of Family Issues* 25, no. 8 (November 2004): 1036, https://doi.org/10.1177 /0192513X04265941.
9. Fingerman, 1044.

10. Carol Hosmer Golly, "Pruning the Family Tree: The Plight of Grandparents Who Are Alienated from Their Grandchildren," *The International Journal of Aging and Society* 7, no. 2 (2016), https://doi.org/10.18848/2160-1909/CGP/v07i02/21-31.

11. Ronald H. Kauffman, "Bleeding Grandparent Visitation Rights," *The Florida Bar Journal* 86, no. 8 (October 2012): 42, https://www.floridabar.org/news/tfb-journal/?durl=%2FDIVCOM%2FJN%2FJNJournal01.nsf%2FAuthor%2FCF21811EAB4729C085257A67004E1340.

12. Kauffman, 43.

13. Kauffman, 44.

14. "Family Law—Grandparent Visitation—California Supreme Court Finds No Infringement of Custodial Mother's Due Process Parenting Interest When Noncustodial Father Supports Grandparent Visitation Petition—*Butler v. Harris (In re Marriage of Harris)*, 96 P.3d 141 (Cal. 2004)," *Harvard Law Review* 118, no. 3 (2005): 1046, http://www.jstor.org/stable/4093355.

15. Marlene Eskind Moses and Jessica J. Uitto, "The Current Status of Tennessee's Grandparent Visitation Law," *Tennessee Bar Journal* 46, no. 1 (January 2010): 24.

16. Moses and Uitto, 25.

17. Lee Dryden, "Court Rules for Parents in Grandparenting Time Case," *Macomb County Legal News*, July 14, 2017, http://legalnews.com/macomb/1445446/.

18. Susanna Schrosbdorff, "The Grandparent Deficit: Fertility Isn't the Only Biological Clock," *Time* 185, no. 11, March 19, 2015. http://time.com/3750528/ biological-clock-grandparents-late-in-life-kids/.

19. Elissa Gootman, "So Eager for Grandchildren, They're Paying for the Egg-Freezing Clinic," *New York Times*, May 13, 2012, http://www.nytimes.com/2012/05/14/us/ eager-for-grandchildren-and-putting-daughters-eggs-in-freezer.html.

20. Arlie Russell Hochschild, *The Outsourced Self* (New York: Metropolitan Books, 2012), 224.

21. Rebecca Flood, "Grandma Says She Was to Blame for Live BBC Interview Gatecrashed by Professor's Children," *Independent* (web page), March 11, 2017, http://www.independent.co.uk/news/world/asia/bbc-interview-professor-children-interrupt-gatecrashed-grandma-south-korea-video-videobomb-a7624211.html.

22. Judith Treas, "Transnational Older Adults and Their Families," *Family Relations* 57, no. 4 (October 2008): 472. https://doi.org/10.1111 /j.1741-3729.2008.00515.x 10.

23. Laura I. Sigad and Rivka A. Eisikovits, "Grandparenting across Borders: American Grandparents and Their Israeli Grandchildren in a Transnational Reality," *Journal of Aging Studies* 27, no. 4 (December 2013): 311, https://doi.org/10.1016 /j.jaging.2013.06.002.

24. Sigan and Eisikovits, 314.

25. Mihaela Nedelcu, "Transnational Grandparenting in the Digital Age: Mediated Co-Presence and Childcare in the Case of Romanian Migrants in Switzerland and Canada," *European Journal of Ageing* 14, no. 4 (December 2017): 381, https://doi.org/10.1007 /s10433-017-0436-1.

26. Miriam Jordan, "Grandparents Win Reprieve from Trump Travel Ban in Federal Court," *New York Times*, July 14, 2017, https://www.nytimes.com/2017/07/14/us/politics/trump-travel-ban-grandparents.html?_r=1.

27. Anup Kaphle, "Do These Grandparents Look Dangerous to You?" *BuzzFeed News* (web page), June 30, 2017, https://www.buzzfeed.com/anupkaphle/muslims-are-tweeting-about-their-grandparents-who-cant?utm_term=.yuNLjOkQl#.tv3YXLzAp.

28. Valerie A. J. Frissen, "ICTs in the Rush Hour of Life," *The Information Society* 16, no. 1 (March 2000): 66, https://doi.org/10.1080/019722400128338.

29. Frissen, 69–72.

30. Taylor Hosking and Lena Felton, "Full Transcript: Senator Jeff Flake Announces He Won't Seek Reelection," *The Atlantic*, October 24, 2017, https://www.theatlantic.com/politics/archive/2017/10/full-transcript-senator-jeff-flake-announces-he-wont-seek-reelection/543846/.

31. Liza Mundy, "Playing the Granny Card," *The Atlantic*, June 2015, https://www.theatlantic.com/magazine/archive/2015/06/playing-the-granny-card/392105/.

32. Mundy.

33. Diana B. Carlin and Kelly L. Winfrey, "Have You Come a Long Way Baby? Hillary Clinton, Sarah Palin, and Sexism in 2008 Campaign Coverage," *Communication Studies* 60, no. 4 (2009): 333–334, https://doi.org/10.1080/10510970903109904.

34. Doree Lewak, "Nobody Does the 'Cool Grandma' Look Like Sarah Palin," *New York Post*, April 22, 2017, http://nypost.com/2017/04/22/nobody-does-the-cool-grandma-look-like-sarah-palin/.

35. Tracie Egan Morrissey, "Sarah Palin: Hillary Clinton Should Open Her Eyes about Abortion," *Jezebel* (web page), May 7, 2014. http://jezebel.com/sarah-palin-hillary-clinton-should-open-her-eyes-about-1572904364.

36. Quoted in Jane C. Timm, "Palin: Being a Grandma Might Turn Hillary Clinton Conservative," *MSNBC* (web page), May 7, 2014, http://www.msnbc.com/msnbc/sarah-palin-being-grandma-will-change-hillary-clinton.

37. Peter Beinart, "Hillary Clinton: Grandmother in Chief," *The Atlantic* (web page), February 6, 2015, https://www.theatlantic.com/politics/archive/2015/02/grandmother-in-chief/385238/.

38. Carlin and Winfrey, "Have You Come a Long Way Baby?" 331.

39. Jake Miller, "Hillary Clinton: Grandmother-in-Chief?" *CBS News* (web page), September 28, 2014, http://www.cbsnews.com/news/hillary-clinton-grandmother-in-chief-2016-presidential-bid/.

40. Tierney Mcafee, "Hillary Clinton Gives a Grandmother's Perspective on Running for POTUS," *People.com* (web page), January 6, 2016, http://people.com/celebrity/hillary-clinton-talks-being-a-grandmother-and-date-nights-with-bill/.

41. Quora (web page), "Question and Answer from Hillary Clinton," December 1, 2015, https://www.google.com/url?q=https://www.quora.com/profile/Hillary-Clinton&sa=D&ust=1519843182261000&usg=AFQjCNE1INRhbHkouoCpB8ER7MRPTIW_5w.

42. Jeremy W. Peters, "How Do You Say 'Vote for Clinton' in Spanish? Ask the Abuelas," *New York Times*, November 1, 2016, https://www.nytimes.com/2016/11/02/us/politics/hillary-clinton-hispanic-support-abuelas.html?_r=0.

43. Sam Sanders, "#MemeOfTheWeek: Hillary Clinton, Not Quite an Abuela," *NPR* (web page), December 26, 2015, http://www.npr.org/2015/12/26/461116160/-.

44. "We Got the Nanny State, Now Welcome to the Granny State," *Virginia Patriot 1776* (blog), February 3, 2015, https://virginiapatriot1776.wordpress.com/2015/02/03/we-got-the-nanny-state-now-welcome-to-the-granny-state/.

45. Lisa Lerer, "GP Talks with Nancy Pelosi," *Grandparents.com*, American Grandparents Association (web page), accessed May 4, 2017, https://www.grandparents.com/food-and-leisure/celebrity/gp-talks-with-nancy-pelosi.

46. Tim Hains, "Pelosi Warns of 'Grandma Living in the Guest Room' if Obamacare Is Repealed," *Real Clear Politics* (blog), January 4, 2017, https://www.realclearpolitics.com/video/2017/01/04/pelosi_warns_of_grandma_living_in_the_guest_room_if_obamacare_is_repealed.html.

47. Robert Laurie, "Pelosi: 'You Want Grandma Living in the Guest Room? Repeal ObamaCare,'" *Herman Cain* (blog), January 4, 2017, https://www.hermancain.com/pelosi-you-want-grandma-living-in-the-guest.

48. Carolyn Lochhead, "Pelosi Ridiculed in New Children's Book," *SFGATE Politics Blog*, November 17, 2009, http://blog.sfgate.com/politics/2009/11/17/pelosi-ridiculed-in-new-childrens-book/.

49. Sara Ruddick, "Maternal Thinking: Toward a Politics of Peace," in *Maternal Theory: Essential Readings*," ed. Andrea O'Reilly (Toronto: Demeter Press, 2007), 96.

50. Dave Itzkoff, "Message to Your Grandma: Vote Obama," *New York Times*, October 6, 2008, http://www.nytimes.com/2008/10/07/arts/television/07sara.html.

51. "Sarah Silverman and the Great Schlep," YouTube, September 25, 2008, https://www.youtube.com/watch?v=AgHHX9R4Qtk.

52. Ann-Christine Diaz, "Jewish Grandparents Promise to Rise from the Dead," *AdAge* (web page), September 22, 2016, http://creativity-online.com/work/bend-the-arc-jewish-action-a-message-from-grandma--grandpa--weve-seen-this-before/49174.

53. Marshall McLuhan, *The Gutenberg Galaxy: The Making of Typographic Man* (Toronto: University of Toronto Press, 1962), 43.

54. Laila Kearney, “Hawaii Grandma’s Plea Launches Women’s March in Washington,” *Reuters*, December 5, 2016, https://www.reuters.com/article/us-usa-trump-women/hawaii-grandmas-plea-launches-womens-march-in-washington-idUSKBN13U0GW.

55. Constance Grady, “The Women’s March on Washington Was Full of Mothers and Daughters,” *Vox* (web page), January 24, 2017, https://www.vox.com/identities/2017/1/24/14352336/womens-march-washington-mothers-daughters.

56. Paola Gianturco, *Grandmother Power: A Global Phenomenon* (Brooklyn, NY: Power-House Books, 2012), 9.

57. Ruddick, *Maternal Thinking*, 137.

58. *Raging Grannies International* (web page), accessed May 17, 2017, http://raginggrannies.org/starter-kit/.

59. Sarah Kaplan, “Meet the 92-Year-Old ‘Raging Granny’ Who Just Got Arrested for Protesting Arctic Oil Drilling,” *Washington Post*, June 10, 2015, https://www.washingtonpost.com/news/morning-mix/wp/2015/06/10/meet-the-92-year-old-raging-granny-who-just-got-arrested-for-protesting-arctic-oil-drilling/?utm_term=.8c202f91a5a5.

60. Dana Sawchuk, “The Raging Grannies: Defying Stereotypes and Embracing Aging through Activism,” *Journal of Women & Aging* 21, no. 3 (2009): 177, https://doi.org/10.1080/08952840903054898.

61. May Chazan and Stephanie Kittmer, “Defying, Producing, and Overlooking Stereotypes? The Complexities of Mobilizing ‘Grandmotherhood’ as Political Strategy,” *Journal of Women & Aging* 28, no. 4 (July 3, 2016): 306, https://doi.org/10.1080/08952841.2015.1017428.

62. Global Grandmothers (web page), accessed May 17, 2017, http://globalgrandmothers.org/linked-giving-2/.

63. Robert H. Binstock, “The Prolonged Old, the Long-Lived Society, and the Politics of Age,” *Public Policy & Aging Report* 14, no. 2 (March 1, 2004): 28, https://doi.org/10.1093/ppar/14.2.1a.

Chapter Four

Grandparenting as Second Chance

When I was a child, my most vivid recollection of a pop culture reference to grandparenting was the Christmas song "Grandma Got Run Over by a Reindeer." Popular in the early 1980s, the song included these lyrics: "She'd been drinking too much eggnog/ And we begged her not to go/ But she forgot her medication/ And she staggered out the door into the snow."[1]

The song poked fun at typical elderly stereotypes, like the crazy old grandma's drinking and medication. I remember singing the song in the car, probably on the way to visit my very own grandparents, without thinking at all about the horrid ideas attached to the song.

My children's first popular culture experience with grandparenting can't be any more different. Their first memory of a TV grandma is *Nina Needs to Go*, a series of animated interstitials featured on Disney Junior. In these short videos, Nina is a little girl out on some adventure (my favorite is the water park), usually with her mother or father. In each episode, she waits too long to go the bathroom, and her parents are unsuccessful in finding an available facility. Just when she's about to wet her pants, her grandmother "Nana" swoops in like a superhero and uses her amazing grandma powers to get Nina to a bathroom just in time.

This chapter examines shifts in how popular culture represents grandparents. Grandparents are plentiful in media representations. At times, like Nina's nana, they are the heroes, saviors, and wise figures. However, many other times they are portrayed as victims, the source of humor, or at the mercy of their children in wanting a role in the lives of their grandchildren. This chapter studies the complicated representations of the grandparent figure, one that can wield power but shoulders many burdens as well. All these representations are related to historical, economic, and sociological changes in our culture regarding aging and family relations.

GRANDPARENTS AND THE AGING TAX

Perhaps the earliest grandparent figure that most people remember is the grandmother in Little Red Riding Hood. Originating around the seventeenth century, the story derives from an older oral tale titled "The Story of Grandmother," itself originating from versions coming out of France, Northern Italy, and Austria. One account, called "The Tiger Grandmother," describes a strange monster possessing the grandmother while her grandchildren are in her care.[2]

In the post-seventeenth-century versions, Grandma is sick in bed and needs Little Red Riding Hood to travel through the woods to deliver her sustenance. Embedded within this story is the sense of obligation to an ailing parent. Little Red's mother wants her own mother to be taken care of, and she sends her daughter to fulfill that duty. The fairy tale affirms the special bond between grandparent and grandchild. Most of all, this tale and its precursors present the grandmother as being in need of caring and rescue.

Images and stereotypes surround aging and the elderly in modern American society. The elderly are a forgotten group and generally are underrepresented in media.[3] In his classic work on television cultivation studies in the 1980s, George Gerbner concluded:

> More older characters are treated with disrespect than are characters in any other age group. About 70 percent of the older men and more than 80 percent of the older women are not held in high esteem or treated courteously, a very different pattern of treatment than that found for younger characters. Similarly, a much larger proportion of older characters than younger characters are portrayed as eccentric or foolish.[4]

Though grandparents comprise a wide range of age groups, their portrayal in many ways has not changed over the last forty years. When the elderly are present, the images are often troubling. Studies indicate that "exposure to television is a significant predictor of more negative stereotypes of aging."[5] In a study on Disney movies, Tom Robinson and Caitlin Anderson found that, though the majority (58 percent) were portrayed in a positive manner, there were still 42 percent that were portrayed negatively.[6] They note, "With 25 percent of the characters shown as grumpy, 12 percent as evil or sinister, 8 percent as helpless, 3 percent as senile or crazy, and 2 percent as the object of ridicule, children are receiving a larger dose of negative portrayals that may help form or reinforce negative attitudes toward older people."[7] Additional research verifies that grandparents in movies and television programs often are portrayed as ailing or sickly. In *Grandparents*, Ursula Adler Falk and Gerhard Falk write, "Grandparents are shown as ill and dying, rarely as healthy, working and contributing adults. Grandparents are also shown as victims of all kinds of misfortunes, seldom as women and men in control of their own lives. Grandparents in movies and television portrayals talk too much but have no substance. They are superficial and superfluous."[8]

More recently, some research has indicated improvement in this representation. For example, many children's books are actively including more diversified and positive messages of grandparenting. One study found that, even when grandparents were represented as physically disabled, they still provided valuable contributions to society.[9]

Grandparents in popular culture are still taxed with additional burdens often assigned to the aging. They overwhelmingly appear as character types that are weak, undervalued, and vulnerable.

THE TICKING GRANDPARENT CLOCK

Expressed throughout many different works in popular media is the strong desire to become a grandparent. The form in which this trope appears varies depending on the period being represented. In earlier periods, grandchildren often served a utilitarian purpose: they could provide more hands for the family farm or, in wealthier families with legacies to protect, carry on the family name. The popular British series *Downton Abbey*, set in the early 1900s, portrayed a noble family that encouraged their eldest daughter Mary to wed and produce an heir in order to keep the family estate intact. Likewise, *Reign*, a fictionalized period piece set during the rule of Mary, Queen of Scots, shows the two queen mothers both pressuring Mary to have grandchildren to secure the monarchy. Throughout the episodes of *Game of Thrones*, royal families face the burden of succession by producing an heir to secure and hold on to power. In these cases, children become a vehicle for securing a legacy rather than a source of purely sentimental attachment.

While some representations illustrate the need for grandchildren to secure the future of the family, other programs depict grandparenting as motivated by affection. What emerges are the nagging grandparents-to-be, who pressure their children to enable them to become grandparents. This "nag" figure becomes popularized in the 1980s and 1990s.[10] Figures include Jesse's parents in *Full House* (1987–1995), Fran's mother Sylvia in *The Nanny (1993–1999),* Daphne's mother Gertrude in *Frasier* (1993–2004), and Robert's mother Marie in *Everybody Loves Raymond* (1996–2005).[11] All these mothers cajole their children to produce grandchildren, offering some comic relief to the program at the same time. For example, in one episode of *Everybody Loves Raymond*, Robert discovers that his mother has been secretly setting the stage to encourage him and his wife Amy to have a baby. After he receives a gift basket with massage oils from his mother, his brother Raymond realizes the truth: "How come Mom's doing all this for you all of a sudden, with the special treatment and candles and wine, massage oil? Oh.

Oh! . . . Grandchildren. She wants grandchildren, and she's doing all she can to grease the wheels."[12]

Sometimes, characters recognize that producing a grandchild can be a way to ingratiate themselves with their in-laws. In *Mad About You* (1992–1999), Paul and Jamie's parents can't wait for grandchildren. When the couple finally starts trying, Jamie can't wait to tell her mother-in-law Sylvia, hoping for a wave of affection.[13] Sylvia, though, dismisses her as trying too hard. In *How I Met Your Mother* (2005–2014), Ted warns his girlfriend Robin about his mother: "She grills every single one of my girlfriends about when we are going to get married and have kids. You'll know it's coming when she mentions my cousin Stacey, six kids in five years." The punch line of the joke comes when Ted's mother doesn't grill Robin, leaving Robin to beg her to pressure her into marrying him and having kids. Robin tells her, "I want you to want me to want to have your grandkids."[14]

As grandchild lust emerges as a theme, the grandparent-to-be nag figure becomes more intrusive. In *Friends*, Monica's father Jack Geller, walks in on Monica and her husband Chandler having sex. When she assures him that this sex is for procreation, he is thrilled and offers advice on positions that might prove helpful for conception. The matriarch in *Reign* offers the fictional Catherine advice on lotions to help Francis impregnate her. In *How I Met Your Mother*, Marshall's father offers him sexual position advice to ensure that he will have a son. As subjects related to sex and procreation become more acceptable to address within popular culture, fertility pressure becomes an acceptable way to discuss sex without having to get into too many details.

As the value of children changes from economic essentiality to emotional value, so does the representation of the grandparent relationship. For many, becoming a grandparent represents commencing the next stage of life. While the biological clock once was ascribed only to women and more recently extended to men as well, grandparents now desire grandchildren to the point that they apply pressure to their own offspring. In an episode of *Teen Mom* that revisits formerly pregnant teens who are now in their twenties, one father tells his son Ryan that he'd like to see him settle down. The father requests, "We want another grandbaby."[15] Ryan's unwillingness to move on to the expected next stage of life—marriage and children—is preventing his own parents from enjoying the fruit of success from their own parenting: grandchildren.

The powerful theme that grandchildren are an expected life stage and are the reward for doing a good job with their own parenting likely stems from common ideologies about motherhood. In American culture, women's worth has been linked with their ability to procreate and nurture.[16] Similarly, fathers now are beginning to face rising expectations of caregiving and nurturing.[17] Men are seen as becoming responsible adults when they have children of their own.[18] These programs reflect the belief that becoming a grandparent is in many ways the mark of success as an adult, as an extension of their parental role. At the same time, grandparenting is more often experienced later in life, as people delay childbearing. It would not be a surprise to see the grandparent nag figure grow, as the pressure to become a grandparent is contrasted with later childbearing by their children.[19]

THE RELUCTANT GRANDPARENT

While some people cannot wait to become grandparents, others feel more hesitation. The antithesis of the grandparent nag is the reluctant grandparent. This theme often appears in programs where the grandparent is forced to assume a grandparent role unexpectedly.

During the 2015–2016 television season, John Stamos played the starring role of Jimmy in the program *Grandfathered*. The title of the program reflects the lack of control Jimmy feels in being assigned the role of grandfather. The premise of the show is that Jimmy is surprised when he learns that he not only has an adult son, but also a granddaughter. Part of his dismay rests with the disconnect he feels in being a grandfather, which interferes with his youthful self-identity. Many of the plots of the show involve Jimmy trying, sometimes vainly, to retain his hip, young, and sexy image while serving his grandfatherly duties. He is self-absorbed and consumed with his own interests rather than others'. For example, in one episode he is so worried, unnecessarily, about having skin cancer that he ignores the fact that his granddaughter needs surgery and that his own child is concerned about her. Finally, he admits, "I'm not used to worrying about people." By the end of the season, becoming a grandparent has helped him assume a more adult role and appreciate the value of family.

Hesitancy to become a grandparent also appears in shows when the parents perceive their child as not ready to become a parent. In *Raising Hope*, Jimmy lives with his parents Virginia and Burt and his grandmother Maw Maw. To Jimmy's and his parents' surprise, a baby he didn't know he had fathered lands at his doorstep. Virginia, the grandmother-to-be, says she doesn't have the time in her life for a baby and wants him to safe-drop the baby at the local firehouse. As people who were teenage parents themselves, they see the baby as a burden on what already is shown to be a harsh, working-class existence. Jimmy tells them, "I can't do this without you guys." He explains how he sees the baby: "It's a chance for all of us to do something good." Virginia finally relents: "What are we going to name it?" They name the baby Hope, indicating the potential the infant has to bond the family and provide all of them with a new purpose. By the end of the episode, Jimmy's parents come into the room, play the guitar and sing a song they sang to him when he was a baby.[20]

In the Freeform television sitcom *Baby Daddy*, Bonnie suddenly becomes a grandmother when Ben is surprised with a baby on his doorstep, much like Jimmy in *Raising Hope*. She rises to her new role by saying, "Your fairy grandmother is here," but she has to battle with her son, who thinks he can take care of the baby on his own. In these shows, the newly minted grandparents at first resist the label foisted upon them. However, in each case they demonstrate an instinctual skill to help care for the baby, as well as the baby's parent. They have not yet finished parenting as they begin their new duties as grandparents. Their caregiving role is continuous and blends uninterruptedly between parenting and grandparenting. The reluctant grandparent is also a common figure in fiction programs about unexpected teen pregnancies. The tension between the grandparents and parents over who will care for the baby becomes a central conflict in many programs. Throughout *The Gilmore Girls*, the main character Lorelai experiences tension with her parents, Richard and Emily, resulting from her teen pregnancy. In the show, Lorelai's daughter Rory is now a teenager, but Lorelai's parents use their financial promise of funding Rory's private high school education to exert control over her upbringing. In the program *Mom*, the female characters experience a generational cycle of teenage pregnancies. The premise of *The Secret Life of the American Teenager* is how the family reacts to the news of their daughter's teen pregnancy. The sitcom *Reba*, starring the country music star Reba McEntire, reveals that her oldest daughter is pregnant around the same time Reba's husband leaves her for a younger woman. The 2017 Disney Channel program *Andi Mack* targets the pre-teen audience with the middle-school character Andi, who discovers that the woman she thought was her mother actually is her grandmother, and her older sister is really her mother.

In these cases, the parents typically are hesitant to assume the duties of grandparenting, in part because they have not yet finished parenting. These programs often deal with the struggles of how much control and support they will provide and the tensions that arise when there is more than one parental figure caring for a child. In *Andi Mack*, for example, Andi's grandmother becomes upset with what she perceives to be a demotion from being thought of as Andi's mother to now her grandmother. Eventually, most of the characters realize their need to rely on their own parents, oftentimes their mothers, to help usher them into the new world of parenting. The grandchild serves to bring the family closer together by reframing the grandparents from antagonists to mentors.

Similar themes resonate in reality television programming about teen pregnancy.[21] The challenges faced by the teen parents on MTV's *16 and Pregnant* and *Teen Mom* have received much attention, but the reluctant grandparent is also a featured character in almost every episode of these programs.[22] On Lifetime, the show *30 Something Grandma* is about women who become grandmothers when their teenagers have babies. The Learning Channel's (TLC) program *My Teen Is Pregnant and So Am I* capitalizes on the awkwardness of women becoming grandparents before they are ready by showing women and their daughters about to be parents and grandparents together. In all these shows, the grandparent figure is seen as reaching this stage of life earlier than imagined and thus unable to perform in normalized roles typical for grandparents.

A major theme of these reality programs is that the grandparent, typically the grandmother, is unable to give up her parental role in order to focus solely on grandparenting. In these programs, the grandparents are obligated to become caretakers, allowing their daughter to remain in their home with the baby, and often inviting their daughter's boyfriend to live with them as well. In *30 Something Grandma*, Prudence says, "I'm in my 30s. . . . I'm not ready to be a grandma. I'm overwhelmed."[23] MTV's *16 and Pregnant* frequently shows parents of teens who have to become caretakers. In one memorable episode, pregnant teenager Jordan is raised by her grandparents, who help out when Jordan has her baby.[24] The grandparents reluctantly fall into the position of raising two subsequent generations after having raised their own children.

The parents often are conflicted between the needs of their own children and those of their grandchildren. Fights over responsibilities and boundaries consistently occur in the programs. In one *Teen Mom* story line, Jenelle fights for years with her mother over custody of her baby. In one memorable scene, Jenelle says to her mother, "Honestly, I should have him full time, not you. I'm the parent. You are not the father either. You are just a grandmother."[25]

Many grandparents express their ambivalence about their status as grandparents by choosing not to be referred to by that name. In *30 Something Grandma*, one grandmother says she would prefer to be called Mimi because she does not feel ready to become a grandparent.[26] Another episode features Patricia, who is about to become a grandmother. She says, "I can't wrap my brain around it yet. And I do not want the baby to call me grandma. That's just too old for me. Maybe Mimi or Nonna. Something. Not grandma. Not grandmother."[27] Likewise, Chantel tells her daughter Caroline, "I'm a young vibrant woman at the age of 37. Don't call me grandma."[28]

These parents reject the term "grandparent" because of both the stigma attached to teen parenthood and the recognition of the financial burden it will have in their lives. The additional, unexpected caretaking these new grandparents must provide destabilizes their livelihood. In *30 Something Grandma,* Patricia describes how she had children so young herself that she was looking forward to having a new stage of life be her time. Now she has to help support her grandchild.[29] Soon after her daughter becomes pregnant, Patricia loses her job. Another new grandmother, Prudence, has to learn how to manage her life with this new responsibility. She worries her own retirement will be pushed back another eighteen years. These shows reflect the financial insecurity of many aging adults, destabilized further by the unexpected responsibility of supporting their grandchildren.

In both fiction and nonfiction depictions, reluctant grandparents face an emotional burden as they try to negotiate the boundaries between parenting and grandparenting. The programs reinforce the blame that these grandparents place on themselves for not raising their children successfully enough to be self-sufficient. This idea is described by Ursula Adler Falk and Gerhard Falk as the "bad seed theory." They define this concept as "the popular stereotype that children who failed to maintain their own families were poorly raised, so the grandparents are at fault, must have been poor parents, and are therefore obliged to raise their grandchildren."[30] Prudence, in *30 Something Grandma*, describes how she was also a teen mother and wanted something different for her children. Prudence's sister tells her that her daughter sees her as more of a friend than a mom, and Prudence feels responsible for not knowing her daughter was sexually active. In *Andi Mack*, the program implies that the grandmother was too restrictive raising her daughter and did not form a strong relationship with her. Grandparenting can also become a source of redemption. Taking care of their grandchildren is positioned by these shows as grandparents' chance to reclaim their success at parenting and complete their assigned responsibility.

It is not difficult to imagine reasons why plotlines that feature reluctant grandparents would resonate today. The ambivalence of moving into the life stage of grandparenting in all these programs reflects societal confusion about the exact role of the grandparent. More adult children between the ages of eighteen and thirty-four are living with their parents.[31] This trend has been influenced by declining economic and job opportunities and financial strain after the Great Recession of 2008.[32] Co-living arrangements, while helpful, blur the lines of parental and grandparent care, thrusting grandparents into ambiguous parental roles. The living and co-dependent relationships become additionally strained, as the generation of parents who are moving into grandparent roles is accustomed to an intensive style of parenting, a habit that may be difficult to shut off when their children become adults. Newer research is exploring how attitudes and behaviors are changing regarding expectations of parental/child ties, intergenerational relationships, and cohabitation. One study exploring expectations of parent/child relationships argues, "Today's cultural narrative is consistent with increased intimacy and dependency of the younger generation, while also disparaging this increased parental involvement."[33] This conflict expands to the grandparent/child-parent/grandchild tryad, becoming fodder for popular entertainment. The recent figure of the reluctant grandparent in popular fictional portrayals has deemphasized the role that class plays in how people feel about becoming a grandparent. For some programs, like *Grandfathered*, the character's reluctance comes mainly from his desire to avoid feeling old. On many reality programs, however, the grandparents' hesitation comes from the drastic financial drain this new role will have on their lives and on their children's lives as well.

GRANDPARENTING AS TRANSFORMATIVE

While some grandparents can't wait to be grandparents and others are more reluctant, another group of older adults is depicted as surprised but ultimately appreciative of the transformative power of grandparenting. In periods before the printing press and widespread literacy, information largely was passed on orally rather than recorded, so those with knowledge of earlier events possessed greater power.[34] Today's information-rich culture has reversed that hierarchy, and the elderly are no longer relied on as much for their knowledge. Wisdom and advice come not from the aged, but from information that can be found easily enough with a quick Google search. In popular media, audiences are reminded of the value the elderly have in the lives of the young. In his research on aging, Robert E. Yahnke argues, "But the primary thrust of the portrayal of old age, in the context of films and videos, is to underscore the abiding resilience and forward-thinking attitudes of the old, especially as they relate to the young."[35] The representations of transformation provide the older figures with moments to shine and reinforce their value.

Grandparents often are featured as part of a road-trip journey that produces a transformation. In the film *Grandma* (2015), Elle, estranged from her daughter, is sought out by her granddaughter Sage, who needs money for an abortion. Elle begins the movie depressed, bitter, and angry, but finds herself unable to deny help to her granddaughter, even if it means asking others for money because she does not have any of her own. Throughout the trip, she mocks traditional expectations people have of the elderly. She jokes, "Don't make me fall; I could break a hip" to her granddaughter. She drives recklessly, not because of her age, but because she enjoys it. She also, at one moment, tells her granddaughter, "Don't call me grandma," but then she later regrets saying it. She's not warm or comforting, but she's committed to supporting her granddaughter, whether it's begging for money from her ex-husband or seeking some old debts. By the end of the journey, though, she has reached new insights about herself. She's wrestled with the death of her long-term partner and makes overtures to reunite with her ex-girlfriend. It's clear that this journey has shifted her internal thoughts.

Bad Grandpa is a road-trip movie that begins when the main character is saddled with a grandson after the child's mother goes to jail. He and his grandson then embark on a journey to locate the child's father. By the end of the movie, he has learned to care for his grandson. Instead of leaving him with an irresponsible father, the grandfather returns and takes his grandson back. The child has given his life meaning and value.

In the YouTube series *Me and My Grandma*, starring Eva Gutowski and Rhea Perlman, Janey and her grandmother set off on a road trip so that Janey can pursue an acting career in Hollywood. As they walk a red carpet, Grandma says, "I'm no longer plain old Grandma. I'm Glamma."[36] The two support each other with advice: Janey teaches Grandma about popular culture, and Grandma offers constant optimism. Eventually, Grandma becomes a social media celebrity while her granddaughter pursues a more traditional Hollywood career path. Grandma reveals, "I thought I'd come out here for you. I figured my ship had sailed. But when we got out here, there were boats everywhere."[37] The grandparents on these journeys become surrogate parents, cheerleaders, and best friends, and they ultimately change as a result of their connection with their grandchild.

At other times, grandparents are needed to help usher a grandchild through an experience or life stage. A popular example of this theme is in the film *Willy Wonka*. Grandpa Joe is bedridden until his grandson wins the golden ticket. He leaps out of bed because only he has the knowledge and ethics to help the child win the contest. Most of Grandpa Joe's knowledge comes in the form of strong values rather than practical advice. A recurring theme is grandparents as wise figures, able to impart wisdom and perspective to their grandchildren. *Grandma's House*, a 1996 film, features a grandmother whose grandchildren come to live with her. She shows them the power of faith and devotion, attributes they were missing until they moved in with her. In the *Princess Diaries* series of films, the grandmother figure is both a manipulator and the only one who can guide her granddaughter through a transformation into becoming a princess.

In some cases, grandparents represent a last hope for grandchildren, as they are the only ones willing to take the children in when they have nowhere else to go. For example, a grandson in the film *Grandma's Boy* is a video game developer. Represented as a man-child, he loses his home and moves in with his grandmother and her two elderly roommates. She provides caretaking duties for him and makes him meals, and he teaches her video games. When he tells her to kill a drug dealer in his game, she says, "I hate violence, but drugs are bad," and shoots. The elderly women unintentionally consume his recreational drugs. While he introduces some fun into his grandmother's life, she helps him develop a relationship with a woman at work by showing her his nurturing side, as well as his baby pictures. When talking about his grandfather, who had passed away, Alex says, "I loved him, and I love you, and I love being your roommate." Later, the grandmother saves his job by showing his bosses that his video game is finished by playing through all its levels.

In some programs, parents have to seek the assistance of grandparents to help them care for their children. In the 2017 Netflix program *Free Reign*, two teens and their mother arrive at their grandfather's home ostensibly to help him, but they find he offers insight and guidance into a new world for the children. At times, these programs show that the bonds between parent and child had been broken, and the grandparents are the last chance for restoring order. In the film *Georgia Rule*, Georgia is estranged from her daughter Lily and is asked to care for her granddaughter Rachel. She has a tough demeanor and strict household rules but clearly loves and wants to help her granddaughter. At one point, Georgia says, "You are a part of me. I don't understand you at all, but I understand me." This reinforces the idea that a genetic connection can serve as both an obligation and commitment between family members. Georgia is able to rescue her granddaughter from a childhood of sexual abuse by giving her a safe haven and forcing her daughter to take responsibility, thereby transforming both her granddaughter's and her daughter's lives.

Many of these programs depict grandparenting as an opportunity to heal wounds from parenting. In the film *Parental Anxiety*, Grandma Diane says, "You know what grandparenting is? A second chance." By the end of the film, the adult children have reformed their relationships with their parents. In *Georgia Rule*, Georgia's work with her granddaughter presents her with an opportunity to heal the estrangement with her own daughter. Likewise, the estrangement between the grandmother and her child in *Grandma* thaws because of the grandparent's involvement with her grandchild. Norman and Ethel are an elderly couple in *On Golden Pond*. They are visited by their daughter Chelsea, who wants to drop off her boyfriend's son to stay with them so Chelsea and her boyfriend can have a European vacation. Bonding with the pseudo-grandchild allows Norman to reconcile his relationship with Chelsea and lessen his preoccupation with dying as he engages in activities with the child. In *Gilmore Girls*, the grandparents provide money to support their grandchild's education, so they are able to demand weekly dinners in order to develop a relationship with her and resolve the estrangement with their own daughter. On the day that Rory graduates from college, her grandmother tries to manipulate ways to continue the weekly dinners. In a heartwarming scene, her daughter reassures her that they will continue. Building a relationship with their grandchild has resulted in a connection with their own child. In some shows, the second chance is presented even more directly. By the end of *Dirty Grandpa* the grandfather attends to the baptism of the new baby he has as the result of a fling with a young college-aged woman. "It's nice to have a second chance," he says. "Maybe it won't take me so long to get the father thing right this time."

These shows present grandparenting as an opportunity to complete the unfinished business of parenting. Since many of these grandparents have children who are not considered successful, they are forced to re-parent as a type of do-over. Grandparents use their relationship with their grandchildren to embark on a new, enlightened life stage. These transformations rest, in part, on stereotypes of aging. The change is based on the premise that their lives have little value without grandchildren. Grandparenting, in these programs, becomes a new stage of life where meaning is dependent on those surrounding them.

LICENSE TO TALK

Another popular image of grandparents is connected to their social status. Grandparents are treated as people who, because of their age, inherently can break cultural boundaries. Their willingness, ability, and obligation to speak truths that others won't share or hear is a central characteristic of many of these characters within popular culture. Grandparents deliver sage advice through their talk and action, but they need grandchildren to uncover that advice and find value in them.

Many grandparents demonstrate their value in their ability to speak a truth that others need to hear. This is represented in the film *Grandma* by the character Elle, who always says what she thinks when she is out with her granddaughter. "She's already pregnant," she says to another boy looking at her granddaughter. Elle talks about abortions publicly and gets thrown out of a coffee shop. In *Georgia Rule*, the grandmother is not afraid to stand up and speak the truth to her granddaughter, her own daughter, and her daughter's husband. The IFC series *Gigi Does It* features a male actor who plays a Jewish grandmother character, often distributing guilt and candor throughout the season. The first episode of the program shows her cajoling her nine-year-old grandson to return her phone calls. She ends up calling him "a little bitch." The brutal, if unnecessarily harsh, truth is treated as shocking but ultimately forgivable because she has reached an age where she can't be controlled by others or by social norms.

On television, the sarcastic and wise grandmother is a popular figure. In *Game of Thrones*, Lady Tyrell plays the witty grandmother who holds much power and plots on behalf of her granddaughter. She is not afraid to talk about her sexual exploits, critique those around her, or speak out to those in power.[38] In *Downton Abbey*, Violet Crawley plays a similar character who is unafraid to speak her mind on behalf of her granddaughters.

Grandfathers are also depicted as having license to say what they want, but their chatter often comes out in sexual talk, which is seen as a failure to respect adult social boundaries. Falk and Falk, in their research on grandparents, describe how grandfathers often fall into the "second childhood stereotype": "Grandpa plays with small children because he is in his 'second childhood' himself, that Grandma is either a helpless old woman who interferes in the lives of younger people or an active 'old lady' who cooks incessantly, bakes endless pies and cookies, says soothing things, and smiles all the time."[39] In *Dirty Grandpa*, for example, the grandfather exists in a childlike/id role and rescues his grandchild from a life of safe predictability. The entire purpose of his journey with his grandson is to reveal the truth about what he thinks is missing in his grandson's life, but other characters do not trust him at first because of the childish behavior he exudes throughout the film. In *Little Miss Sunshine*, Grandpa Edwin has been forced to live with his children and their family when he is thrown out of his retirement home for using and selling drugs. He is treated as needing a babysitter himself, but he ends up becoming a central figure in the family. He imparts an important truth to his granddaughter: "A real loser is someone who's so afraid of not winning he doesn't even try." His wisdom trumps his other misbehavior and breaking of social norms. These representations present grandfathers as Cassandra-like figures, able to see the truth but not believed at first. However, they often are redeemed by the end of the film because of their knowledge, while still retaining their childlike qualities.

The grandparents do not perform their truth functions with words alone. Grandmothers also use physical intimidation. The films *Grandma* and *Georgia Rule* both feature scenes in which the grandmothers beat up men who have mistreated their grandchildren. The scenes illustrate the grandmothers' devotion to their grandchildren and the rage they can muster without care for the law or other social codes of behavior. If an adult hits another adult, one might expect retribution, but an elderly person hitting someone at least half their age is seen both as nonthreatening and humorous.

Sexuality becomes a way to elicit humor by having the grandparents cross lines of propriety with their honesty. Most of the sexual representation of grandparents falls into two different extremes: absence or obsession. *Bad Grandpa* is produced by the MTV Jackass film series, where people are filmed performing dangerous stunts or acting crudely to strangers. The main character is a bad driver, steals, is sexually inappropriate (he pulls down his pants in public), and tries to use his grandson to hook up with women. In *Little Miss Sunshine*, Grandpa Edwin teaches his granddaughter Olive an inappropriate burlesque dance to perform at a beauty pageant, unbeknownst to the rest of the family. Before another member of the family runs into a store at a rest stop, he asks if Edwin wants anything. "Yeah, get me some porn," Edwin replies. "Get me something really nasty too, I don't want any of that airbrushed s**t." He brags about his sex life at the retirement house and quizzes his teenage grandson about his sex life. The other characters in the film disapprove of his behavior, but they put up no real resistance. When he is finally challenged and the family threatens to kick him out of the road trip, he fights back: "So, pull the truck over! You're not gonna shut me up! F**K YOU! I can say what I want!"

While the film portrays this behavior as inappropriate, it is also presented as one of the consequences of aging and senility. Most of *Dirty Grandpa* involves the grandfather acting recklessly and in a childlike manner. Like Grandpa Edwin, he seems overly invested in his sexuality, and he constantly looks for women to sleep with. His irresponsibility spills over to his grandson, and he encourages him to drink, frolic with women, and causes him to end up in jail. To convince his grandson to help him hook up, he says, "The greatest gift a grandson can give his grandfather is a hot college girl who wants to have unprotected sex with him before he dies." In these representations, oversexualized grandfathers are consumed by their id, with sex serving their self-gratification. They have gone too far in expressing their internal desires.

While the grandfathers' overt sexuality is treated as inappropriate and perhaps a result of senility, grandmothers often serve to provide humor by being sexual, contrasting with the chaste image typically associated with older women. The humor for these grandma figures rests in treating their hypersexuality as a punch line. For example, when an adult grandson in the film *Grandma's Boy* moves in with his grandmother and her roommates, one of his friends loses his virginity to one of his grandmother's roommates. When comparing partners, the elderly roommate admits, "Let's see, you were my, uh, I don't know, 3,000 something." The friend then mutters, "I should have worn a condom." The humor is derived from inverting the expectation of who typically is more sexually experienced. After her husband's death in *Gigi Does It*, Gigi graphically describes sex acts and searches for a sexual partner.[40] These representations conform to the stereotypical dualism that typically surrounds depictions of female behavior. Women are confined to either maternal, asexual, and nonthreatening portrayals or they are oversexualized women not suited for maternity.[41]

More recently, programs have featured grandmothers who use sexuality to express their identity. In *Grandma*, Elle losing her lover is a major theme in the film, and her granddaughter's sexuality and pregnancy force her to acknowledge her own sexuality. At one point in the film, she is even willing to prostitute herself to a former love to earn money for the abortion her teenage granddaughter needs. The sitcom *Mom* showcases teen pregnancy over three generations. In a particularly poignant episode, Bonnie realizes she is going through menopause. She's heartbroken and thinks her life is over. Her daughter suggests that she could focus instead on being a grandmother. Later Bonnie agrees: "I woke up in the middle of the night and realized, since I'm clearly not a sexual being, I needed a new identity." However, she looks ridiculous as "the caregiver, the nurturing crone," as she calls it. By the end of the show, she uses hormone therapy to return to her normal state of craving sex.[42]

Many of these stories begin with elderly characters who have no place to go, such as Grandpa Edwin, who is forced to live with his children; or they are isolated figures, such as the grandmothers in *Georgia Rules* and *Grandma*, who live alone and are left behind with little or no relationship with their own children. With so little to lose, they often become liberated. They can say what they want, and sometimes they are able to speak to more difficult truths in society, like the grandmother in *Grandma* who discusses women's lack of power in society. At the same time, they also violate social norms by not reining in truths, like when they openly express their sexual urges. At other times, they speak out on behalf of the most marginalized members of their families, their grandchildren. As the elderly lose power and respect in society, they can align themselves with others who have a similar social status, often their grandchildren. Yet, their truth comes with the price of not always being believed, or of others realizing their value only after their death.

POWER PLAYS

Representations of grandparenting in these programs illustrate the power clashes and symbiotic relationships between grandparents and their extended families. In some shows, the grandparents must move in with their children, while in others, the children must move in with their parents. In a few stories, the conflict is over grandparents who do not live with their children and must fight for access to their grandchildren. Most programs represent battles over power and the culture clashes that ensue. A common tactic in television programming is assembling different groups of people and watching them interact. Therefore, it is not surprising that television programs often show grandparents living with their grandchildren or grandchildren living with their grandparents. Throughout different periods, however, the representation of these familiar relations change.

The 1970s television program *The Waltons* was set in the earlier period of the Depression and World War II; however, the representation of the family nostalgically imagines rural families from earlier historical periods living intergenerationally, under one roof. The grandparents are valued and needed to help maintain and support the family. Depictions of grandparents in later periods, intermingled with family members living with or near them, reflect more complicated social interactions. Often, a grandparent is the cranky or meddling figure, such as in the programs *Mama's Family* (1983), *All in the Family* (1971), and *Everybody Loves Raymond* (1996). These shows rely on plots in which the grandparents cause problems for the parents by interfering with the raising of the grandchildren. For example, in one episode of *All in the Family*, Archie is upset about his daughter and son-in-law's disinterest in religion, so he defies their wishes by secretly baptizing his grandson Joey. The first episode of the television program *Family Matters* (1989) is about the dad's fear of his mother, who is about to move into the family's house. His fear proves true when she sides with her grandson over him in an argument about whether the teenager can stay out late at a party. In *Full House*, the brother-in-law and best friend move in to help a widower take care of his daughters. In one episode, the grandmother is thinking of moving in, and they all find the idea horrifying. Later, recognizing her need to have value in her life, they offer to set her up nearby. The shows during these earlier periods represent grandparents as both a threat and an inevitable part of the family. The obligations of family mean that grandparents must be tolerated, but family members try to keep them at a distance.

More recently, perhaps reflecting the needs of the sandwich generation of caregivers, programs have been representing the dual caregiving that adult children perform, with different generations sharing one roof. Both the grandparent and the middle generation express their frustration and love. For example, in *Young Sheldon* (2017), set in the late 1980s and early 1990s, the grandmother, Connie Tucker (Meemaw), lives across the street. Connie is presented as both a quirky character and someone who speaks the wise truth. She cares greatly for her grandchildren, but she does not want to be overburdened with caring for them. In one episode, Connie declines to take on further after-school care. Her daughter says, "But you love your grandchildren," and Meemaw replies, "I love ice cream too, but I don't want to eat it from 3 o'clock to 6 o'clock five days a week."[43] Grandma Saracen in the series *Friday Night Lights* ostensibly cares for her grandson Matt, but he takes care of his grandmother himself, as she suffers from dementia. Much of the humor in the program *Mom* derives from the woman taking care of both her children and her mother, though she accepts help from her mother when offered. In the Showtime series *The Chi*, Ronnie cares for his elderly grandmother while she looks out for his best interest. Compared with shows produced in earlier periods, these programs present the tensions and mutual dependence between grandparents and their children from both perspectives.

The grandmother character can sometimes even supplant the couple relationship in a show. For example, when Mindy becomes pregnant in *The Mindy Project*, her boyfriend Danny's mother, Annette, realizes it and is more excited than her son. If Danny is Mindy's "baby daddy," then Annette is Mindy's "baby granny." Annette acts as Mindy's nanny while he is away, but Mindy fires her because she finds her too intrusive. Annette threatens to sue Mindy for lost wages, reflecting a modern idea that childcare should be recognized as valuable labor. Later, Mindy realizes that her newly hired nanny is problematic (she's an anti-vaccinator, for example) and asks her baby granny to come back.[44] After coming to terms, Annette resumes watching the baby. Later, even when Danny is no longer involved romantically with Mindy, Annette and Mindy remain bonded.

Similarly, in *How I Met Your Mother*, Lily does not want her father, whom she believes was a miserable caretaker for her during her childhood, to be her nanny. She keeps looking for alternative choices, finally settling on a "perfect" nanny, until she realizes that she's not willing to leave her baby with a stranger. After she falls asleep and wakes to find her father compassionately taking care of the baby on his own, she finally admits that he would make a great nanny.[45] These programs reflect an acceptance among family members of the need to work together to raise the next generation, and they recognize the symbiotic relationship between parents and grandparents. The programs also illustrate grandparents' challenges in finding the right balance of having access to their grandchildren without meddling in their children's affairs.

Often the battle for control manifests in the conflict over access to grandchildren. In *Gilmore Girls*, the grandparents' wealth does not guarantee they can see or have influence over their grandchild. Their daughter, teenage mother Lorelai, had run away from home with her baby and remains estranged from her parents Richard and Emily until she needs their financial support to send her daughter to a prep school. When they require weekly family dinners to guarantee their financial support for Rory's schooling, they enforce a connection to the family. Similarly, access to grandchildren is a major theme in the film *Parental Guidance*. The grandparents, Artie and Diane, depend on the parents to let them into the lives of their grandchildren. When their children call them to ask them to babysit for a weekend, the grandmother is excited. She becomes anxious, though, when she sees pictures of the children's paternal grandparents on the mantel, but none of her or her husband. She worries that they have become the "other grandparents," saying, "They have their real grandparents that they love and put on the mantel, and then there's us." During the remainder of the film, she sets off to prove her worth as a grandparent.

Other representations show grandparents competing with other sets of grandparents for attention and access to their grandchildren. Grace visits her daughter Mallory to help with the grandchildren after Mallory is prescribed bed rest while pregnant with twins in an episode of the Netflix sitcom *Grace and Frankie*. Once there, she becomes upset when she finds Grandma Jean, their paternal grandmother, already there. Grandma Jean says, "I can stay as long as she needs. My house plants are plastic, and my husband's dead." Grace is uninterested in playing the games the children want, and she finds herself unable to connect with them. Later, she laments to her friend Frankie that she's a bad grandmother. Frankie offers a grandmother pet metaphor, advising: "Not all hamster grandmas need to run around in the wood shavings making forts out of toilet paper tubes. Some keep the little ones from eating their poop." When Grace finally accepts her grandma personality, she finds value in her own attributes. She teaches her grandchildren to play cards and tells them the truth about where babies come from.[46] These programs reinforce grandparents' feelings of dependency on their children over seeing their grandchildren and the pressure they sometimes place on themselves to conform to high expectations.

Despite grandparents on these programs wanting to be a part of their children's lives, sometimes what stands in the way is a culture clash of age and values. In *Parental Guidance*, the grandfather Artie is told that he's been fired because he doesn't have enough of a connection with today's youth, especially without a social media presence. Much of this film contrasts the parents and grandchildren embracing technology with the grandparents' lack of knowledge. The grandparents can't figure out how to operate most of the household appliances, drive the car, or even use the children's car seat. Later, the grandson helps the grandfather by teaching him about ESPN's X Games and other extreme sporting events to prepare him for a job interview. Age is not seen as a path to wisdom but a weakness that needs to be overcome.

Another culture clash emerges from grandparents' different values for raising children. A recurring theme in programs is that past parenting styles are simply inferior. Many stories contrast the current focus on more intensive parenting with the laissez-faire style of earlier periods. Episodes of *Raising Hope* find humor in contrasting the son's ideas on the right way to parent with his parents' unwillingness to change, like his mom constantly smoking in front of the baby or flashbacks that show the father as a baby riding in a car without a car seat and a hole in the floor.[47] In *Parental Guidance*, Artie calls his son soft for not being willing to discipline his children through spanking. He also introduces "old school" parenting to the family: "We all sit at one table, and we all eat the same thing," he announces at dinner. He ignores his daughter and son-in-law's rules, feeds his grandchildren sugar, and uses his own method to solve his grandson's speech impediment. In the ABC television series *Black-ish*, Grandma Ruby ignores all of her daughter-in-law Bow's instructions when she babysits the children, feeding them sugar and letting them play violent video games. Bow, having just dealt with her father-in-law Pop's health scare, forgives her and tells her, "You're a bad person, but you're a fantastic grandma. It's okay that you spoil them. Every moment we get with you is a gift."[48] Grandparenting is sometimes seen as a threat to parental authority, but one that is often resolved after the adult children realize that the older generation has something to offer.

In some programs, grandchildren prefer the company or advice of their grandparents to that of their own parents, generating a threat to the parental figure. For example, in the television sitcom *The Goldbergs*, set in the 1980s, the character Pops is an involved grandfather. His grandson Adam, who also narrates the show, describes him as "my grandfather, Pops, 80 years of pure awesome." Pops often "rescues" his grandchildren from the decisions made by their parents. Adam narrates, "He was always cooking up a plan in that brilliant mind of his." Throughout the episodes, Pops often disagrees with a parental rule and instead does what he wants. He buys his grandson a car, despite his parents having said no to one. He pretends to take his youngest grandson to the gym, but really takes him to the mall to give him lessons on how to pick up women. In the first episode, when his daughter takes away his car because of a recent accident, he says, "If you take away my car, you take away my time with my grandson. Getting waffles with that little guy, it's the best part of my week." This character illustrates the grandparent as a figure who colludes with his grandchildren against a common enemy: the parents. He also is dependent on his children to give him access to his grandchildren. In *Black-ish*, Pops becomes a threat to Bow when he bonds with her teenager daughter Zoey, despite Bow's attempts to do the same. Zoey tells her mother, "I talked to Pops. He gave me some awesome advice. You should cherish him more." When Bow presses him about his advice, he replies, "I listened to her, gave her some generic advice in a deep, soothing voice. I Morgan Freeman-ed her."[49]

The grandparents in these programs strive to prove their value as grandparents. Much of the humor occurs when the elderly characters accidentally offer value to the family. The shows also imply a natural link between grandchild and grandparent, serving oftentimes to counter, balance, or threaten parenting approaches and philosophies.

GRANDPARENT CULTURES

Given that the elderly, and grandparents in particular, face the problem of a lack of representation in television programming, minority grandparent characters face an even greater obstacle, as television historically also has less representation of minority characters as well. A 2010 study on representation of minorities in television found:

> the vast majority of Latino (91 percent) and white (77 percent) characters were in main roles, while only 61 percent of African Americans were depicted in such a television role. Thus, the few Latino actors that appeared in prime time were in main roles. While African American characters were three times more likely than Latinos to appear on television, they were more likely to be depicted in minor roles. Still, the sheer representation of minority characters is lacking—especially Latino and other minority characters.[50]

While grandparents can pose a threat to the power structure of a nuclear family, they also can be valuable in their role as transmitters of culture.

Sociologist Patricia Hill Collins argues, "Motherhood, whether bloodmother, othermother, or community othermother, can be invoked by Black women as a symbol of power."[51] Often, popular representations of minority characters represent grandparents as holding important patriarch and matriarch roles within the family. An example of this is the character Mabel "Madea" Simmons, played by Tyler Perry. Madea speaks the truth and refuses to conform to the rules of society, and she imposes her own form of justice. She's frequently brought into courts of law because of her tendency to threaten others, but she also is a nurturing figure. Her motivations are good, in that her decisions are made in efforts to protect her family. She often takes her grandchildren into her home as a refuge when they have no other place to go.

Madea's representation fits the dominant and stereotypical image of women of color in popular culture. Collins discusses how the Mammy image consists of a black woman taking care of white children through nurturing of the children and subservient behavior to her employers, while often needing to leave her own children in the care of others. In contrast, the Matriarch figure represents a colder, harsher black woman caring for her own children, who often is more preoccupied with economic survival than nurturing, and is perceived to emasculate the men around her.[52] Marilyn Yarbrough and Crystal Bennett describe a third stereotype—the "Sapphire"—as "evil, bitchy, stubborn, and hateful."[53] The Sapphire often takes out her anger on the black males around her, according to these authors. The character of Madea seems to combine the images of Mammy, Matriarch, and Sapphire. She is ultimately a caretaker, but she offers a rougher, hard-nosed approach. The grandmother image also allows Madea the freedom to speak freely while retaining her authority and power over her family. Because Tyler Perry plays the role in drag, Madea comes to represent a more inclusive voice, speaking ideas that many may think, but that only a grandmother could get away with saying.[54] However, some may argue that Perry contributes to the invisibility of the black grandmother because he plays the role in drag rather than casting an actual elderly woman.

Like the black grandmother, the black grandfather role on television also serves the function of portraying elderly folks who speak their mind. The program *Black-ish* treats the live-in grandfather Pops as an essential member of the family. Pops is often portrayed as grumpy and in disagreement with the modern parenting style of his son and daughter-in-law. In particular, he sees a problem in the way his grandchildren are not being taught about the difficulties of surviving while being black in a white world. He regularly expresses distrust of institutions such as the medical profession and the IRS. For example, Pops tells Bow, "My daddy told me there ain't but three things in life a black man's got to do: stay black, pay taxes, and die. . . . The IRS came after my daddy, scared his black a** white as a ghost."[55]

Animated films that focus on different cultural groups often follow similar patterns of portraying grandmother figures as the characters who are thought of as crazy or dismissed but speak the truth. In the Disney film *Moana*, Gramma Tala is set apart from the tribe both physically, as she lives isolated from the other members, and in her beliefs and practices. She imparts stories and ideas to her granddaughter Moana that the rest of the tribe rejects. She is thought of as strange to the tribe, but the story frames her ideas, in part because of the virtue of her age, as holding value for Moana and the tribe as a whole. Gramma Tala has a special relationship with her grandchild, understanding her when others do not. Similarly, the character Abuelita in the film *Coco* serves as the matriarch to the family. In her role as protector of the family, she hits Miguel on the head with a shoe to enforce the family's ban on music. Only after reconciling the history of his ancestors can Miguel move the family forward. In these films, the grandparents possess great, if unrecognized, power through their knowledge of their cultural and family history.

Some programs have the grandparents showcase their knowledge as they transmit it to their grandchildren. The cultural influence of grandparents resides in programs that highlight these close intergenerational relationships. Particularly in immigrant families, grandparents represent a connection to a heritage that parents have left behind as families settle in a new land. Some researchers have explored the role that grandparents play in minority families as historians of the family and preservers of their traditional cultures. Yoshinori Kamo writes that Asian American children, in particular, "learn to be Asians mostly from their family members including grandparents, while they learn to be Americans mostly from people outside their family."[56] The Taiwanese family in the sitcom *Fresh off the Boat* has their Grandmother Jenny live with them. The show frequently uses the gag of forgetting about the grandmother, as when the family leaves without her when going on trips. The humor comes from the depiction of the grandmother as a part of the scenery and an easily forgotten member of the household. She leads a full—if invisible—life, and her family is surprised when they see her friends and activities. Yet, she's also an integral part of the household, often giving advice and counsel that the family members do not always want but realize they need.[57] In *Dr. Ken*, a sitcom about a Korean American doctor and his family, the grandfather, DK, moves in during the beginning of the second season and becomes a regular presence in the lives of his grandchildren.[58]

In the reboot of the 1970s sitcom *One Day at a Time*, a Cuban American single mom named Penelope lives with her two teenage children and her mother Lydia. Lydia keeps their Cuban heritage and culture alive for her grandchildren with rituals and religious references, but she also is immediately accepting of their lives, particularly when her teen granddaughter Elena comes out as gay. In *Jane the Virgin*, Jane has grown up with her mother

Xiomara (Xo) and her grandmother Alba. Flashbacks show that Jane had often served as a mediator between her mother and grandmother when the two could not agree. Yet they remain an important presence in each other's lives. Alba watches telenovelas and shares them with her daughter and granddaughter. She's religious, and though she can understand English, she speaks Spanish on the show, encouraging an appreciation for the language and culture.[59]

Researchers note that grandparents can play important roles in preserving religious beliefs across generations.[60] These programs represent grandparents as invested in their obligation to pass on cultural traditions to their grandchildren. While at times their advice might seem silly or ill-advised, they are frequently depicted as loyal. Most of the grandparents reveal their value to their children and grandchildren, who eventually appreciate what they have to offer. The grandparents here are willing to sacrifice their own freedom and livelihood for the survival and happiness of their families and their descendants' future.

GRANDPARENT AS SUPERHERO

Increasingly, fictional stories are portraying grandparents as superheroes or magical, with supernatural powers. These grandparents often have not only a personal relationship with their grandchild, but also serve as a larger, general grandparent figure. These representations reflect emerging trends in aging and questions about the status of grandparents today.

In *Just Add Magic*, an Amazon original series for children, a grandmother is a central figure in the program. She lives with her son's family and often cooked with her granddaughter, but she has lost her voice now and seems unable to function. In the program, she is the victim of a magic cooking spell and is unable to use her voice. During the first season, the granddaughter and her two friends work to find a magic cure for her condition. While the grandmother is without a voice during the first season, she holds within her the knowledge of magical spells. After the spell is broken, she discourages her granddaughter and her friends from using the cookbook of spells. The magic represents both power and danger, something that may be used but should be feared. The grandmother's condition resembles dementia, and her granddaughter desperately wants to find a way to understand her. Magic in the show is a tool the granddaughter uses to help her grandmother find her voice and restore her power.

The magical powers of grandparent characters give them agency over their lives and others. *Uncle Grandpa*, a Cartoon Network show, features a superhero character described as "not just *your* Uncle Grandpa, but he's everybody in the world's Uncle Grandpa." His purpose is to bring fun and reassurance to children and other characters in the program. "I believe in you," he tells a kid who is sad because his shirt doesn't fit over his belly.[61] His magical powers include being able to duplicate himself, solve problems, fight wolves, and rescue tigers. He can help children overcome their fear of the dark or take them on an exciting adventure. Nana, the grandmother in *Nina Needs to Go*, can sense when Nina needs rescuing, and she has superhero-like tools at her disposal, such as her trusty umbrella, which she uses to fly in like Mary Poppins. She always finds a bathroom for her granddaughter in time, even when the task seems impossible. Unlike Nina's parents and older brother, Nana never judges Nina for waiting too long.

Another powerful grandfather/grandson team shows up in the surreal program *Rick and Morty*, part of the Adult Swim lineup on Cartoon Network's nighttime programing for adult viewers. Television critic Neil Genzlinger describes *Rick and Morty* as "grandparenting at its unhinged finest."[62] In the show, the mad scientist grandfather takes his often-reluctant grandson on absurdist adventures. Like other magical grandparent characters, he exposes his grandchild to new worlds. Their difference in age does not impede their ability to work together. In contrast, they show few physical constraints and often engage in aggressive, superhuman physical activities. By the very nature of their age, these superhero grandparents have the time, patience, and knowledge to provide experiences—or in the case of Nina, bathrooms—for the grandchildren in their lives.

Magical grandparents have their counterpart in popular entertainment: evil grandparents. Much of the dark humor or horror arises from reversing common stereotypes about weak or innocent grandparents. Examples of these evil grandparent figures can be found in films such as *Grandma's House* (1988) and *Flowers in the Attic* (2014), where children are left in the cruel care of their grandmother. In *Grandpa's Psycho* (2015), the grandfather's love and care for his granddaughter contrasts with his torturing and murdering women he believes are sinful. Children visiting their grandparents during the summer in *The Visit* (2015) begin to notice their disturbing behavior. In *Paranormal Activity 3* (2011), Grandma Lois makes a deal with a demon that impacts her grandchildren in the future. The grandmother is not herself evil in the 2015 horror film *The Chosen*, but she has to be sacrificed to save her family from a demon. Instead of serving as an essential connection to their family's traditions and culture, these grandparent figures are to be feared or must be sacrificed for the good of the family.

These two opposing archetypes make visible a struggle with the idea of aging. On the one hand, these characters resonate with the fact that people are living longer and more often are engaged in physical activity, resisting the stereotype of frailty. These magical and superhuman characters illustrate to children a grandparent figure that is post-age, existing in a world that values their mythical powers and ability to seek unique adventures. On the other hand, the characters are cast in a fantasy world, suggesting the limits their age would impose in reality. The evil grandparent reverses the power of the elderly, turning them from something that is celebrated into a power that should be feared. Evil grandparent characters play into anxieties about the struggles over differing values, family control, and shifting political power and competition for resources as people live longer and demand more visibility.

CONCLUSION

In many ways, the image of grandparents has come quite far from the song in which a reindeer runs over a drunk grandma. These days, that grandmother, and her grandfather counterpart, are much more likely to be traveling to some magical place, embarking on a grandparent/grandchild road trip, or offering wise counsel to children or grandchildren during a moment of need. Simultaneously, stories in popular culture often show that the grandparent character needs a grandchild in order to have a second chance, resolve unfinished business, and become valuable again to society. In some representations, grandparents move from being occasional visitors to having an integral role in a grandchild's life, sometimes at the expense of the parents. Humor from many of these programs often reinforces stereotypes of aging. The grandparents are sage truth-tellers, but only because they do not seem to know when to be quiet. They are having their own sexual revolutions, but they treat them as public experiences.

These representations position the maturity of the grandparent somewhere between that of the unruly child and the seasoned adult. They have childlike tendencies to satisfy their own urges that violate social norms, but they are endowed with wisdom gained from years of living. They are valuable but also can pose a threat. Grandparents often transform their grandchildren and help to make their world better in these stories. While they maintain that grandparents are needed and valuable, that value comes not from what they can contribute to the world themselves but how they can help the next generation flourish.

NOTES

1. Elmo Shropshire and Patsy Shropshire, "Grandma Got Run Over by a Reindeer," written by Randy Brooks, released January 1, 1979.

2. Jamshid J. Tehrani, "The Phylogeny of Little Red Riding Hood," *PLOS ONE* 8, no. 11 (November 13, 2013): e78871, http://dx.doi.org/10.1371/journal.pone.0078871.

3. JoEtta A. Vernon et al., "Media Stereotyping: A Comparison of the Way Elderly Women and Men Are Portrayed on Primetime Television," *Journal of Women & Aging* 2, no. 4 (1990): 55–68, https://doi.org/10.1300/J074v02n04_05; Tom Robinson and Caitlin Anderson, "Older Characters in Children's Animated Television Programs: A Content Analysis of Their

Portrayal," *Journal of Broadcasting & Electronic Media* 50, no. 2 (June 2006): 295, https://doi.org/10.1207/s15506878jobem5002_7.

4. George Gerbner et al., "Aging with Television: Images on Television Drama and Conceptions of Social Reality," *Journal of Communication* 30, no. 1 (Winter 1980): 45, https://doi.org/10.1111/j.1460-2466.1980.tb01766.x.

5. Margie M. Donlon, Ori Ashman, and Becca R. Levy, "Re-Vision of Older Television Characters: A Stereotype-Awareness Intervention," *Journal of Social Issues* 61, no. 2 (June 2005): 314, https://doi.org/10.1111%2Fj.1540-4560.2005.00407.x.

6. Robinson and Anderson, "Older Characters," 208.

7. Robinson and Anderson, 209.

8. Ursula Falk and Gerhard Falk, *Grandparents: A New Look at the Supporting Generation* (Amherst, NY: Prometheus Books, 2002), 168.

9. Robert M. Beland and Terry L. Mills, "Positive Portrayal of Grandparents in Current Children's Literature," *Journal of Family Issues* 22, no. 5 (July 1, 2001): 639–651, https://doi.org/10.1177/019251301022005006.

10. It is even recognized on TV.com's list of popular tropes as part of the "I want grandkids" plotlines.

11. "I Want Grandkids," TV Tropes (web page), accessed December 5, 2017, http://tvtropes.org/pmwiki/pmwiki.php/Main/IWantGrandkids.

12. *Everybody Loves Raymond*, "A Job for Robert," Season 2, Episode 8, CBS, November 29, 2004, directed by Gary Halvorson.

13. *Mad About You*, "The Good, the Bad, and the Not So Appealing," Season 4, Episode 4, NBC, October 29, 2005, directed by David Steinberg, written by Paul Reiser and Danny Jacobson.

14. *How I Met Your Mother*, "Brunch," Season 2, Episode 3, CBS, October 1, 2006, directed by Pamela Fryman, written by Carter Bays and Craig Thomas.

15. *Teen Mom OG*, "Put a Ring on It," Season 6, Episode 1, MTV, August 22, 2016, produced by Carly Rhodes; *Teen Mom OG*, "Tweet Tweet," Season 6, Episode 2, MTV, August 22, 2016, produced by Carly Rhodes.

16. For more about mothers and ideology, see Shari Thurer, *The Myths of Motherhood: How Culture Reinvents the Good Mother* (New York: Penguin Books, 1995).

17. Janice Kelly and Laura Tropp, "Changing Conceptions of the Good Dad in Popular Culture," in *Deconstructing Dads: Changing Images of Fathers in Popular Culture*, ed. Laura Tropp and Janice Kelly (Lanham, MD: Lexington Books, 2016): xi–xx.

18. Laura Tropp, "Who's Your Daddy: Sperm Donation and the Cultural Construction of Fatherhood," in *Deconstructing Dads: Changing Images of Fathers in Popular Culture*, ed. Laura Tropp and Janice Kelly (Lanham, MD: Lexington Books, 2016): 31–50.

19. Anne Tergesen, "The Long (Long) Wait to Be a Grandparent," *The Wall Street Journal*, March 30, 2014, https://www.wsj.com/articles/the-wait-to-become-a-grandparent-gets-longer-1396020375.

20. *Raising Hope*, "Pilot," Season 1, Episode 1, FOX, September 21, 2010, directed by Michael Fresco, written by Gregory Thomas Garcia and Lucas Neff.

21. Though labeled reality programs, the people within these programs do become characters, with their construction within the program created and shaped by producers. Having said that, the real aspects of their lives that are blended with the construction of their characters still lead to interesting understandings of how aging and relationships between grandparents and their children are seen.

22. Laura Tropp, "What's a Baby Daddy to Do: Fathers on the Fringe in MTV's *16 and Pregnant*," in *MTV and Teen Pregnancy: Critical Essays on* 16 and Pregnant *and* Teen Mom, ed. Letizia Guglielmo (Lanham, MD: Scarecrow Press, 2013), 161–176.

23. *30 Something Grandma*, "Adventures of Prudence," Season 1, Episode 2, A&E, November 22, 2016, produced by Jennifer Duncan.

24. *16 and Pregnant*, "Jordan 2011," Season 3, Episode 1, MTV, April 19, 2011, produced by Dia Sokol.

25. *Teen Mom 2*, "Expect a Miracle," Season 6, Episode 10, MTV, September 10, 2015, produced by Alexis Charizopoulos.

26. Julia Halewicz, "Accidental Grandparents," *Grandparents.com* (web page), accessed October 27, 2016, https://www.grandparents.com/family-and-relationships/family-matters/accidental-grandparents.

27. *30 Something Grandma*, "Adventures of Patricia," Season 1, Episode 1, A&E, November 15, 2016, produced by Ali Mansfield.

28. *30 Something Grandma*, "Adventures of Chantal," Season 1, Episode 3, A&E, November 29, 2016, produced by Ali Mansfield.

29. *30 Something Grandma*, "Adventures of Patricia."

30. Falk and Falk, *Grandparents: A New Look*, 58.

31. Richard Fry, "For First Time in Modern Era, Living with Parents Edges Out Other Living Arrangements for 18- to 34-Year-Olds" (Washington, DC: Pew Research Center, May 24, 2016), http://www.pewsocialtrends.org/2016/05/24/for-first-time-in-modern-era-living-with-parents-edges-out-other-living-arrangements-for-18-to-34-year-olds/.

32. Fry, *For the First Time,* 20.

33. Karen L. Fingerman and J. Jill Suitor, "Millennials and Their Parents: Implications of the New Young Adulthood for Midlife Adults," *Innovation in Aging* 1, no. 3 (November 1, 2017): 5, https://academic.oup.com/innovateage/article/1/3/igx026/4643095.

34. Walter Ong, *Orality and Literacy: The Technologizing of the Word* (New York: Routledge, 1991), 41.

35. Robert E. Yahnke, "Intergeneration and Regeneration: The Meaning of Old Age in Films and Videos," in *Handbook of the Humanities and Aging*, ed. Thomas R. Cole, Robert Kastenbaum, and Ruth E. Ray, 2nd ed. (New York: Springer Publishing Co., 2000), 295.

36. *Me and My Grandma*, "Elderboo," Season 1, Episode 2, YouTube Red, March 22, 2017, written by Cynthia Adarkwa and Liz Rivera.

37. *Me and My Grandma*, "Elderboo."

38. *Game of Thrones*, Seasons 3-4, HBO, 2012–2013.

39. Falk and Falk, *Grandparents: A New Look*, 147.

40. *Me and My Grandma*, "Barfelona," Season 1, Episode 5, YouTube Red, March 22, 2017, written by April Quioh.

41. For more on dualism, see Amber E. Kinser, *Motherhood and Feminism* (Berkeley: Perseus Books, 2010), 9–11.

42. *Mom*, "Estrogen and a Hearty Breakfast," Season 1, Episode 7, CBS, November 14, 2013, directed by James Widdoes, written by Chuck Lorre and Eddie Gorodetsky.

43. *Young Sheldon*, "Potato Salad, a Broomstick, and Dad's Whiskey," Season 1, Episode 14, CBS, March 1, 2018. Directed by Howie Deutch, written by Chuck Lorre, Steven Molaro, and Tara Hernandez.

44. *The Mindy Project*, "Mindy and Nanny," Season 4, Episode 7, FOX, October 27, 2015, directed by Roger Kumble, written by Mindy Kaling and Lang Fisher.

45. *How I Met Your Mother*, "Nannies," Season 8, Episode 3, CBS, October 8, 2012, directed by Pamela Fryman, written by Carter Bays and Craig Thomas.

46. *Grace and Frankie*, "The Negotiation," Season S2, Episode 3, Netflix, May 6, 2016, directed by Trent O'Donnell, written by Marta Kauffman and Howard Morris.

47. *Raising Hope*, "Pilot."

48. *Black-ish*, "Dr. Hell No," Season 2, Episode 3, ABC, October 7, 2015, directed by Millicent Shelton, written by Kenya Barris and Gail Lerner.

49. *Black-ish*, "The Talk," Season 1, Episode 2, ABC, October 1, 2014, directed by Rebecca Asher, written by Kenya Barris and Vijal Patel.

50. Elizabeth Monk-Turner, Mary Heiserman, Crystle Johnson, Vanity Cotton, and Manny Jackson, "The Portrayal of Racial Minorities on Prime Time Television: A Replication of the Mastro and Greenberg Study a Decade Later," *Studies in Popular Culture* 32, no. 2 (Spring 2010): 108, https://www.jstor.org/stable/23416158.

51. Patricia Hill Collins, "The Meaning of Motherhood in Black Culture and Mother-Daughter Relationships," in *Maternal Theory, Essential Readings*, ed. Andrea O'Reilly (Toronto: Demeter Press, 2007), 281.

52. Patricia Hill Collins, *Black Feminist Thought: Knowledge, Consciousness, and the Politics of Empowerment*, 2nd ed. (New York: Routledge Classics, 2009), 85.

53. Marilyn Yarbrough and Crystal Bennett, "Cassandra and the Sistahs: The Peculiar Treatment of African American Women in the Myth of Women as Liars," *Journal of Gender, Race and Justice* 3 (Spring 2000): 638.

54. *Big Momma's House* (Twentieth Century Fox, June 2, 2000) also uses granny drag. Martin Lawrence stars as an FBI agent who dresses up as a grandmother to conduct his investigation.

55. *Black-ish*, "Switch Hitting," Season 1, Episode 20, ABC, April 22, 2015, directed by Ken Whittingham, written by Kenya Barris.

56. Yoshinori Kamo, "Asian Grandparents," in *Handbook on Grandparenthood*, ed. Maximiliane Szinovácz (Westport, CT: Greenwood Press, 1998), 110.

57. *Fresh off the Boat*, Seasons 1–4, ABC, 2015–, created by Nahnatchka Khan.

58. *Dr. Ken*, Seasons 1–2, ABC, 2015–2017, created by John Fox, Ken Jeong, and Jared Stern.

59. *Jane the Virgin*, Seasons 1–4, CW 2014–, written and developed by Jennie Snyder Urman.

60. Casey Copen and Merril Silverstein, "Transmission of Religious Beliefs across Generations: Do Grandparents Matter?" *Journal of Comparative Family Studies* 38, no. 4 (Autumn 2007): 497–510.

61. *Uncle Grandpa*, "Pilot," Season 1, Pilot, Cartoon Network, May 7, 2010, created and written by Peter Browngardt.

62. Neil Genzlinger, "A Warm and Fuzzy Grandpa? Well, Not Exactly '*Rick and Morty*' on Adult Swim," *New York Times*, December 1, 2013, http://www.nytimes.com/2013/12/02/arts/television/rick-and-morty-on-adult-swim.html.

Chapter Five

Performing Granny and Pop

A widely shared YouTube video features grandparents misidentifying the phrase "Netflix and Chill," which has become new youth slang for hooking up.[1] A video of a Canadian grandmother's New Year's greeting to her grandchildren went viral after her grandchild placed it on YouTube.[2] Yet another set of grandparents also received much attention on YouTube for their video where they pick out a date for their grandson.[3] None of these activities alone are particularly unusual, but when these actions are done by a grandparent and shared publicly, they have the power to attract attention.

Grandparents can inspire, motivate, and entertain. Part of the appeal of the grandparent on social media, within reality television, or in celebrity or political worlds is the surprise of a person who is a grandparent still being an active player in worlds typically associated with younger people, like digital culture. These unexpected moments, though, also serve to reify common stereotypes associated with aging, serving to contrast these "hip" grandparents with those who do not have the same vibrancy or coolness. Grandparent images often are branded on the internet, reality television, and social media. These worlds sometimes become places where grandparents are able to reinvent the image of the elderly, reclaim a new image for themselves, or gain popularity, sometimes intentionally but sometimes not. At the same time, despite attempts to defy stereotypes associated with aging, these newer images often retain problematic representations from the past.

OUTING GRAM AND GRAMPS

Many elderly people use the image of the grandparent while embracing social media to become celebrities within digital worlds. Sometimes they use stereotypes of aging, but then turn them around to gain new power. At other times, they purposely counter images of the elderly by showcasing versions of themselves that defy stereotypes. Occasionally, their children or grandchildren thrust them into unexpected worlds. Once in these worlds, they are offered to the audience as a source of amusement, entertainment, or nostalgia.

One popular genre of YouTube posts is dancing grandparents. A quick search using the phrase "grandma dancing" in YouTube brings over two million results ("grandpa dancing" brings over one million). These videos often quickly attain viral success.[4] For example, BuzzFeed featured a viral video of Lady Gaga's Grandma Ronnie dancing while watching her granddaughter perform in concert.[5] CNN reported on another "Dancing Nana" video that a granddaughter made of her grandmother dancing to oldies music.[6] Grandmas breakdancing are particularly popular, with one video receiving over 100,000 views.[7] Most of these videos rest on the surprise that the grandparent is able to both appreciate popular culture and participate in it. Oftentimes, it is not the grandparents themselves posting the videos but their relatives, frequently a grandchild. They showcase their grandparents by contrasting them with the typical image of the more dormant, restful, rocking-chair grandparent. Grandchildren like to show that their grandparents are "cool." One video showing a great-grandmother dancing to Bruno Mars even made the *Today Show*.[8]

The dancing granny is not just an American phenomenon but an international trend. In China, so many dancing nannies have used outdoor public performances as opportunities to get exercise and express themselves that the Communist government has begun to see them as a political threat and started to rein them in.[9] In this example, one can see the appeal of the image of the grandparent. Dancing without worry of what others think is a sign of liberation and freedom. In China, a place where freedom is constrained, the dancing grandma becomes a symbol of autonomy. The United States is constrained less by political restrictions than by cultural expectations of certain ways to dress, act, and live, and grandparents remain one of the last groups, aside from children, who can express themselves however they want without fear of judgment.

Sometimes, though, the image of the grandparent shifts from being about self-expression to an inability to control impulses. The YouTube channel *The Angry Grandpa Show* has over three million subscribers. The show is hosted by a son, Michael "Pickelboy" Green, but features his father Charles Green, whom he labels "Angry Grandpa." Angry Grandpa may suffer from bipolar disorder; he has done everything from revealing to his grandchildren in a fit of rage that there is no Santa Claus, to expressing extreme political views, to actually breaking things.[10] After some of his initial videos, Angry Grandpa became an internet meme. He and his son often play pranks on each other. While some of his initial videos seem more genuine, the later ones have more of a performative feeling. The figure of Angry Grandpa plays into the aging stereotypes he represents. He seems unable to control his impulses, and while mental illness may be influencing his rage and anger, people laugh at it. He, like the dancing grandmas, represents those who can finally speak their mind with nothing to lose. He tends to go over the top, but his age makes him seem ultimately unthreatening, which allows others not to take him too seriously.

In other videos, grandparents find new technology empowering. A 79-year-old woman named Shirley Curry has over 100,000 subscribers on her YouTube channel, where she's known as Gamer Grandma. In her videos, she plays the online role-playing game the Elder Scrolls. Her videos have become an entirely new profession for her: she has to answer emails, deal with requests from media, and devote time to recording her gaming videos regularly.[11] In her gaming introduction, she introduces herself as "Grandma Shirley" and asks if you would like to join her while she plays Skyrim. Just like other gamers, she takes viewers through her playing of the game. She describes the reason why she plays: "What I really enjoy most in the game is traveling across the country, looking in all the caves, discovering places, fighting, killing things, looting—that's my preference."[12]

Curry usually opens her videos by referring to her subscribers as grandkids. She wasn't expecting the fame that she received, and now she feels at times that it's a bit like a job. Interviewed in *PC Gamer*, she says about her fans of all ages, "I'm Grandma to all of them . . . all of them call me Grandma."[13] YouTube artists often refer to their fans as "friends." While many different YouTube channels and television programs offer the image of the grandma for audiences to consume, in this case, Gamer Shirley has gone further in thinking of and treating her fans as if they were her grandchildren.

Many other grandparents ask their grandchildren for assistance in using social media. After Hillary Clinton received the Democratic nomination for president, many young women posted pictures of their grandmothers on social media to demonstrate their connection to the historic moment. One woman wrote, "My grandmother in Maryland asked me to share this. She was born during the Woodrow Wilson administration." In the picture, the grandmother holds a sign that says, "I've been waiting 95 years for this." Other women posted pictures of taking their grandmothers with them to vote in the primaries. One Tweet read: "Today I took my 85y/o gram to vote in PAs primary for the first time ever! #loveinpa #imwithher."[14]

In other cases, grandchildren express both shock and pride at their grandparents' actions. One grandmother was on vacation when she spontaneously decided to do shots with a group of young women on spring break. She posted the picture on Twitter, but it was her granddaughter's retweet with the caption "My grandma is in Mexico taking shots with random girls on the beach and posting pics of it with captions like they're bff's" that ended up with over 20,000 retweets.[15] Another grandson shared his Italian grandmother's frustrated efforts to work her Google Home device, mispronouncing "Google" as "Goo Goo."[16] The grandparents are simultaneously mocked and appreciated for what they do not know. Our culture's expectation of elderly grandparents rests in their knowledge of the past and not their awareness of current trends. When they do express knowledge of fads or popular culture, they provide shock, surprise, and comic relief.

Within social media, grandparents sometimes actively defy aging stereotypes. Scholar Hilde Van den Bulck says of the perception of aging: "Aging—and particularly influencing and resisting it—is today presented in popular and celebrity culture as a life choice rather than a biological certainty."[17] These YouTube videos can change people's perspectives of the elderly. One can be older but still be a gamer. One can be older but still enjoy the music of today. One can be older but still do shots on the beach. While this may counter a definition of popular media as only for the young, it also puts pressure on older people to adopt "girlish" or "boyish" attitudes in order to be seen as still valuable and visible within popular media. These grandparents are valued when they do something that counters the dominant stereotypes of aging.

Different levels of agency exist in the way these stories are told. Sometimes grandparents get help in making their voices heard, but at other times, they are being outed. For example, though one does not get the impression from the dancing videos that the grandparents were coerced to dance, it seems clear that their intention in that moment was not to become a viral video sensation. Just as young children become viral hits by way of their parents, in a similar way the elderly become viral hits because of the younger people in their lives. While it used to be grandparents were the ones showing off pictures of their grandchildren, now grandchildren are sharing images and videos of their grandparents. Many, of course, have good intentions, wanting to legitimately preserve these memories. The women posting pictures of taking their grandmothers to vote are preserving what feels like an important historical moment. Others, though, such as Angry Grandpa, seem to use the videos to showcase the absurdity and out-of-bounds behavior of their grandparents. Only in later videos does the grandfather seem to be in on the joke in Angry Grandpa. Sometimes the grandparents themselves have full agency in creating the videos, often to defy a stereotype associated with aging. Other times, a component of their presence is used by younger people as either comic relief, a means to tell their story, or just a way to show the world something about their grandparents that they find interesting or peculiar.

GRANDPARENTS AS DIGITAL RESPITE

One grandmother received national attention when she sent a text to the wrong person, accidentally inviting a teenage stranger to Thanksgiving dinner. When the teenager realized the mistake, he texted back, "You not my grandma. . . . Can I still get a plate tho?" She replied, "Of course you can. That's what grandma's do . . . feed everyone."[18] The tweet exchange went viral, and so did news coverage of their dinner and the Thanksgiving meal they shared the following year as well. Media coverage of "real" grandparents often features the theme of their failures to master new technology or their flat-out rejection of our digital world.

Some of the more popular videos of Angry Grandpa show him destroying technology, such as a clip with over twenty-two million views in which he smashes a Playstation 4 to show his anger after his grandson does not show up to bake Christmas cookies. He also destroys a Samsung Galaxy S7, a Nintendo Switch, an iPhone, and an iPad Pro, among other gadgets. His destruction of new technology showcases his wrath, but it also demonstrates his power in rejecting the appliances of the digital world. In a more mild-mannered way, the short HBO Latino web series *Gran'pa Knows Best* also features a grandfather who rejects technology and offers old-fashioned, traditional advice. Voicemail messages from his grandfather left on his answering machine were what inspired William Caballero, the creator of *Gran'pa Knows Best*, to make a program around the wise musings of his grandfather, Victor Muriel. Muriel represents both his Puerto Rican upbringing and the views of his generation in his commentaries on his program.[19] *Gran'pa* uses 3-D printed models of the grandfather set in different poses but uses the actual voice of his grandfather. Each episode begins with a question and follows with Muriel answering them with his views on subjects such as drugs, politics, and technology. People are encouraged to pose their own questions to him at @Ask_Granpa. Gran'pa's answers often are simple, with conservative advice, including "Don't do drinks" and "Support your country." He can sometimes be political: "Republican is no good. They want to be with the wealthy people," but more often his advice is generic, like "Be good citizen, vote." Gran'pa himself rejects digital technologies: "I never used the computer. I never used a mouse. . . . My computer is in my head."[20] Gran'pa Muriel offers a working-class ethos that values traditions passed on from generation to generation rather than new technology. His advice offers a connection to the past.

Other programs highlight both the relationship and the digital divide between grandparents and their grandchildren. PBS and WNET launched a series they advertised as featuring "intergenerational duo Kevin and Grandma Lill Droniak." Titled *The ChatterBox with Kevin and Grandma Lill*, the series contrasts the age difference, perspectives, and love between Kevin and his grandmother.[21] One segment titled "Drunk History" features Grandma Lill declining to drink but happy to share her stories with Kevin. Kevin even visits her senior center to "see her in her natural habitat." Grandma Lill shares stories of the games she played growing up, like a "Ouija board warning of wars with Russia." Her grandson tries to get her onto Snapchat, even inviting an expert on the show to help her. When she tries out Snapchat, she is surprised that her message disappears so quickly, although she's reassured by the expert teaching her that this is supposed to happen. The episode ends with her learning the technology but questioning its usefulness.

Grandparents unwilling to embrace or appreciate new technology are common themes in these videos. Studies of grandparents and technology use indicate that they do, especially at the urging of their children and grandchildren, embrace new technology, yet they also play an important role in questioning the technology and respecting existing social and cultural etiquette regarding technology. In their work on "remote grandparenting," Kim Sawchuk and Barbara Crow found that "discussions over habits, rules of conduct, and behavior in the home were moments when some grandparents asserted their role as teachers—not of the technologies—but of values and intimate practices deemed in jeopardy. In some instances, this closed the generational gap, drawing grandparents and grandchildren into a circle of mobile and mediated intimacy."[22]

In these videos, the audience sees the generational tug-of-war over technology. Much of what makes *Grandma Lill* and *Gran'Pa Knows Best* stand out is the contrast of the elders' enduring wisdom with the ephemeral knowledge of the younger generation, which is consumed by an appreciation of popular culture and the use of technology like Snapchat that emphasizes short-lived knowledge. Within a culture so reverent toward technology, these grandparents offer a respite from the digital and popular culture world. Gran'pa Muriel shows off knowledge that comes from his experience and heart rather than technology. Grandma Lill is open-minded but quietly questions the need for new technology. Angry Grandpa demonstrates his visceral and physical rejection of technology. In some ways, these images illustrate a stereotype of the elderly being dismissive of technology, but they also offer a respite. The elderly appearing in these programs offer a competing value system: an opportunity to reject technology that is beginning to feel more invasive in our lives.

Of course, they must be part of the digital world in order to send this message, but that's where their children and grandchildren step in. Pål André Aarsand's research on digital divides between grandparents and grandchildren and gaming found that this supposed "divide" is sometimes used strategically by the grandparents, "where children's competence is celebrated and where the child is cast at the centre of the attention."[23] In the YouTube videos, the grandparents do seem to be using the divide strategically, with an interesting twist. By allowing themselves to become the center of attention in the videos, they are performing for the camera and audience, but also for the attention of their grandchildren. Grandparents serve as reminders to question the technological world we live in, reminding audiences that newer isn't always better. They have an important message to give about technological skepticism, but it can be missed when they are simply laughed at for their lack of knowledge or aversion to new technology.

THE GRANDMA MASK

A popular trope for reality television programs is the depiction of competing contestants. Pitting grandmothers against each other is the latest way to showcase the grandmother on reality television. Producers likely employ it because of the tension and drama that it creates. At the same time, the image of grandmother rivalry is contrary to the typical image of the sweet, quiet grandmother out to promote everybody's best welfare.

In the program *Chopped*, the host, the judges, and the contestants themselves position the grandmothers as experts full of wisdom from the beginning of the program. The host begins by announcing, "With experience and expertise to spare, no one cooks like grandma." One grandma says, "My five grandchildren want me to win, and I'm not going to let them down." Another claims, "I've changed over 49,000 diapers, and I figure anyone who can do that can do anything." In describing her role as a grandmother, one woman says, "Grandchildren are like little nuggets of heaven." The show references the nurturing characteristic of grandmothers even when judging: one judge says, "I definitely feel the love in this dish." The grandmothers in the show use the traits of aging to defend themselves and their decisions. For example, in one episode a grandmother forgets her popovers; she says it is because she's older and her mind is not the same. The judges often go easy on the grandmothers in their criticism, using the cultural expectations of grandmothers in their decision-making. One judge offers, "I feel like we are going to get nurtured and fed today." Even the grandmas describe the judges as nice: "Did you see?" one grandmother exclaims. "They couldn't say anything bad about anything."[24]

Similarly, in *Clash of the Grandmas* on the Food Network, the grandmothers in the program use the stereotypes of aging to their advantage. One contestant warns, "We might look meek, mild, and sweet. We are the five best grandma cooks in America, and this grandma is not going down without a fight."[25] Because of their age, they can claim to be ignorant of trends. The host asks if they know what a "food hack" is, and they answer, "No, we're grandmas."[26] The grandmothers also work to defy expectations of aging in their performance of the grandma role. They act competitively and sometimes perform counter to the stereotype of having a sweet, nurturing nature. One grandma proves her competitive worth by doing push-ups, which, of course, doesn't seem necessary in connection to a cooking competition. Another one claims her food is better than sex. One grandma stores items she needs to carry in her bra. They also sweet-talk the judges and challenge the norms of the competition reality television genre. When a judge pressures one contestant to finish her dish in time, she says, "We're grandmas, and you are going to give us all heart attacks." As in *Chopped*, they also persuade the judges to be nicer just because they are grandmas. Their identity as grandmas is present throughout the episodes. For example, one episode shows videos of their grandchildren indicating their favorite color and asking their grandmothers to make a dish using that color.[27]

The competitive grandmothers articulate power in these roles. They take on the grandma persona, which often can be limiting, and use it to manipulate judges or challenge other contestants. In their research titled "Older Women and 'Frailty,'" Amanda Grenier and Jill Hanley study grandmother empowerment and resistance. They find that "older women may use oppressive stereotypes and perceptions imposed upon them to subvert the system."[28] In these competition shows, contestants use the grandma image to shame someone into treating them better. At other times, they can get a laugh by challenging a grandma stereotype. To this end, they subvert the dominant stereotypes by treating the grandma role as a mask that they can put on and remove at their disposal.

What is also interesting about these programs is the very premise of putting grandparents into a competitive role in the first place. Grandparent competition is moving outside the realm of reality television and into real life. As grandparenting becomes a longer and more distinguishable phase of life, some are treating it in much the same way as these reality programs do: yet another game in which to be the best, something to win. In this case, the prize is often the affection of their grandchildren.

A couple told me about how they were sightseeing in China and met an older couple who complained about the challenges of being grandparents in a country that restricts how many grandchildren they can have. The older couple said one of their biggest battles was with the other set of grandparents as they competed for the attention of their one grandchild. Grandparent competition had become an issue in China ever since the country began strict population control. China's one-child policy, which has since been somewhat relaxed, has shifted the influence, power, and competition of grandparents. As families were limited in the number of children they could have, they began to develop a "little emperor" phenomenon in which one child, often a boy, was doted upon by both parents and grandparents. Research suggests that children in China who live with their grandparents are more likely to become obese. Critics claim that a contributing factor is grandparents who spoil their only grandchild.[29] Another study found that paternal and maternal grandparents compete for their grandchild's affection, resulting in a gamified atmosphere. Researchers observed, "Apparently there were no hard feelings between the two women, who playfully competed to be the child's choice of sleeping partner each night. The competition provided a platform for the two caregivers to unreservedly display their affection for the child."[30] In this way, the grandparent experience mimics the fun and good-natured spirit found in the cooking reality shows.

Grandparenting competition is migrating beyond China. The popular press and social media are shocked but also delighted to tell stories of grandparent rivalry. One video, shared widely on YouTube, shows grandmothers fighting in the delivery room over their newborn baby grandchild.[31] In another incident in which police were called, a television news story in Pittsburgh reported, "Fist Fight between Great Grandmothers in Hospital Maternity Ward."[32] Another article was titled, "Grandmother vs. Grandmother: A Shocking Rivalry."[33]

Advice columnist Dr. Karen Rancourt, also known as Dr. Gamma, is a specialist on intergenerational relationships. She told me that she is seeing more cases of grandmothers competing with each other. "The competition can take many forms," she said. "Typically it takes the form of material items, showering the grandchildren with gifts." Rancourt points out, though, that this can become a serious problem: "This becomes especially problematic when one set isn't in the financial position to compete at that level." She also sees the problem as gendered: it is the grandmothers, not the grandfathers, who often are competing. This gendered display is connected to the mediated stereotype that women are naturally aggressive toward each other, as expressed in the slang term "frenemies," referring to female friends who are also competitive adversaries.[34] This contrasts with the expectation of women, especially of a certain age, to behave demurely and ladylike. As grandparenting becomes a more recognizable stage of life, and more products and images are marketed to grandparents, the idea of needing to compete for the most idealized image is no longer surprising. The competing grandmother, in both real life and represented on reality programs, creates a safer version of the aggressive female to be consumed and watched by the public. Grandparenting is treated as a point in which to assert status and power. While this can be empowering at times, extreme images, such as the competitive grandmother, do not truly counter stereotypes but rely on previous images of the grandmother as sweet and innocent to create a new extreme. Neither image truly acknowledges the complexities of people.

WORKING FOR VISIBILITY

While many images that appear online are created for the purpose of attracting visitors, the web can also serve to mirror unequal representations that already exist in real life. Researchers note that, though the internet has the promise to offer alternative viewpoints and more representations of minority groups, much of the content tends to mimic previous content established in traditional media.[35] This is particularly disappointing for minority groups like black grandparents, who have limited and sometimes problematic depictions, as explored in the previous chapter. It is important, then, to recognize those who are working to change those depictions.

I interviewed Dr. LaShawnDa Pittman, assistant professor at the University of Washington and founder of the website RealBlackGrandmothers.com, who discovered a real need for the website while she conducted research exploring slavery narratives. One day her students came up to her and said, "We don't know how to tell you this but when you Google black grandmothers, a lot of porn comes up." This was something I had observed as well, but for Dr. Pittman, it became an opportunity to correct a long history of misrepresentation. She said, "This misrepresentation of all these women over time—from the mammy figure to the post–Civil War era, to the matriarch. . . . Where can you go to get a sense of who these women really are? I don't see my grandmother reflected in any of these grandmothers." She found the site especially important because she knew through her own research that "these are a group of women that carry families and communities on their backs."

Dr. Pittman had no trouble finding people to share their stories; she describes them as "hidden in plain sight." Unlike many constructed grandmother images online, the women featured on her site lack artifice in their narratives. Instead, people submit stories about their grandparents, share details of their lives, and reflect upon the impact they had. One woman describes attending church with her grandmother and putting her hair in rollers later at night. Many of the stories depict sacrifice, cooking, and advice grandparents gave to their grandchildren. "You are getting their truth," Dr. Pittman said. "You aren't getting it from all these other perspectives. You are not getting black men in drag. Their truth is complex. I wanted to show their humanity, their struggles, their interests. They are museum-goers. They love opera. They send their granddaughters Robert Frost when they are in college. They are lesbians. They are not all Christians. They are thirty-something and ninety-something."

THE WISE SAGE

One Latina grandma uses her YouTube channel to show off her craft projects. She became so popular, with her All Crafts Channel having over half a million subscribers, that she was featured on NBC News.[36] Many programs use the grandparent image to connote preservation or offer advice and survival skills. Grandparents in these programs are positioned as having something to offer just by virtue of their age and longevity, and they are valued for the traditional skills they can show off.

Grandma's cooking holds a special place not only in American folk culture, but also within the realm of televised cooking programs, which have memorialized and idolized recipes and traditions. The Food Network's *Southern at Heart* produced a special episode titled "Grandma's Cookbook," where host Damaris Phillips inherits and updates her grandmother's recipes.[37] Likewise, the Food Network program *Trisha's Southern Kitchen* featured its second episode titled "Grandma Knows Best," in which the host prepared her favorite recipes from her grandmother. The popular food show *The Chew* had a special grandma edition, "paying homage to the women in our lives who pass down their stories, recipes, and love." The show titled the special episode "Grandma's Greatest Hits." In a segment called Chew Tank, the show featured a special "Grandma Edition," where each grandmother brought in her favorite recipe to compete. One contestant was introduced with the declaration, "Sylvia is a grandmother who has more gusto than grandchildren."[38] They ended the episode by sharing social media posts featuring viewers' grandma moments.

In some programs, the entire premise rests on the importance of learning how to cook just like grandma. In the program *Grandma's Boy*, on Fox International, the host, Chef Donal Skehan, travels throughout the world and learns families' secret recipes. He then makes each recipe and tries to win the seal of approval from the family's matriarch. In this program, the grandmother is valued as the head of the family and ultimate judge of the food prepared for the family. *Mom's Cooking* on Lifetime has Chef Joe Corsano watch daughters learning how to prepare their favorite childhood recipes from their own mothers, so they can pass those recipes on to the next generation. In *My Grandmother's Ravioli*, on the Cooking Channel, television personality Mo Rocca goes from kitchen to kitchen to learn how to cook family dishes and listen to stories from grandparents. Grandmothers' recipes are treated as artifacts and connections to family heritage that are to be preserved, and children and grandchildren are enlisted in the preservation process.

The value of survival skills is showcased in other programs featuring grandparents. For example, in the web series *Great Depression Cooking*, 91-year-old Clara tells her audience how to make Depression Era meals. Filmed by her grandson, Clara cooks in her own home with a simple kitchen, in contrast to the glamorous kitchens usually found in cooking programs. While she cooks, she tells viewers about her family, but also what life was like during the Great Depression. As she makes her first dish, pasta and peas, she says, "It's not expensive, but it's nourishing." She offers viewers an understanding of cooking when one is restricted to buying inexpensive food. She tells viewers, "The Depression was bad." Grandma Clara talks about the need to eat pasta every night with a different vegetable mixed in it. To the American middle class, for which food appears to be plentiful, she offers insight to a lost skill: how to build a meal with little money. In fact, many of her fans praise her advice on cooking within a set budget, and she is featured on survivalist websites.[39]

Grandparent survival skills have become a popular trend. The website *Off the Grid News* features an article titled "10 Survival Skills Your Great-Grandparents Knew (That Most of Us Have Forgotten)." The list includes gardening, blacksmithing, and butchering an animal.[40] Another article on *Huffington Post* discusses "4 Life Skills Only Grandpas Can Teach," including auto repair and carpentry.[41] Grandparents in earlier times were critical to the survival of the family because of the knowledge they possessed. Now, they appeal to those committed to living off the grid or planning for an uncertain future. As society appears to become more economically and politically unstable, and people become aware of their dependence on technology, their simple-living skill sets are gaining attention. Instead of just providing wisdom to their own families, grandparents can become the matriarchs and patriarchs to anyone with an internet connection.

Grannies on Safari on PBS showcases grandmothers taking on the opposite of a sedentary lifestyle. Part of the appeal of the show is these elderly grandmothers maintaining an active lifestyle.[42] The grandmothers use their travels as elderly women to teach viewers an appreciation for treasures that can be found anywhere. The grannies received attention when they were in Egypt during its political turmoil, and they have been featured on a segment titled "Not Your Ordinary Grannies" that highlighted their nonconformity to the typical granny image.

Some grandparents have built a following based on the wisdom and advice they can offer others. Barbara and Harry Cooper's granddaughters encouraged them to set up an advice blog to give them something meaningful to do when they moved to an assisted living complex in Los Angeles. Their blog, *The OGs (Original Grandparents)*, originally was meant for family members only, but they found that strangers came to the blog looking for advice. Barbara, who died in 2016, went by the name Cutie and developed a large following on Facebook.[43] Their video blog, *Ask Grandma Anything*, included questions about romance and relationships. She advised a woman who was hesitant to get married or have children to just do it, as she will not regret the decision. Similarly, NYU adjunct social media professor Mike

Mathews set up a Skype account to allow his neighbors to talk with his 100-year-old grandmother in Washington State. It turned out that people regularly wanted advice from what they saw as a distant but wise figure. Besides asking advice, often about their own relationships, callers treated his grandmother like a therapist who kept their conversations confidential.[44]

The endurance of grandparents is packaged as a trait to learn from in different forms in many of these programs. Some have skill sets in cooking, a craft, or travel. Others have the ability to survive in tough times. In all these cases, their age signifies wisdom that younger people are expected to learn from and pass on.

THE GRAND BRAND

While the internet and reality programs help some grandparents become stars as a result of their grandparent status, celebrities who are already in the public eye still have to figure out how to handle the grandparent rite of passage. In her article "Nothing Less Than Perfect: Female Celebrity, Ageing and Hyper-Scrutiny in the Gossip Industry," Kristy Fairclough explores the challenges of aging while being a celebrity:

> Ageing is configured in contemporary society as a kind of narcissistic problem and exists as an embarrassing reminder to a celebrity-obsessed transformation focused society that ultimately there is no successful way to fight it. . . . The roots of youth are deeply woven into culture, where there is an obsessive need to hold onto markers of youth as long as possible to the point that youth now appears to stretch out farther into middle age than ever before.[45]

A quick Google search for celebrity grandparents reveals articles such as "20 Celebrity Grandmas Who Are Not Only Banging, but Fabulous," "Famous & Fabulous Grandmas of Hollywood," "19 Celebrity Grandmas That Look Fabulous and Far from Frumpy," and "Hollywood's Hottest Grandpas." The numerous headlines about celebrity grandparents set up the expectation that celebrities resist the negative associations with aging when they reach this phase in their lives.

While many of the visible components of aging are related to the body, the grandparent phase is different in that it is outside the control of the celebrity and disconnected from the physical aging process. Since people come into grandparenting at different ages, the celebrity media machine sends mixed messages in its attempt to both define what being a good grandparent is while setting expectations to retain the vitality attached to youth. This, in turn, creates challenges for celebrities as they shape their image.

The value of youth is prevalent especially in professional sports. Being called "gramps" in the sports world usually signals nearing the end of a career. Chicago Cubs player David Ross was given the title by his younger fellow baseball team members. They acknowledged his last year playing on the team by opening an Instagram account titled "Grandparossy_3." Since then, strangers shout out "Gramps" to him on the street.[46] Clearly, this is part of a good-natured hazing ritual, as Ross was only thirty-nine at the time, with young children of his own. However, it also shows the burden sports figures face as they age. When Vikings NFL player Brett Favre became a grandfather, sports media pointed out that he was "the only grandfather in the NFL."[47] Mark Hendrickson was the subject of national news stories with his attempts to make a comeback as a Major League Baseball player after becoming a grandfather at 49.[48] Coaches also face scrutiny as they get older. Anna Sofia Botha, coach of Olympic South African runner Wayde van Niekerk, was a seventy-four-year-old great-grandmother when she was initially turned away from greeting van Niekerk at the finish line because no one could believe she was his coach, despite her credentials. She simply looked too old to the officials.

Some celebrities have responded to the challenge of aging by treating grandparenthood as a new phase of life that gives them both pleasure and acceptance. Kirstie Alley, for example, used the birth of her grandson to tweet about her plans to spoil him. She wrote, "When your son has a son…bliss."[49] The Police lead singer Sting sees the ability to have moments with his grandchildren as "a sign of real wealth."[50] Marie Osmond says it is a chance to make peace in her life, quoting advice from her own mother: "You know that you are successful when you can honestly say that you are a happy grandma. That means that your children love you, that you have put family first and that your grandbabies love you."[51] Grandparenting also becomes a marketing opportunity and a new chance to showcase their image. Some celebrities use their grandparent status to offer themselves up as authorities on grandparenting. Television journalist Lesley Stahl used her expertise as a journalist to write *Becoming Grandma*, a book that is both a memoir and a research study about grandparenting. In it, she discusses how grandparenting helped transform her life: "Becoming a grandmother turns the page. Line by line you are rewritten. You are tilted off your old center, spun onto new turf."[52] When actress Jessica Lange became a grandmother, she wrote the children's book *It's about a Little Bird*, about two girls who visit their grandmother's farm. The illustrations inside are modeled after her own grandchildren.[53]

Other celebrities find that the moment they become grandparents necessitates rethinking the image they are about to embrace. This reinvention allows celebrities to retain a more youthful image, which is especially important when battling the prejudice they may face within the entertainment industry as they grow older. However, they often are met with ridicule in these attempts. Kris Jenner, the matriarch of the Kardashian family, was attacked online when she announced through the media that she prefers the name "Lovey" over "Grandma." Jenner indicated that too many people were calling her Grandma by the time she had her third grandchild.[54] One blog post asked, "Is Kris out of line here? 'Lovey' seems a little bit excessive of a demand to place upon one's grandchildren."[55] Likewise, when Gwyneth Paltrow appeared on the television talk show *Chelsea Lately*, she and the host chuckled over how her mother, actress Blythe Danner, asked to be called "Woof" by her grandchildren because she thought of herself as "still hot." Kristy Fairclough describes the challenge celebrities (particularly female) have in maintaining cultural expectations of a beauty standard while aging. She writes, "Indeed, in a post-feminist, neoliberal society, ageing is not something to be feared, but must be both celebrated and fought; women must battle nature in order to look much younger to adhere to and maintain the fantasy of the sexualised middle-aged woman."[56] Many celebrity grandmothers face the dual challenges of meeting maternal expectations of being "grandmotherly" while also managing the celebrity media standard of projecting a sexy youthfulness.

Though many celebrities work hard to combat the negativity associated with aging that "Grandma" or "Gramps" implies, others reaching this new life phase use it as an opportunity to shift their image. For example, Charlie Sheen, often in trouble because of his bad behavior, was able to reposition himself as a more settled person as a grandparent. In a television interview on ABC, he said that becoming a grandfather "kind of blew my mind. But what a gift."[57] For others, being a grandfather poses an opportunity for a second chance, both on a personal level and with the public. When Kiefer Sutherland spoke to *People* magazine about becoming a grandparent, he said that he was not always the best dad but would be a better grandfather. Rapper Snoop Dogg rated himself only a "7-plus" as a father, but was enthusiastic about being a grandfather, saying he easily has become "a gullible, get-away-with-everything kind of grandpa."[58] Suzanne Somers has said that being a grandmother is a chance to correct mistakes she made as a parent.[59] When Bernie Sanders ran for the 2016 Democratic nomination, he was assigned the label "grumpy grandpa," but found that the moniker could work for him. The *Washington Post* listed "7 Ways Bernie Sanders Reminds Us of Our Grumpy Grandpa," including that "he's always right," and he "gives history lessons to young people."[60] Sanders himself uses the grandpa image to show off a more playful side. In a *People* magazine article, his children described the fun he has playing "monster" with his grandchildren.[61]

Though celebrity grandparents may have problems defining themselves at this juncture in their lives, for young celebrities, having an adoring grandparent becomes a purely positive publicity opportunity. In fact, they frequently post about their relationship with their grandmothers, much to the approval of their fans and entertainment media. Lady Gaga used Instagram to show her talking with her grandmother right before her performance at the Super Bowl halftime show.[62] Cindy Crawford shared a picture of her with her grandmother, and *Us* magazine observed that her "family is genetically blessed."[63] Miley Cyrus tweeted a picture of her tattoo, which was a portrait of her grandmother, accompanied by the caption "because I am her favorite and she is mine."[64] Actress Jennette McCurdy regularly uses social media to show off her grandma. During her appearance on *The Tonight Show*, the posts became the subject of her interview. Jimmy Fallon shared a picture of her "cutest grandparents," and he talked with her about how they watch her new show. He then read an email from them complimenting the show and asking if she needed a ride from the airport.[65] Actor Matt Bomer credits his grandparents as role models. "I sort of take cues from my grandparents," he said.[66] Katy Perry regularly brings her grandmother to events, including the Grammy Awards, where she told *E!* host Ryan Seacrest, "If I don't go home with any Grammys, I still go home with my Grammy."[67]

In the popular music world, grandparents can be the inspiration for songs. Justin Timberlake created the music video "Mirrors" to demonstrate his love for his grandparents and celebrate their long-standing relationship with each other by showing the progression of their courtship.[68] The rapper Macklemore (Ben Haggerty) put his grandmother in his music video "Glorious." The video showed them enjoying their time together in a convertible and engaging in various activities in honor of her 100th birthday.[69] Celebrities publicizing their relationship with grandparents is not just a phenomenon in the United States. Lay, lead singer of the South Korean boy band EXO, released a song celebrating his grandparents' 50th anniversary. Like Macklemore, he included his grandparents in the video.[70] Irish musician Ed Sheeran honored his grandparents' love story in his song "Nancy Mulligan." His grandmother helped publicize the song when she allowed a news crew into her home to watch her reaction when she listened to it for the first time.[71] The grandparents here help to extend their grandchildren's fandom by showing the sweet and gentle side of the stars' lives.

Celebrity grandparenting is filled with both pitfalls and possibilities. The grandparent image can be positive, as seen in the way young celebrities find approval by touting their grandparent relationships. But, for the celebrities who are becoming grandparents themselves, media coverage of their transition can be problematic. Kristy Fairclough distinguishes between celebrities who are labeled "desperate" by the media and those who are "sanctioned" as aging appropriately.[72] If grandparent celebrities navigate this media gauntlet successfully, they are marked as valued. However, if grandparents are perceived as attempting to retain a youthful image, they are judged or ridiculed as failing to cross into the grandparent phase gracefully. Thus, celebrity grandparents are stuck in a no-win paradox: they are pressured to buy into the ideology of beauty and youth so that media coverage perceives them as successful, but in doing so, they may be labeled as not accepting their new life phase. Those that receive positive coverage are able to successfully navigate this challenge. Grandfathers often find this journey easier, as they can show how grandparenting has tamed them and allowed them a second chance to parent. For women, who were expected to parent well the first time, the second chance is not as easy an image to manage. Though actors and sports figures often attempt to hold on to their youthful image, being a grandparent helps politicians show they are seasoned veterans who have the wisdom and experience that comes with age.

THE GRANDMA GAZE

Scholar Deborah Jermyn explores how aging women celebrities are expected to relinquish their starring roles and acquiesce to the loss of their youth and sexual allure:

> These are roles in which ageing itself is rendered as a horrifying process of inexorable decline, with female ageing and the ageing of female stars particularly, figured as grotesque and traumatic. The refusal to properly relinquish the expectation of public attention which fame has afforded—but which our culture demands older women must surrender as their sexual allure fades and they enter into invisibility—is figured as both the source and evidence of mental instability.[73]

In these representations, elderly women sometimes challenge cultural assumptions of aging by engaging in activities that many would not associate with the elderly, including the frank discussion of sexuality. At other times, they reject modern culture's obsession with popular culture and question the assumptions we make about the elderly. Often, these women perform and use these stereotypes in order to gain attention and recognition from a culture inclined to ignore them.

Perhaps one of the best-known elderly Hollywood actors challenging aging stereotypes with her persona is Betty White. Instead of stalling her career, aging has allowed her to transform herself into a new role that offers an alternative to the chaste grandmother figure. She has appeared in guest spots on popular television shows such as *30 Rock* and *Young and Hungry*, and she hosted an episode of *Saturday Night Live* where she surprised viewers with an act that included sexual innuendo. One television critic writes, "She was unsettling the expectations of her audience even as she played to them."[74] In her hidden camera show *Off Their Rockers*, she enlists the support of other elderly folks to play pranks on younger people, most of whom counter or play into a stereotype of older people. The warning at the beginning of the program illuminates the role reversal the show engages in: "The following program contains imagery which some of you may find shocking, hilarious, or hilariously shocking, depending on how you feel about seniors pulling pranks on youngsters. Frankly we hope you're all for it; it's kind of our thing."[75] The show often has an elderly person act like a grandma and ask for help from an unsuspecting younger person. One woman asks a couple for help writing a birthday card for her grandchild. Dictating to them, she says, "Happy Birthday, Billy. Now that you're 12, you should know you are adopted. Enjoy your cake." She has them sign the card, "Not your real grandmother."[76] In another episode, a grandma tells a man that she has read her granddaughter's diary and needs him to explain to her what certain slang phrases mean. As she goes on, the phrases become more sexually explicit.[77] In this program, older people use the stereotype of the elderly needing assistance to catch people off guard and provide a shocking reveal.

Like White, another great-grandmother uses media to offer opposing connotations for the aging grandmother. Helen Ruth Elam Van Winkle, known as "Baddiewinkle," has more than three million followers on Instagram and the tagline, "Stealing Your Man Since 1928."[78] Many of her posts subvert the typical image of a great-grandmother. One picture shows her in a bathing suit with the caption "On my way to steal your man." In another, she is wearing a tie-dye shirt that says, "Acid: Just drop it." She has posed with waitresses at Hooters, the restaurant known for its cleavage-showing servers. Baddiewinkle dresses in clothing more often associated with younger women, including a sexy leather dress and lingerie. She is a transgressive figure, flouting the conventional age boundaries, and she has become an Instagram star. She is invited to premieres, award shows, and regularly hangs out with other celebrities.[79]

The YouTube channel 3GoldenSistersTV features three elderly sisters dressed in "grandmotherly garb" who mock popular culture. The stars of this program were first noticed for their video commenting on the Kim Kardashian sex tape. Part of their draw is the shock value of seeing them in their roles as grandmas eating lunch but discussing the sex tape in graphic terms. Another aspect of their humor derives from their attempts to understand, connect, or question the value of popular culture. For example, one grandma immediately rejects a pair of popular shoes from Kanye West's line of sneakers, calling them "clumsy and stupid looking." She then is shocked at their $200 price. The grandma even critiques the packaging, contrasting it with the good old days: "It's such a simple box. It's not even a beautiful box with velvet where it looked good. What a generation we have. Just stay on line. For a pair of shoes like this, take it back. I'm sorry, Kanye West. I love your rapping, but I didn't even know you were a designer." At other times, they slip into popular grandma tropes such as asking, "Are you hungry?"[80] They have become so popular that they now have their own television show on the

OWN cable network. These grandmas embody the power to expose and reject the frivolity of popular culture.

The glamorous grandmother is an emerging image. A quick Google search reveals products such as shirts, pillows, and bags that feature phrases like "I'm her Glamma, not her Grandma." More broadly, the grandmother figure is becoming a fashion trend that mimics the Yummy Mummy fad that took hold in the early twenty-first century. Scholar Jennifer Musial describes the Yummy Mummy as "a consuming and consumable neo-liberal subject. On one hand, she is the ultimate consumer of goods, services, and clothing that mark her socio-economic status. And on the other hand, she is a consumable sexual object. The Yummy Mummy is an appropriate site of desire because she is safe."[81] The Glamma extends the sexual object persona into later years while communicating that one's worth is still connected to one's sexual desirability. Like the Yummy Mummy, the "Yummy Granny" is encouraged to seek her empowerment through style and purchasing, becoming a consumable object while consuming.

In London, the *Daily Mail* cited a survey that showed many grandmothers make an effort to look stylish when picking up their grandchildren from school. According to the article, the survey revealed, "The majority have said they consciously aim to dress well without looking over the top or calling too much attention to themselves, yet one in ten admitted that a father has chatted them up whilst they waited in the playground."[82] Not everyone, though, is happy with the image of the Glamma. One woman writes about her own problems with the label: "Glamma, to me, sounds fake, pretentious and desperate. It smacks of someone who is terrified of aging, of being old enough to have grandchildren."[83] The writer instead encourages her fellow grandmothers to embrace aging and the grandparent experience.

The idea of the fashionable and sexy grandparent extends to grandfathers as well. Irvin Randle, a grandfather and teacher from Texas, became a viral sensation when a stranger asked permission to share photos of him on social media to show off his fit and well-dressed body. The photos were posted on Twitter with the hashtag #MrStealYourGrandma. They ended up with over seven million likes, which surprised Randle.[84] Another group of elderly men have obtained online fame thanks to the Instagram account @fashiongrandpas, created by fashion public relations executive Christina Belchere. Belchere told a reporter at *Business Insider* that she was beginning to notice "dapper old men scuffling about around her office on 57th and Madison."[85] She started posting pictures of these men, who did not seek out this exposure and may not actually be grandfathers. By labeling them "grandpas," Belchere sets up the contrast of fashionably dressed older men with the familiarity and frumpiness usually associated with grandfathers.

The male gaze refers to women being positioned to be looked at, so that men can consume their projection of sexuality.[86] Now, the gaze is extended to the granny and grandpa. These elderly figures are watched and enjoyed, but much of their success is connected to viewers' surprise when they subvert expectations. When it comes to expressions of sexuality, grandparents usually are ignored and invisible, providing nothing worth watching anymore. Efforts to claim the Glamma brand, look fashionable, and be sexy are ways to re-empower grandparents, yet it creates the paradox that, if they are successful, they succumb to the trap of the gaze, where they exist, in some part, for the pleasure of others.

GRANDMAPRENEURS

While some use the grandma persona to reinvent their image, others see it as an opportunity to begin a new stage of life and develop a new identity. In the early twenty-first century, women who made businesses out of their experience and wisdom as mothers became known as Mompreneurs. Now, grandmothers are engaging in some of these same practices. Taking on the identity of grandparent entrepreneur, many are starting websites, blogs, and businesses that highlight their status as a grandparent. Implicitly recognizing the shifting life stage for themselves, many outwardly celebrate it with their public activities.

Monira and her mother Naomi are the co-owners of "reBlossom Mama and Baby Center," a combination parent-child community center and shop in Georgia. It has become a one-stop place to buy baby items while taking classes and socializing with other visitors. Monira told me about the bonding time she and her mother had after she gave birth to her first child. "I remember the moment when we were driving around our town looking for a nice place to buy gently-loved items for our new baby," she said. "I turned to my mom and said, 'Do you want to open a shop with me?' And she said, 'Yes,' just like that." Her mother was serious about helping out any way she could, even selling her car to help raise some cash for the business.

Naomi used the skills from her previous business background to serve in a consulting position. "My mom was our advisor from the start, always bringing up points we may not have thought of," Monira added. "She was the ultimate bargain shopper. . . . She always was able to pull from her years of experience to help guide us. In the early days she helped me buy everything. She was wonderful at looking through garments. She taught me about what brands were higher-end and how you could tell the difference in fabrication." As the business took off, Monira focused more on the day-to-day tasks of the business, and her mother stayed around to help with childcare. Now that the children are school-aged, during the summer Naomi runs "Nana Camp" for them, and she still comes into the store on a weekly basis.

Teresa, creator of the successful blog *Nanahood: The Second Half of the Motherhood Journey*, describes herself online as "the bloggy-est nana in the hood (the NanaHood that is)."[87] Her blog has become a place to learn about activities and events for grandparents, read the latest news about celebrity grandparents, and follow her musings and experiences as a nana herself. She is a magazine columnist and author of several books. When she became a grandmother, she viewed it as an opportunity to reinvent herself with this new identity, which she saw as a necessary part of getting older. Teresa told me about her delight at becoming a grandmother: "I never suspected the power of a grandmother's love for her grandchildren. It didn't occur to me that being a grandmother would be so awesome. It's something I'm very passionate about." She began to host her blog to provide grandmothers more information and resources for being a nana. Her biggest audience is on Facebook, where her page has over 35,000 members. Teresa describes herself as a small to mid-size blog, but her visitors are engaged, and she often reaches 60,000 to 100,000 homes. Companies looking to build connections with these audiences have approached her, and most respect that her blog is a business. However, she is dismayed that "sometimes they don't see it as a business and they think I should be honored just to do it for free." She recognizes her power in connecting companies to a new and potentially strong market. She also has been a leader in mentoring other grandmothers who want to start businesses like hers.

Lisa, writer of *Grandma's Briefs*, frames her blog as focused "On Life's Second Act." Lisa told me in an interview that she sees grandparenting as just a part of the next phase of life for her, "the second act beginning once my children were fully grown and gone and the first act of adult life—parenting—was over. The second act allows me to focus on myriad interests: grandparenting, writing, hobbies I put on the back burner during parenting, spending 'couple' time with my husband, now that it's just the two of us." Lisa treats her blog as a business and expects to generate some revenue for the amount of time she puts into it. Lisa says that one of her goals is to let her audience "know they're not alone in the various aspects of grandparenting and/or life after the nest empties, and to share with them some of my ideas, opinions, successes and failures along the way." Her blog has allowed her to travel more and book more freelance writing gigs. She now meets women across the globe. Lisa finds that the articles that get the most interaction and comments from her readers are the DIY posts. She adds, "especially one in which I show how to make a 'pillow lounger' for kids. It's the most-visited post on my site. A close runner-up is an article on how to write personalized inscriptions and sentiments for grandkids, things grandparents want to express to their loved ones but don't quite know how to find the right words. And then there are those posts in which I simply share a silly aspect of my life that resonates with others, makes readers say, 'Me, too!'" Since she posts pictures of her grandchildren on her blog, she's hoping that they will appreciate the record of their childhood that she is leaving behind.

With these businesses, older women are experiencing a period of life that used to go unnoticed and make themselves not only visible, but also profitable.

USURPING GRANDMA

When popular images become ubiquitous, they can become opportunities for others to use and profit off the brand. As the grandparent brand emerges, there is evidence that others outside the grandparent age range use it for their own messaging and purposes.

One young Cuban American Millennial comedian, Jenny Lorenzo, became a viral hit when she created the character "Abuela," modeled after her grandmother. Her first video, "What Abuela Wants You to Eat," drew appreciation from the Latino community and immigrant grandmothers across cultures.[88] In most of the videos, she dresses up like her grandmother and engages in shopping outings, cooking, judging a new boyfriend, or giving "weird pregnancy advice." The videos poke fun at the grandma figure, but they also relish in the affection and traditions she represents. Similarly, the IFC series *Gigi Does It* features David Krumholtz, a male comedian who plays a Jewish grandmother in the program.

The creators of these programs often discuss their character performances as tributes to their own grandparents. Krumholtz says that his character, "in looks and in personality, is a tribute to his late grandma."[89] Lorenza notes that others have told her that her grandmother character helps to keep the memory of their own grandmothers alive.[90] To be sure, it is difficult to object to honoring and preserving the memory of a grandmother, but they also are using the grandparent role to comment on and commodify it. The grandmother image ultimately loses its connection to the original grandparent and becomes a figure of entertainment to be watched.

Other activities that used to be the domain of the elderly are now becoming fads among younger people. Knitting, for example, is not just for grandma anymore. In her chapter titled "Knitting, Sewing and Grandma's Retro-Style," Elizabeth Nathanson observes about craft shows on television:

> While the image of the warm, sensitive and creative grandmotherly type populates a number of these programs about crafts and crafts projects, recent years have seen the rise of a new kind of crafter, a younger, arguably more hip craftswoman. These women appeal to a youthful audience interested in appropriating and adapting traditional crafts to a modern sensibility.[91]

The universalizing of grandparent experience borrows the activities of aging in order to dissect them, satirize them, and then re-share them. Some may see this as providing a service to the aging population, allowing a greater visibility and celebration of aging culture. The crafts and activities that might have been relegated to the shadows now have become popular with others. Old and young can knit alongside each other. At the same time, the power of grandparents is supplanted by outside groups. Some scholars have explored how using a group identity can give power to individuals.[92] These bloggers can use the grandparent brand to reach an audience and develop power in the marketplace. However, when others outside the group use these labels for their own purposes, even in an attempt to honor or share in an elderly pastime, the power of the grandparent is usurped.

CONCLUSION

Grandparenting within the public eye provides both possibilities and challenges. Writing about electronic media in the 1980s, Joshua Meyrowitz argued: "By severing the traditional link between physical location and social situation, for example, electronic media may begin to blur previously distinct group identities by allowing people to 'escape' informationally from place-defined groups and by permitting outsiders to 'invade' many groups' territories without ever entering them."[93] With the internet and social media, the blurring of worlds becomes even more pronounced today as elderly people can not only enter new worlds, as with television, but also embrace completely new identities that they can choose to share. The grandparents featured here are aware of the public image they maintain, and they sometimes use tropes and stereotypes associated with aging to disarm the public. Whether in cooking programs or on a YouTube channel, they can gain attention by playing to or going against the granny type. Activists can counter opponents by using the granny image or contrasting it with their message. In all these cases, the grandparenting image can provide power. At other times, grandparents and the people and organizations associated with them recognize their inherent power to impart wisdom. However, the celebrity grandparent reminds us of the stereotypes associated with aging and social pressure in popular culture to retain a youthful image. Once labeled a grandparent, celebrities need to actively work to reposition themselves in this new role while maintaining a perception in the public as still young enough to offer value. Some grandparents have successfully carved out an identity for themselves in this new role, but too often many grandparents are represented as caricatures, not interesting enough on their own but valued only in what they have to offer from their past experiences or in the characters they can perform for others.

NOTES

1. Yagana Shah, "Grandparents Hilariously Struggle to Define 'Netflix and Chill,'" *Huffington Post* (blog), June 15, 2016, https://www.huffingtonpost.com/entry/grandparents-hilariously-struggle-to-define-netflix-and-chill_us_57616f13e4b05e4be8605662.

2. "Grandma's New Year Message Tops YouTube," *CBC News*, January 3, 2007, http://www.cbc.ca/news/canada/montreal/grandma-s-new-year-message-tops-youtube-1.651225.

3. Yagana Sha, "Grandparents Hilariously Struggle."

4. Megan O'Neill, "Top 10 Dancing Grandma & Grandpa Videos on YouTube," *Ad Week* (web page), June 30, 2010, http://www.adweek.com/digital/top-10-dancing-grandma-grandpa-videos-on-youtube/.

5. Christian Zamora, "Watching Lady Gaga's Grandma Dance," *BuzzFeed* (web page), August 24, 2017, ttps://www.buzzfeed.com/christianzamora/lady-gagas-grandma-slays-seat-choreo?utm_term=.djlAbXEPk#.qbd2yNa93.

6. "Dancing Nana Becomes Viral Sensation," YouTube, reported on *CNN*, March 14 2013, https://www.youtube.com/watch?v=lmWTL2-_TDg.

7. "Breakdancing Grandma," *FRK DanceSchool*, YouTube, October 23, 2006, https://www.youtube.com/watch?v=IIBEaN80YVs.

8. Rima Abdelkader and Scott Stump, "Watch This Adorable Great-Grandma Dance to Bruno Mars at Her 100th birthday," *Today.com*, March 3, 2017, https://www.today.com/parents/watch-adorable-great-grandma-dance-bruno-mars-her-100th-birthday-t108811.

9. Serenitie Wang, "Beijing Gets Tough on Dancing Grannies," *CNN World* (web page), February 28, 2017, http://www.cnn.com/2017/02/28/asia/china-gets-tough-on-dancing-grannies/.

10. Paul Bowers, "Why Is This Man so Angry?" *Charleston City Paper* (web page), March 27, 2013, https://www.charlestoncitypaper.com/charleston/why-is-this-man-so-angry/Content?oid=4595072.

11. Xiaroan Shi, "Meet YouTube's 79-Year-Old Grandma Gamer," *Vice* (web page), February 2, 2016, https://www.vice.com/en_us/article/youtubes-best-celebrity-gamer-is-a-79-year-old-grandma.

12. Shirley Curry, *SkyrimSE*, Episode 1, YouTube, accessed May 12, 2017, https://www.youtube.com/channel/UCzkY7wa8Ksxv4M5NyUYgTmA.

13. Steven Messner, "What It's Like to Become a YouTube Gaming Celebrity at 80 Years Old," *PC Gamer* (web page), November 30, 2016, http://www.pcgamer.com/shirley-curry-gamer-grandma-interview/.

14. Julia Reinstein, "People Are Sharing Pics of Their Grandmas Celebrating Hillary Clinton's Nomination," July 27, 2016, https://www.buzzfeed.com/juliareinstein/grandmas-for-hillary?utm_term=.qkD736Q16#.dd4Rv5xE5.

15. Gina Mei, "Badass Grandma," *Cosmopolitan*, March 14, 2017, accessed February 27, 2018, https://www.google.com/url?q=https://www.cosmopolitan.com/lifestyle/a9129308/badass-grandma-doreen-grett-spring-break-mexico/.

16. Josh K. Elliott, "'Ok Goo Goo!' Italian Grandma Struggles with New Google Home," *CTV News* (web page), January 3, 2018, https://www.ctvnews.ca/sci-tech/ok-goo-goo-italian-grandma-struggles-with-new-google-home-1.3743876.

17. Hilde Van den Bulck, "Growing Old in Celebrity Culture," in *Aging, Media, and Culture*, ed. C. Lee Harrington and Denise Bielby (Lanham, MD: Lexington Books, 2014), 68.

18. Jennifer Earl, "Grandma Who Texted Wrong Teen Last Thanksgiving Invites Him Back for Dinner," *CBS News*, November 27, 2017, https://www.cbsnews.com/news/grandma-who-texted-wrong-teen-last-thanksgiving-invites-him-back-for-dinner/.

19. *Gran'pa Knows Best*, Del Valle Productions (web page), accessed May 3, 2017, http://www.granpaknowsbest.com/contact-us.

20. *Gran'pa Knows Best*, Seasons 1 and 2, 2015–2016, directed by William D. Caballero.

21. *The ChatterBox with Kevin and Grandma Lill*, PBS (web page), accessed May 3, 2017, https://www.youtube.com/channel/UCKvWRakjdSbtK-4phfY2gjQ.

22. Kim Sawchuk and Barbara Crow, " 'I'm G-Mom on the Phone': Remote Grandmother, Cell Phones and Inter-Generational Dis/Connections," *Feminist Media Studies* 12, no. 4 (December 1, 2012): 503, https://doi.org/10.1080/14680777.2012.741863.

23. Pål André Aarsand, "Computer and Video Games in Family Life: The Digital Divide as a Resource in Intergenerational Interactions," *Childhood* 14, no. 2 (May 2007): 252, https://doi.org/10.1177/0907568207078330.

24. *Chopped*, "Chopped Tournament of Stars: Sports Stars!" Season 19, Episode 3, Food Network, March 9, 2014, produced by Linda Lea.

25. *Clash of the Grandmas*, "Thanksgiving at Grandma's," Season 1, Episode 1, Food Network, November 13, 2016, produced by Mark Freed.

26. *Clash of the Grandmas*, "Christmas at Grandma's," Season 1, Episode 4, Food Network, December 4, 2016, produced by Mark Freed.

27. *Clash of the Grandmas*, "Granny Family Food Fight," Season 1, Episode 3, Food Network, November 27, 2016, produced by Mark Freed.

28. Amanda Grenier and Jill Hanley, "Older Women and 'Frailty': Aged, Gendered and Embodied Resistance," *Current Sociology* 55, no. 2 (March 2007): 221, http://doi.org10.1177/0011392107073303 .

29. Linda Poon, "Some Chinese Grandparents Are Making Their Grandkids Fat," *NPR.org*, July 29, 2015, http://www.npr.org/sections/goatsandsoda/2015/07/29/427066070/chinese-grandparents-are-making-their-grandkids-fat.

30. Esther C. L. Goh and Leon Kuczynski, "Agency and Power of Single Children in Multi-Generational Families in Urban Xiamen, China," *Culture and Psychology* 15, no. 4 (December 2009): 528, https://doi.org/10.1177/1354067X09344881.

31. "One Born Every Minute: Grandma's Fighting," *Lifetime*, YouTube, December 2, 2011, https://www.youtube.com/watch?v=IMCY7WO8zgM.

32. Amy Wadas, "Police: Fist Fight between Great Grandmothers in Hospital Maternity Ward," *CBS Pittsburgh*, October 10, 2014, http://pittsburgh.cbslocal.com/2014/10/10/police-investigate-fight-between-great-grandmothers-in-maternity-ward/.

33. Dorene Weinstein, "Grandmother vs. Grandmother: A Shocking Rivalry," *MomZette* (web page), February 10, 2016, https://www.lifezette.com/momzette/grandmother-vs-grandmother-a-shocking-rivalry/.

34. For more information on frenemies and depictions of aggressive behavior within media, see Sarah M. Coyne et al., "'Frenemies, Fraitors, and Mean-Em-Aitors': Priming Effects of Viewing Physical and Relational Aggression in the Media on Women," *Agressive Behavior* 38, no. 2 (March 1, 2012): 141–149, http://doi.org/10.1002/ab.21410.

35. Riva Tukachinsky, "Where We Have Been and Where We Can Go from Here: Looking to the Future in Research on Media, Race, and Ethnicity," *Journal of Social Issues* 71, no. 1 (2015): 191, doi: 10.1111/josi.12104.

36. Lorraine C. Ladish, "This Latina Abuela's Crocheting Tips Made Her a YouTube Sensation," *NBC News* (web page), March 17, 2016, https://www.nbcnews.com/news/latino/latina-abuela-s-crocheting-tips-are-youtube-sensation-n538816.

37. *Southern at Heart*, "Grandma's Cooking," Food Network, Season 5, Episode 3, October 18, 2015, directed by Kevin Lezak.

38. *The Chew*, "Grandma's Greatest Hits," ABC, February 7, 2017, produced by Gordon Elliott.

39. "*Great Depression Cooking*: Get Budget-Minded Meals from the Online Cooking Show Created by 93-Year-Old Clara Cannucciari," in *Food, Drink, History, Life, Open Culture* (blog), November 23, 2015, http://www.openculture.com/2015/11/great-depression-cooking.html and "Depression Cooking: A Visit to Clara's Kitchen," *Backdoor Survival* (blog), accessed May 23, 2017, http://www.backdoorsurvival.com/depression-cooking/.

40. Rich M., "10 Survival Skills Your Great-Grandparents Knew (That Most of Us Have Forgotten)," *Off the Grid News* (blog), accessed January 27, 2018, http://www.offthegridnews.com/extreme-survival/10-survival-skills-your-great-grandparents-knew-that-most-of-us-have-forgotten/.

41. Chris Pummer, "4 Life Skills Only Grandpas Can Teach," *Huffington Post* (blog), July 4, 2014, https://www.huffingtonpost.com/2014/07/04/grandfather-relationship-_n_5533839.html.

42. Leslie Baldacci, "These Grannies Are on Safari," *AARP* (blog), May 11, 2011, http://www.aarp.org/entertainment/television/info-05-2011/grannies-on-safari.html.

43. Huma Qureshi, "Got a Problem? Just Ask Grandma," *The Guardian*, September 28, 2012, https://www.theguardian.com/lifeandstyle/2012/sep/29/barbara-cutie-cooper-grandmother-blogger-advice.

44. Joe Marino and Natalie O'Neill, "Who Needs a Shrink When This Grandma Will Listen for Free," *New York Post*, October 6, 2017, https://nypost.com/2017/10/06/who-needs-a-shrink-when-this-grandma-will-listen-for-free/.

45. Kirsty Fairclough, "Nothing Less Than Perfect: Female Celebrity, Ageing and Hyper-Scrutiny in the Gossip Industry," *Celebrity Studies* 3, no. 1 (March 2012): 92, https://doi.org/10.1080/19392397.2012.644723.

46. "Cubs Give 'Grandpa Rossy' Grand Send-Off as Career Nears End," *Chicago Tribune* (web page), September 14, 2016, http://www.chicagotribune.com/sports/baseball/cubs/ct-david-ross-grandpa-rossy-instagram-20160914-story.html.

47. "Vikings' Favre Welcomes Grandchild," *ESPN* (web page), April 6, 2010, http://www.espn.com/nfl/news/story?id=5061588.

48. Susanna Kim, "Grandpa Pitcher Aiming to Be Rare MLB Player," *ABC News* (web page), January 16, 2015, http://abcnews.go.com/Sports/grandpa-pitcher-aiming-rare-mlb-player/story?id=28278436.

49. Isabelle Khoo, "Kirstie Alley Kids: Actress Shares First Photo of Grandson Waylon Tripp Parker," *Huffington Post* (blog), June 22, 2016, http://www.huffingtonpost.ca/2016/06/22/kirstie-alley-kids_n_10611690.html.

50. Janine Rubenstein, "Sting and Wife Trudie on Life as Grandparents and Empty-Nesters," *People.com* (web page), September 16, 2016, http://people.com/music/sting-and-wife-trudie-on-being-grandparents-and-empty-nesters/.

51. "Marie Osmond on Life with Her 3 Grandkids—'I'm the Happiest I've Ever Been.'" *Closer Weekly* (web page), May 4, 2016, http://www.closerweekly.com/posts/marie-osmond-life-grandmother-grandchildren-exclusive-101177.

52. Lesley Stahl, *Becoming Grandma: The Joys and Science of the New Grandparenting* (New York: Blue Rider Press, 2016), 1.

53. Claire Kirch, "Jessica Lange Publishes First Children's Book," *Publishers Weekly* (web page), October 1, 2013, https://www.publishersweekly.com/pw/by-topic/childrens/childrens-book-news/article/59331-jessica-lange-publishes-first-children-s-book.html.

54. Andy Neuenschwander, "Kris Jenner Talks North West, Doesn't Want to Be a 'Grandma,'" *E! Online*, July 24, 2013, http://www.eonline.com/shows/chelsea/news/442007/kris-jenner-talks-north-west-doesn-t-want-to-be-a-grandma-watch-the-interview.

55. Bedhead, "Kris Jenner Refuses to Be Called 'Grandma' at Age 57: Understandable or Odd," *celebitchy* (blog), July 25, 2013, http://www.celebitchy.com/312076/kris_jenner_refuses_to_be_called_grandma_at_age_57_understandable_or_odd/.

56. Fairclough, "Nothing Less Than Perfect," 92.

57. Sarah Kunin and Catherine Thorbecke, "Charlie Sheen Discusses His New Film, 'Mad Families,' and Life as a Grandfather," *ABC News* (web page), January 11, 2017, http://abcnews.go.com/Entertainment/charlie-sheen-discusses-film-mad-families-life-grandfather/story?id=44643201.

58. Ranee Dawn, "What Kind of Grandpa Is Snoop Dogg? The 'Get-Away-With-Everything' Kind," *Today.com*, May 13, 2015, http://www.today.com/parents/what-kind-grandpa-snoop-dogg-get-away-everything-kind-t20886.

59. Molly O'Neill, "Suzanne Somers Talks about Grandchildren," *Grandparents.com*, American Grandparents Association (web page), accessed May 20, 2017, http://abcnews.go.com/Entertainment/charlie-sheen-discusses-film-mad-families-life-grandfather/story?id=44643201.

60. Amber Phillips, "7 Ways Bernie Sanders Reminds Us of Our Grumpy Grandpa," *Washington Post* (web page), July 22, 2015, https://www.washingtonpost.com/news/the-fix/wp/2015/07/22/7-times-bernie-sanders-reminds-us-of-our-grumpy-grandpa/?utm_term=.0cc75b849052.

61. Sandra Sobieraj Westfall, "'Fun Grandpa' Bernie Sanders," *People.com* (web page) January 23, 2016, http://people.com/celebrity/bernie-sanders-is-fun-grandpa-5-things-we-learned-at-his-home/.

62. Joyce Chen, "Lady Gaga FaceTimes Her Grandma Ahead of Super Bowl Halftime Show," *US Weekly* (blog), February 5, 2017, http://www.usmagazine.com/celebrity-news/news/lady-gaga-facetimes-her-grandma-ahead-of-super-bowl-halftime-show-w465060.

63. Rachel Togerson, "Cindy Crawford's Grandma, 97, Proves Her Family Is Genetically Blessed," *US Weekly* (blog), September 21, 2016, http://www.usmagazine.com/stylish/news/cindy-crawfords-grandma-97-proves-her-family-is-genetically-blessed-w441346.

64. Jessica Dysart, "Celebrities Who Are Best Friends with Their Grandparents," *Huffington Post* (blog), June 5, 2014, http://www.huffingtonpost.com/2014/06/05/celebrities-grandparents-_n_5411773.html.

65. "Jennette McCurdy Has the World's Cutest Grandparents," *The Tonight Show Starring Jimmy Fallon*, YouTube, June 12, 2015, https://www.youtube.com/watch?v=1TUyhDzbkYA.

66. "Matt Bomer Thanks Grandparents for Thriving Marriage with His Husband," *People.com* (web page), August 21, 2016, http://www.peoplemagazine.co.za/celebrity-news/international-celebrities/matt-bomer-thanks-grandparents-for-thriving-marriage-with-his-husband/amp.

67. Alison Schwartz, "Katy Perry's Grammy Date: Her Grandma!" *People.com*, February 13, 2011, http://people.com/awards/grammy-awards-katy-perry-brings-her-grandma/.

68. James Montgomery, "Justin Timberlake Premiers Emotional 'Mirrors' Video," *MTV News*, March 19, 2013, http://www.mtv.com/news/1704004/justin-timberlake-mirrors-music-video/.

69. Sara M. Moniuszko, "Macklemore Marks his Grandma's 100th Birthday with 'Glorious' Video," *USA Today* (web page), July 7, 2017, https://www.usatoday.com/story/life/entertainthis/2017/07/07/macklemore-gives-his-grandma-glorious-100th-birthday-new-video/458335001/.

70. Yonhap, "In New Album, EXO's Lay Sings to Mark His Grandparent's Love," *The Korea Herald*, September 25, 2017, http://www.koreaherald.com/view.php?ud=20170925000787.

71. Anna O'Donoghue, "Watch Ed Sheeran's Nan," *Irish Examiner* (web page), March 3, 2017, https://www.irishexaminer.com/breakingnews/entertainment/watch-ed-sheerans-nan-listen-to-the-song-he-wrote-about-her-for-the-first-time-779898.html; Nicole Pomarico, "Ed Sheeran's Grandma Hears 'Nancy Mulligan' for the First Time & Her Reaction Is Adorable," *Bustle* (web page), March 2017, https://www.bustle.com/p/ed-sheerans-grandma-hears-nancy-mulligan-for-the-first-time-her-reaction-is-adorable-video-42847.

72. Fairclough, "Nothing Less Than Perfect," 97–99.

73. Deborah Jermyn, "'Get a Life, Ladies. Your Old One Is Not Coming Back': Ageing, Ageism and the Lifespan of Female Celebrity," *Celebrity Studies* 3, no. 1 (March 2012): 4, https://doi.org/10.1080/19392397.2012.644708.

74. Laura Bennett, "Betty White Is Not a Sex Machine," *The New Republic* (web page), June 16, 2013, https://newrepublic.com/article/113296/betty-white-and-our-cruel-obsession-dirty-old-women.

75. *Betty White's Off Their Rockers*, "Taking Advantage," Season 3, Episode 1, Lifetime, February 28, 2014, written by T. J. Chambers.

76. *Betty White's Off Their Rockers*, "Betty's New Chef," Season 3, Episode 2, Lifetime, February 28, 2014, written by T. J. Chambers.

77. *Betty White's Off Their Rockers*, "Taking Advantage," Season 3, Episode 5, Lifetime, March 14, 2014, written by T. J. Chambers.

78. "86-Year-Old Is the Baddest Great-Grandmother on Instagram," *BoredPanda* (blog), accessed July 5, 2017, http://www.boredpanda.com/baddie-winkle-instagram-grandma/.

79. Julija Nėjė, "Remember the 86-Year-Old Badass Grandma? Now She's 88 and Even More Badass!" *BoredPanda* (blog), accessed February 4, 2018, https://www.boredpanda.com/badass-grandma-instagram-baddie-winkle/.

80. Grandma Mary's YouTube Trailer (web page), *3GoldenSistersTV*, accessed July 12, 2017, https://www.youtube.com/user/3GoldenSistersTV.

81. Jennifer Musial, "From 'Madonna' to 'Whore': Sexuality, Pregnancy, and Popular Culture," *Sexualities* 17, no. 4 (June 2014): 404–405, http://doi.org/10.1177/136346071351633.

82. Bianca London, "Are Glam Grannies the New Yummy Mummies?" *DailyMail.com* (web page), November 6, 2012, http://www.dailymail.co.uk/femail/article-2228605/Are-glam-grannies-new-yummy-mummies-Grandmothers-join-school-run-style-wars.html.

83. Melissa Charles, "The Problem with 'Glamma,'" *Huffington Post* (blog), May 20, 2016, https://www.huffingtonpost.com/melissa-charles/the-problem-with-glamma_b_7315096.html.

84. Joy Sewing, "Local Man Trending as #MrStealYourGrandma Surprised by Instafame," *Houston Chronicle* (web page), July 1, 2016, http://www.chron.com/life/style/article/Local-man-goes-viral-as-MrStealYourGrandma-8334823.php.

85. Megan Willett, "The World Is about to Fall in Love with the Fashionable Grandpas of Instagram," *Business Insider* (web page), June 9, 2014. http://www.businessinsider.com/fashiongrandpas-instagram-sensation-2014-6.

86. Laura Mulvey, *Visual and Other Pleasures*, 2nd ed. (New York: Palgrave MacMillan, 2009).

87. Teresa Bell Kindred, *Nanahood* (blog), accessed February 2, 2017, http://nanahood.com/.

88. Victoria Moll-Ramírez, "Comedian Jenny Lorenzo 'Channels' Her Abuela, Makes Her a Viral Hit," *NBC News* (web page), May 12, 2017, http://www.nbcnews.com/news/latino/comedian-jenny-lorenzo-channels-her-abuela-makes-her-viral-hit-n757361.

89. Kate Stanhope. "IFC's 'Gigi' Team on Turning David Krumholtz into a Jewish Grandma: 'He's a Very Handsome Woman,'" *The Hollywood Reporter*, July 31, 2015, https://www.hollywoodreporter.com/live-feed/ifcs-gigi-team-turning-david-812509.

90. Victoria Moll-Ramírez, "Comedian Jenny Lorenzo 'Channels' Her Abuela, Makes Her a Viral Hit," *NBC News* (web page), May 12, 2017, http://www.nbcnews.com/news/latino/comedian-jenny-lorenzo-channels-her-abuela-makes-her-viral-hit-n757361.

91. Elizabeth Nathanson, "Knitting, Sewing and Grandma's Retro-Style," in *Television and Postfeminist Housekeeping: No Time for Mother* (New York: Routledge, 2013), 109.

92. Mary Bernstein, "Celebration and Suppression: The Strategic Uses of Identity by the Lesbian and Gay Movement," *American Journal of Sociology* 103, no. 3 (November 1997): 531–565, http://doi.org 10.1086/231250.

93. Joshua Meyrowitz, *No Sense of Place: The Impact of Electronic Media on Social Behavior* (New York: Oxford University Press, 1986), 57.

Chapter Six

The Grandparent-Industrial Complex

My mother came home from a store one day annoyed and carrying a bunch of "Grandma's Cookies." When I tried to ascertain the trouble, she said she thought it was unfair for the cookie brand to use the grandma image. Her biggest concern was that it stereotyped grandmas as bakers; since she didn't like to cook, the cookies made her feel like she wasn't satisfying her grandma duties. She brought home the cookies to show me as evidence, but also as a treat for her grandchildren.

While I easily reassured my mother that she's a wonderful grandma, regardless of her cooking skills, she was raising a fair point. Grandparents have shifted from just being a member of the extended family to a brand of their own. The use of the titles "Grandma and Grandpa" is interesting in part because of their lack of a clearly defined role; it can refer to someone who has a grandchild or another who is simply old enough to be a grandparent. This is something my mother intuitively grasped, and rejected, in her cookie episode. In recent years, the grandparent label has emerged to sell products and help the surge of a new life stage. It also is used as a branding tool and to market products that advertise a cultural respect and appreciation of grandparents. The commodification of grandparent culture has defined a group for whom products are designed, marketed, and branded, which affects how grandparenting itself is perceived.

MARKETING COHORT

In 1978, President Carter signed a proclamation that created Grandparents Day as a formal holiday. His primary goal was to bring attention to senior citizens and those performing the caretaking role of grandparents. The law was a way to highlight an often forgotten group. Marketing to an older population had not been popular, unless an advertiser was selling a specific product to them. Many marketers adhered to a consumer strategy that noted older people were less likely to spend money. Others may have been less intentional, as they were out of touch with the older population, which some critics have attributed to a decline in relationships between grandparents and their grandchildren. Avoiding older audiences was also connected to the stigma of aging: many agencies reasoned that advertising to an older population might be counterproductive because people don't like to feel old.[1] Today, though, this group is no longer overlooked, at least from a marketing perspective.

Now companies and organizations see this cohort as an opportunity to invent new products, create new services, and to build a new target market. The marketing and consumer industries realize the power of a target audience that reveres and enjoys a newfound role that often accompanies growing older: the grandparent.

To companies and marketers, grandparents represent a new market full of potential. More grandparents today have disposable income, which is ideal for marketers looking to identify new groups to buy products.[2] Grandparents nationwide spend an average of $27.5 billion on their grandchildren every year.[3] A new statistic now accompanies the perennial figure of how much it costs for a parent to raise a child into adulthood: being a grandparent costs about $2,383 per year, not including unreimbursed childcare.[4] Researching the grandparent market, Dennis H. Tootelian and Sanjay B. Varshney found that the "amount spent on grandchildren by baby boomer grandparents is double that of earlier generations."[5] Grandparent markets are differentiated as well. The researchers concluded, "Entertainment and travel and vacations apart, grandparents over 75 years old spend more than those aged 50 or below in all product categories."[6]

Marketing specialist Lori K. Bitter writes about the marketability of grandparents who are in the Baby Boomer generation. Those born between 1946 and 1964 have had new products marketed to them at every life stage all their lives: "Post-war optimism and high fertility rates created a huge generation of young people, and a corresponding marketplace of products and services to meet their needs."[7] Consequently, Boomers have become accustomed to entering each life stage with their own designated products, markets, and rituals. Grandparenting as another life stage is becoming its own market.

Marketers are developing additional strategies to target grandparents. Like other demographic groups, including parents and children, grandparents are becoming more narrowly defined. Pamela Paul has examined marketing strategies to target grandparents as consumers. Marketers, for example, are now distinguishing between traditionalist grandparents, who are more patriotic and cautious with spending, and makers, who are more independent achievers that are more concerned about social status. She notes that a new group, "thinkers," has emerged: "Currently 16 percent of the grandparent population, they are more intellectually curious, active and globally oriented, and will start to replace the other three groups as Baby Boomers begin to dominate the grandparent population."[8]

Those within the advertising and marketing industries are beginning to move away from a focus on youth culture and shift their energy to targeting grandparents. One columnist laments the opportunity companies have missed: "Many retailers and brands typically focus on parents (the spenders) and children (the influencers) but the often overlooked grandparent—mostly Baby Boomers—might get you more bang for your marketing buck this year."[9] In admiring the market potential of this group, another industry specialist writes: "Along with caregiving and empty-nesting, grandparenting represents a Boomer life stage with the most 'consumer moments' and an openness to trying new products and services that they may have not considered in the past."[10] When *Grandparents.com* was building its website and searching for an advertising agency to help with branding and marketing, one of its key requirements was the ability to distinguish between senior citizens and grandparents.[11] In the past, an older person may have been labeled a "grandma" or "grandpa" as a universal term of appreciation—or derision. Today, being a grandparent is recognized as having specific desires and habits.

Grand magazine was created twelve years ago. Its subtitle defines its purpose: "The Lifestyle Magazine for Awesome Grandparents." The magazine recognizes this period as a life stage and offers opportunities to experience that stage better. It exists to be the go-to place for everything grandparent related. Christine Crosby is the founder and editorial director of *Grand*. When she became a grandmother, she realized that grandparents were invisible in the consumer market. "There was nothing out there addressing the day-to-day lifestyle for grandparents," she said. "We gathered together some investors, friends, and families." Crosby remembers that the early phase of the magazine was challenging: "At first it was very difficult because people really had a notion of what a grandparent was, which was so stereotyped and inaccurate. . . . Then, all of a sudden, everybody realized that Baby Boomers were becoming grandparents." More businesses became interested in this emerging market: "Grandparents buy everything not only for themselves, including entertaining and travel, but then there's a level in which they help their children, and that third level with the grandchildren: funding education and school books." Crosby describes grandparents as "mega consumers, and they have disposable income." This year *Grand* has encouraged grandparents to move online, she says, "because that is where your grandchildren are. Do it, because if you don't, you will be left behind. It is an imperative. Become educated." Crosby says she has seen the perception of aging shift: "Today we don't call it old like it's a four-letter word. It's just a new stage of life."

Grand treats the life stage of grandparenting as more than simply having grandchildren; it is an entire lifestyle. One issue of the magazine covers grandchild-related issues, such as how to deal with money and spending with grandchildren, and advertises books and other gifts to purchase for both readers' grandchildren and themselves. There is even a section for expecting grandparents, offering a quiz for grandparents-to-be to determine "what kind of grandparent will you be."[12]

Likewise, the American Grandparents Association and its companion website feature stories, advice, and articles designed to be of interest to this group. *Grandparents.com* posts stories that are shared an average of over three thousand times per day. Started in 2007 to guide grandparents toward activities they can do with their grandchildren, the site was sold in 2010 and went public in 2012 with a larger focus, including the ability to host communities for exchanging ideas.[13] These sites represent the ability to target a group of people sharing a new life stage that brings with it new challenges and opportunities.

PURCHASING POWER

Just like the transition to parenting, a novel world of consumer opportunity opens up for parents becoming grandparents. There are apps to buy, toys to purchase, and college financing to consider. Retailers are using what they call "grandma grabbers" to encourage grandparents to shop in stores. One marketing group employs sweepstakes offers targeted to the elderly to collect marketing data on grandparents.[14] Stores now are marketing directly to grandparents, including hosting grandparent events and grandparent nights.[15] On Grandparents Day every September, grandparents around the country can receive free admission to zoos, amusement parks, and museums. Some businesses offer special treatment to grandparents throughout the year. CoCo Key Water Park offers a "CoCo Cares Grandparents Pass," which permits grandparents to enter the water park free on Sundays after they pay for their grandchild's admission.[16] At Carter's children's clothing stores, grandparents get a special 10 percent discount on Wednesdays.[17] One furniture store even advertises "Farm Tables for Grandparents Saying 'No' to Downsizing."[18] It is becoming commonplace now for grandparents in a wealth bracket that can afford it to open up Section 529 college savings accounts for their grandchildren. Websites that explain the rules and regulations of these accounts and offer college investment advice are devoted exclusively to grandparents. Financial rules and structures will need to catch up to this new cohort, who is investing in its grandchildren from the very beginning of their lives. For instance, some financial counselors warn grandparents of the unintended consequences of opening 529 accounts in their grandchildren's names, reducing their chance of qualifying for financial aid.[19] Schools are already recognizing the fiscal power of these grandparents, and more of them are targeting them to spend money on behalf of their grandchildren. Preparatory schools, for example, are now reaching out to grandparents to solicit donations. It is becoming more common to invite grandparents to sit on boards and increase their involvement during the year with grandparent events.[20] Colleges are hosting Grandparent Days more often, recognizing not only the nurturing bond they have with their grandchildren, but also the investment they have put in their grandchildren being there.

Grandparents also have new opportunities to buy products, some designed specifically for them. The toy industry is one industry category that is expanding its target market to intergenerational marketing.[21] Studies indicate that many grandparents love spending money on their grandchildren: about 25 percent of grandparents reported spending over $1,000 in the past year.[22] Toys "R" Us offered coupons specifically to grandparents, with the knowledge that they are major toy consumers.[23]

Grandparents can purchase the UsTyme app, which was developed by grandparents who wanted to keep their grandchildren's attention on Skype. The app does so by allowing them to share activities like reading books and playing games over the video call.[24] The Entertainment Software Association (ESA) reports that 26 percent of gamers are 50 years of age or older, and 29 percent are 18 years of age or under.[25] Another study commissioned jointly by the ESA and AARP found that "close to four in ten adults aged 50-plus are gamers (38%) while 62% are non-gamers."[26] Game platform makers, like Microsoft's Xbox, propose that their devices should be used as media portals not only for children, but for their parents and grandparents as well.[27] Nintendo has marketed particular games directly to grandparents, including Brain Age and Wii Bowling, promising that they could engage with their grandchildren while playing.[28] Encouraging this trend are studies that indicate playing with video games can improve the cognitive abilities of elderly people.[29]

Elderly adults have the potential to be a large market for gaming because of their disposable income, the free time they have in retirement, the benefits associated with increased brain activity, and the way they can use video games to connect with their grandchildren. Some criticize game developers for not focusing enough on this market.[30] Scholars have noticed the potential for gaming to promote multigenerational connections and learning.[31] In the future, grandparents may be key players in gaming.

Even industries beyond those traditionally associated with children are keeping the grandparent market in mind. One grandmother described to me her need to buy a new car after she and her husband began shuttling their grandchildren around and taking them on long trips. *Consumer Reports* now offers guidance on the "Best Cars for Families with Grandparents" and includes advice to consider that grandparents can get in and out of some models of cars better than others.[32]

Book publishers also have become more aware of grandparents, both as a defined consumer market and as a subject matter. A quick search for grandparent books on Amazon brings up over 2,500 options. Advice books are sold as gifts to new grandmothers, just like parenting books, to help them adjust to becoming a grandparent.[33] Some advice books available include titles like *Today's Grandmother: Your Guide to the First Two Years* and *Extreme Grandparenting: The Ride of Your Life*. Other books chronicle authors' experiences or serve as reflections on being a grandparent, such as Anne Lamott writing about her teenage son's firstborn child in *Some Assembly Required: A Journal of My Son's First Son* or *The Granny Diaries*. Some offer activities that you can do as a grandparent, such as *The Grammie Guide* or *Creative Grandparenting*. Grandparents as subjects in children's books have surged in the last few years.[34] *My Grandma Can Do Anything* (2005), *Here Comes Grandma* (2005), *The Grandma Book* (2006), *Henry and Mudge and the Great Grandpas* (2006), *Silly Frilly Grandma Tillie* (2012), *I Love You, Grandpa* (2012), *How to Babysit a Grandma* (2014), *My Grandpa Is Not Grumpy* (2014), *My Grandparents Love Me* (2016), and *Grandma Loves You* (2017) are just a few examples. Rosemary Mastnak's book *Cooking with Grandma* was successful enough to launch two sequels, *Adventures with Grandpa* and *Dancing with Grandma.*

One scholar who studies the depiction of grandparents in children's literature writes about the benefits of these books for the grandparent-grandchild relationship:

> Children's understanding of their grandparents can be reinforced as they learn to appreciate and verbalize the importance of the grandparent role as heard in stories and seen in books. Tales about a grandparent's era or youth bind generations together through a common understanding of the similarities and differences across experiences and generations.[35]

Some books deal with how to handle the death of grandparents, which is not unexpected now that grandparents increasingly are playing key roles in the lives of children. Grandparents today look for books to use as guidance in how to perform that role. At the same time, grandparents are becoming central characters in children's libraries.

Grandparents also are participating in their own activities with their grandchildren. Monira, the owner of a store that targets parents, noticed that more and more grandparents were bringing their grandchildren to play groups and activities at her store at different times than when parents showed up. She decided to tag a grandmothers' group meeting on to the end of one of the children's scheduled story times to give them an opportunity to meet and network. At these meetings, she discovered that the grandparent experience is not uniform. Talking with them, she realized that their reasons for spending time with their grandchildren varied. Monira said, "I feel like there are always the type of grandparents that fall into grandparenting because of a need. Maybe the partner is not involved anymore, and there is a single mom, and it's really out of a very necessary situation. But I think there is also a rising group of grandparents that are choosing to really take part in their grandchild's life in a more active role." Some grandparents at the meetings were looking for opportunities to connect with other moms or grandparents, while others preferred to focus on being with their own grandchildren. Monira said that many grandparents had a different view than parents on childcare. "From the grandparent perspective, they have that experience. They know the child will survive," she said. "They have a wider, broader perspective. They seem more grounded and not so worried." Many grandparents are taking advantage of their free time to enjoy relationships with their grandchildren without experiencing the anxiety of parenting. Businesses are sprouting up to offer them spaces to have these opportunities.

Surely, this explosion of goods and activities has made grandparents more visible to the public, and it may even be reconfiguring their position within their own families. Richard A. Settersten, a scholar on aging, writes about the concept of subjective aging, which does not always provide clear markers to define stages of aging:

> Subjective aging is also rooted in social processes that extend beyond interpersonal relationships. Although social ties are especially important, appraisals of aging are shaped by opportunities and constraints presented by demographic, epidemiological, and historical contexts; the welfare state and social policies; cultural ideas about the phases of life and the transitions that punctuate them; and cultural ideas related to age, aging, and gender.[36]

The marketplace, then, becomes another space where people can think subjectively about their age.

MARKETING TO GRANDPARENTS

In addition to marketing products to grandparents, advertisers are using the grandparent image to sell products and services to consumers in other age groups. Commercials that feature grandparents are becoming popular among some large companies.[37] Sometimes these commercials acknowledge or reinforce age stereotypes, but increasingly they offer insights into new roles that are emerging for them.

Some advertisements that target the elderly imply that grandchildren are the reason to value life and stay healthy. In an ad for Humana's medical plan, little children talk about their relationship with their grandparents, with statements like "Grandma just makes me happy," "Grandma is the best," "The total package," and "Grandpa spoils me rotten." These ads use grandchildren's love and devotion to motivate investment in health services and products. A Cheerios commercial shows a grandmother talking to her little grandbaby in a highchair as she feeds her. She makes a map out of the Cheerios and shows the baby where all their relatives live. A Polish commercial viewed and shared globally features a man painstakingly learning English so that he is able to greet his American grandchild with the phrase, "Hi. I am your grandpa."[38]

Many of these advertisements focus on the bond between grandparents and their grandchildren. One London ad for Heathrow Airport, titled "Coming Home: The Greatest Gift of All," had over three million viewers online. It follows elderly grandparent teddy bears on their airplane journey and through the airport. Waiting relatives and overjoyed grandchildren meet them at the arrivals area, and the bears transform into happy human grandparents. The commercial shows attributes of aging, as the bears rely on each other and the help of others at the airport to manage their travels.[39] In these commercials, grandchildren are treated as a lifetime achievement reward.

The rite of passage that comes with being a grandparent is another feature of these commercials. In some, this rite is positioned as facing the exhaustion of having grandchildren visit. This is a theme in a Campbell's soup commercial: grandparents try to keep up with their grandchildren, concluding with the line "Grilled cheese and Campbell's tomato soup go together like grandchildren and chaos." Another campaign for Medicare both targets and features grandparents who are subjected to trials and tribulations, from the kids playing tricks on them to having to listen to the children practice their instruments. They finally watch their grandchildren leave and exhale, "Well, we survived."[40] These commercials showcase the challenges and joys of grandparents acting as babysitters.

Automobile commercials are showing grandparents who possess important generational knowledge to pass on to the their descendants. In a 2016 Subaru commercial, a "hippie" grandmother accompanies her child and granddaughter on a road trip to Woodstock. The commercial contrasts the grandmother's connection to nature (smelling the air), belief in the mystical (thinking she can talk to the universe), and her frank talk (about her early sex life) with the parents rolling their eyes at each other. Yet it's also clear that they are taking this road trip because the grandmother can provide her grandchild with a sense of wonderment and idealism that the entire family values. By the end of the commercial, the whole family is hugging the tree under which the grandmother met her husband.

Volkswagen also used a self-described "family-oriented" marketing campaign for their 2017 Atlas SUV. Their ad featured a grandmother as the source of family connection and generational memory. In the commercial, she had just lost her husband, and his dying wish was for the family to take a road trip on his behalf. Along with her children and grandchildren, the grandmother crosses the country while she imparts a sense of the family's history and an appreciation of the beauty of the country's landscape. The advertising agency chose to cast a "real grandma" with little acting experience but who had a real-life loyalty to the Volkswagen brand. The commercial used a real photo of her and her husband as she described the day they met. The tagline said, "Life's as big as you make it. The all-new seven seater Volkswagen Atlas."[41] The commercial sent the message that a grandmother can provide a reflective break from everyday life, but it also illustrated that more families need larger vehicles to accommodate grandparents in their everyday lives. Both of these car ads featured grandparent images to target not only grandparents but also other groups that appreciate their existence.

More ads bring to light aspects of grandparenting that may not have been as visible before, such as grandparents raising their grandchildren full time. After the recession in 2007, the number of children being raised by grandparents increased: 39 percent of the seven million grandparents who live with their grandchildren serve as the primary caregiver.[42] An Angel Soft commercial received media attention for its spot titled "Grander Parents." It tells the story of a young girl named Hailey who is taken in by her grandparents when her father ends up in jail. The grandmother says, "We want to be the grandparents, knowing that we have to be the parents." This particular commercial followed others in a series called "Be Soft. Be Strong." The campaign focuses on moments where people are "rising to the occasion," according to the company's brand manager, and was inspired by people whom the ad team knew were raised by their grandparents.[43] At one time in the past, a family in which grandparents had to take over raising their children's children would have been labeled an incomplete or failed family. Now, it is recognized as a new type of family. Reports indicate that since 2009, the rate of grandparents raising grandchildren is increasing.[44] Emerging from the shadows, this issue is now recognized by consumer brands.

The idea of the grandparent as necessarily completing the family shows up in some commercials. For example, a Ridgewood Savings Bank ad focuses on the desire for physical proximity among family members. It features a couple shopping for a home, and the wife surprises her mother with the fact that she bought a house close to her. When her mother asks what they will do with the extra room in the house, the daughter reveals a picture of an ultrasound to let her mother know that she is about to become a grandma.

Some of these commercials assume stereotypes of aging, while others challenge these ideas. An Oscar Mayer ad depicts a grandfather as too candid in his responses and interactions with his grandchildren. It comments, "Sometimes being too transparent can be a bad thing." The notion of a senile elderly main, unable to restrain his impulses, becomes the butt of the joke. An Ally Bank commercial uses grandparents who depend on their grandchildren to negotiate a digital world. The commercial narrates, "No branches equal great rates. It's a fact, kind of like grandkids equal great tech support," implying they are just happy to see their grandchildren so they can operate their digital appliances.

In contrast, an Amazon Kindle for the holidays ad is among a newer group that celebrates older generations embracing digital technology. It features a grandmother buying her grandson a Kindle so she can encourage his love of reading. Unlike other ads that feature technically illiterate elderly people, this one shows a grandmother perfectly capable of browsing the internet and making a technological purchase for her grandson. In one commercial for the telecommunications provider Xfinity, different sets of grandparents are shocked to discover social media posts from their grandchildren complaining about their upcoming holiday visits because of their lack of technology. "Entering the gates of hell where there's no wi-fi and no shows. AKA grandmas." The grandfather tells his wife, "She means we aren't up-to-date." Their house is full of "old" technology, like a tube TV and a basket full of remote controls, until they completely upgrade it to the grandchildren's surprise. Technology serves to help the grandparents reconnect with their grandchildren, from posing with them for Facebook pictures or having their granddaughter use a digital filter to remove wrinkles from the picture. By the end of the commercial, the grandparents are rewarded for their efforts with a post from their granddaughter professing her love for grandma's house and the hashtag #BestHolidayEver. Once the grandparents discover they are digital outcasts, they upgrade and are able to reconnect to their family through this technology. The commercial shows elderly couples not only adopting technology, but also embracing it and brushing off the stereotype of being technophobes.

Some of these commercials address the larger theme of aging, but typically they are reassurance that having grandchildren is the reward for a life well lived or that one's legacy will be carried on through their grandchildren. Other ads use the image of the grandparent or the elderly as a punch line to sell products to grandparents laughing at themselves, as well as to a larger audience. Shyon Baumann and Kim de Laat argue that media seldom portray elderly characters as buying products for themselves: "Instead, the characters engage in consumption within their relationship as parents/grandparents or employees. The focus is not on the self or indulgence, as is often the case with younger characters."[45] This idea is extended to grandparents reaching fulfillment through their relationship with their grandchildren in most of these commercials. The purpose of any of the products they buy is to reinforce that relationship, rather than indulging in consumerism to satisfy themselves. Whether it is using the best vehicle to take an extended family trip or buying technology so that grandchildren will want to visit, the grandparents use products and services in these commercials to strengthen family ties and not be deemed irrelevant.

BRANDING GRANDMA

Some companies have evolved from simply selling a specific product to grandparents to using their image to market an entire brand. One grandfather in China reached worldwide recognition when he began modeling clothes for his granddaughter's store, Yuekou. Though the clothes were designed for teen girls, he wore the clothes and adopted a feminine style. Using her grandpa to sell clothing ended up being promotionally successful, bringing her line international attention.[46] Another Chinese grandfather, Wang Deshun, received the moniker "China's hottest grandpa" when he showed off his fit body during Beijing Fashion Week. Now Reebok plans to capitalize on his fame by using Deshun as a model in a new ad campaign centered on the theme "Be More Human." The brand recently recognized a fan who posted a picture of his grandmother wearing a red pair of its Ultra Boost 3.0 shoes.[47]

While the grandpa branding is only beginning to receive attention, the grandma moniker has long been capitalized on for the many possibilities it represents. The designation certainly is not new, as anyone who has frequented a "Grandma's restaurant" can attest. However, using the image of grandma in branding to market goods has swelled. For example, a series of ads for Grandma's Cookies encourages people to "unleash that inner Grandma power." The commercials play on the *Are You My Mother?* children's book by having people who eat the cookies take on stereotypical grandma activities like knitting.[48] The ads do more than tell people to buy Grandma's Cookies; they encourage them to relish the nostalgia of being grandma.

Businesses continue to convert the grandma image into a marketable brand. Jody Scaravella created the restaurant Enoteca Maria in Staten Island, New York, where he hires grandmothers to do all the cooking. His idea was born out of the restaurateur's memories of his own grandmother in the kitchen. He says, "Growing up I realized that my grandmother had been the repository of our family culture and identity."[49] Initially, he placed an ad to hire Italian housewives to do the cooking but then broadened their grandma roster by hiring more women from other regions.[50] The restaurant has a website that introduces potential restaurant-goers to the grandmothers who do the cooking, offering a personal link to those making the meal. These days, people aren't paying for meals just like grandmas used to make; they are buying the labor of grandmas themselves to make those meals.

Like Enoteca Maria, a company called Wooln hires grandmas to do the knitting.[51] Wooln describes itself as bringing together "talented New York grandmothers and people who want to know where their dream knits come from and who made them."[52] They see their company as providing needed services, including bringing retirees back to the workforce and making intergenerational connections. When I interviewed Margaux Rousseau, one of the co-creators of Wooln, she described her move from France to the United States when she and her co-partner Faustine Badrichani were both young moms. They were interested in creating a business that involved social economy and wanted to bring value for elderly women. She felt that the work of mothers and grandmothers often was devalued in American culture and thought their business could bring a new appreciation to an old-fashioned hobby and an elderly group. They didn't find it easy at first to locate granny knitters, despite thinking that since these women were already knitting, they would appreciate being paid for their work. Eventually they found a network of women, with their first knitter being 96 years old.

Rousseau describes the draw of their business: "People want to wear something with a story and know stitch by stitch who was working on this piece." One challenge was positioning what many saw as the conflicting images of grannies participating in an old-fashioned business with the youthful image portrayed for their line. In fact, they found that when they posted a picture of one of their granny knitters, they received more traction on social media with younger consumers than when they produced more youth-directed advertisements. Rousseau describes her knitters as "a granny with a story," and they bring these stories right to their website. The granny branding encourages customers to recall when they had a connection to their products and the people who created them.

Another connection between old and new can be found in dating websites. The Jewish matchmaking service Jdate has created a marketing campaign that uses grandmothers and great-grandmothers in their ads. The campaign, called "Powered by Yentas," implies that grandmothers are helping to design the algorithms that make the matches for users. These ads borrow from the historical tradition of Jewish grandmothers playing a significant role in finding mates for their children.[53] One ad shows a grandmother figure sitting in front of a computer. The ad says, "She knows JavaScript, Python, and Shirley Finkelstein's grandson. Sign up already." Another ad features three grandmothers sitting at a table and working on laptops. The caption reads, "Kvetch all day. Code all night."[54] The ad's humor comes from the juxtaposition of recognizing the traditional value grandmothers provide in matching couples with the unexpected attribute of grandmothers who know how to code.

Marketing expert Jerry Useem describes a new digital marketing environment where online retailers can predict consumer spending habits and adjust prices at an hourly rate.[55] When people have lost connection with the producer of a product and its price, and only have a brand image as a frame of reference, these grandma businesses promote a reconnection with the maker and product in a new way. Consumers may not be trading with a neighbor or building their own products, but these businesses allow them to feel as if they are.

At one time, grandmother clothes were mocked, and their cooking was taken for granted. Now they have become something to desire. The company Rent-a-Grandma appeared in an episode of the popular television program *Shark Tank*, where aspiring entrepreneurs pitch ideas to a panel of celebrity funders.[56] Capitalizing on people's notions of the grandmother archetype as warm and caring, founder Todd Pliss created his company with this image in mind. In his *Shark Tank* pitch, he contrasted a teenager engaged in social media on the couch with one of his grandmas focused on nurturing and caring for a client's children. His idea was that people would prefer a "grandma" to a younger person as a babysitter or tutor. He recognized a potential market in renting out grandmas on an hourly or weekly basis, and he wrote the tagline "Always Trust Your Grandma."

When I spoke with Pliss, he articulated his recognition of two groups that needed to be served: working parents who were having trouble finding steady babysitters who could commit to a family for a period of time, and older women who couldn't find jobs, often because of age discrimination. Pairing the two together made sense to him because people wanted what he labeled "the grandma experience to have a loving, caring older woman in their life." At first, he had to explain to clients that the women who work for him did not adhere to the stereotype of a grandma sitting in a rocking chair. Eventually, he found that people appreciated what this particular group could offer: "They are the ones with the experience," he said. "They are going to be very loyal. They are not running off somewhere. They are more settled in life." Pliss has found that some parents call his company because they had loving relationships with their own grandparents, but because of reasons like death or distance, their own children have not been able to have that same experience. They use his service not only to put their trust in mature caregivers, but also to set up what they see as an important relationship that should exist in the lives of their children. Pliss adds that parents like, for instance, how grandparents tend to be more willing to take kids to the park and let them play than having them sit and play video games. The grandma here is positioned as an antidote to our digital world. His company has since extend beyond the United States to a global market.

Rent-a-Grandma and Wooln illustrate how digital culture shifts the concept of grandparenting. Until now, grandparenting has always been geographically bound and connected to a specific family. Now, services can sprout up to connect those without family ties. The grandmother brand represents authenticity. People believe that they can trust grandmas to provide quality products and honest services. In a world where so much is manufactured, there is a desire to connect with the homemade.

Once a figure like the grandma becomes a brand, more people feel free to adapt the image in new, sometimes surprising ways. Last year, the British advertising agency Mother began a rebranding of grandma during the holiday season. During the month of December, they temporarily named themselves "Grandmother" to bring awareness to issues of aging. They redecorated their reception area with photos of the staff's grandmothers and ran initiatives that celebrated older people and defied stereotypical images of the aging. For example, they set up a "Red-Hot Grannies" phone line, where people could pay to hear older women reading erotic lines from classic literature.[57] The advertising agency also hosted a debate and information session on portrayals of the elderly in the media.[58] The agency capitalized on the shock value of contrasting the typical conservative grandma image with a sexually empowered one.

Some are using the grandma image to correct misperceptions of the elderly, while others attempt to draw in new consumers. Once controlled primarily by those in the role, the grandma image has become an opportunity for those outside the role to manage and assign new meaning to it, and new markets for it.

THE GRANDPARENT EXPERIENCE

Grandparenting occupies a new life stage today, and new traditions, rituals, practices, and even names for grandparents, are emerging and are marketed back to them and their families.

When I was born, most of my family focused on what name I was to be given. In many families today, however, much attention is also given to what to name the new grandparent. As a child, I had fewer choices available as to what to call my grandparents. My default choice was Grandma and Grandpa. Since we are a Jewish family, I imagine I could have chosen the names Sadie or Bubbe, but those options were never offered to me. Later, my younger cousin began calling my grandfather "Poppy," and I was puzzled that we didn't use the same name.

This naming process used to be more organic. Names for grandparents were given based on what the family traditionally had used as their endearment of choice for grandparents. Names varied by region and ethnic heritage. Today, though, the options for what to call a grandparent seem endless. In her article "Mamaw Got Run Over by a Combine," Susie Shy Thompson studies naming practices in the South. She points out that grandchildren, by the very nature of their birth, create the role of a grandparent, and oftentimes the grandchildren themselves assign the name to the grandparent.[59] Other times, the grandparent chooses a name but then allows the child to reassign a nickname.[60] She argues that the naming process for grandparents illustrates their special relationship with children: they are seen as figures of power as matriarchs and patriarchs of the family, but they willingly share that power with their newest descendants. The idea that a grandparent has so many options for an endearing name is a newer cultural phenomenon. When grandparents were simply extended relatives, what to name them was not that important; they typically followed the traditional name passed on through their families. Now, what was once an organic process has become a more orchestrated and constructed one.

Celebrities have moved into the naming game, often inventing, with varying degrees of success, new ones. Since the terms "grandma" and "grandpa" are already associated with being old, many begin their journey toward grandparenting by rejecting or reinventing the name. Lionel Richie told an entertainment reporter about his misgivings about becoming a grandfather: "Let me tell you, grandpa scared me a little bit. When Nicole came to me and said: 'You're going to be a grandpa,' I thought that sounded quite . . . old."[61] He ended up taking the name Pop-Pop instead. Martha Stewart's daughter, Alexis, announced on her radio show that her mother would just be referred to by her first name. She said, "Martha is going to be called Martha."[62] Susan Sarandon asked to be called "Honey."[63] In her memoir *Goldie: A Lotus Grows in the Mud*, Goldie Hawn discusses her excitement in waiting for her grandchild but also her ambivalence about the name: "But was I really a 'grandmother'? A word that had so many connotations of old age and decrepitude. My son Oliver decided I should be called 'Glam-Ma,' which I thought was quite brilliant and made us all laugh so hard."[64] Hawn's "Glam-ma" has since made it into the *Urban Dictionary*, defined as "the new generation of grandmas, who are stylish in the way they live and dress. These women do not fit the typical cardigan-wearing, permed hair granny stereotype, they are glamorous."[65]

More and more grandparents are spending time finding their perfect grandparent name.[66] Almost as soon as the option for inventing new names for grandparents became popular, people began offering services to help others with the naming trend. Like the many books of baby names sold to parents-to-be, new books now offer advice on what name to choose as a grandparent. *The New Grandparent Name Book* promises many options for names, including "heritage names that celebrate ethnicity or families ties, as well as names that reflect personality traits or simply the desire to be called by a name that is as unique and special as the person who chose it."[67] One can also use the Grandparent Name Generator, sponsored by the American Grandparents Association, to find a unique grandparent endearment. When I tried out the digital tool, the name it gave me was "Soosa Lauramo."[68]

The shift in the naming process is connected to changes in our history, culture, and buying and consuming practices. As grandparenting becomes a more clearly defined phase of life, people search for a new name to go with it. Many associate the traditional grandparent names with old age; as people live longer, they don't want to be saddled with a moniker that designates them as an elderly person. Grandparents want to divorce from the generic names "Granny" and "Pops" that traditionally have been used to refer to any elderly person, whether they have grandchildren or not. Instead, they want to recognize their life stage that has associations beyond age. As families become larger due to second marriages, and as more grandparents live longer and become great-grandparents, more names are needed to distinguish between the multiple matriarchal and patriarchal family members.

It is hard to imagine a time when pregnancy was not filled with months of to-do lists and medical and consumer experiences in which women play only a partial role. In past periods, however, women alone had to determine if they were pregnant, then would gradually let others in on the secret. Today, the announcement of a pregnancy is filled with all manner of rituals, from custom birth notices to gender reveal parties to announce the sex of the baby. Announcing to one's parents that they are becoming grandparents, while always significant, has taken on a level of planning and public declaration like never before.

Many expectant parents plan special moments and later post the surprised reactions of their parents on YouTube or other social media. The couples I spoke with often shared stories about the moment they found out they were going to become grandparents. One grandmother was told, "Get Your Knit On." Another set of grandparents received "notes" from their grandchild-to-be. One note the couple shared with me read:

> Dear ?*
> There are so many things I want to do together like go for walks and picnics, sing songs and let you teach me about the world. I can't wait for you to read me books like this one before bed. I love you bunches!
> Love,
> Your Grandbaby
> *We will have to decide together what I will call you.

Another grandmother-to-be discovered boxes mailed to her. Inside was a little plastic egg. When she opened the egg, she found a little chick and a note that read, "My favorite grandparent" and "Coming soon—in November."

Some of these moments are so popular that they become viral hits or make the national news. One such example includes a soon-to-be grandfather who thought he was participating in a game night. As he played, the game revealed that he was going to become a grandparent. This surprise received over six million views on YouTube. In one announcement that "failed" but made *America's Funniest Home Videos*, a family tried to tell a woman she was about to become a great-grandma, but she kept thinking they were just paying her a compliment as to how "great" a grandmother she was.[69] ABC News featured a couple who decided to wait and surprise the grandmother-to-be just two days before giving birth. The grandmother, whose grandson was born in a scheduled Cesarean section on the grandmother's birthday, said it was the best surprise she ever had.[70] Today, parents can consult blogs that offer suggestions as to the best ways to tell their parents that they will become grandparents, including baking a cookie cake with "Grandparent-to-be" written on it.[71]

Waiting to become a grandparent is emerging as a new consumer experience. Grandma showers are becoming a ritual designed to usher grandparents into this life stage, and they receive presents they can use when grandchildren visit their home.[72] One can find "grandparent starter kits," which include bottles, diapers, and even photo frames filled with sonogram pictures. Sometimes, these events create conflicted feelings about whether they should be entitled to such a ritual. Some see it as "stealing the thunder" of the expectant mom.[73]

While grandparents often have kept to the background of family life, they are now moving to more prominent places within the family. One trend that shows this change is the grandparent photo shoot. Families are choosing to hire photographers for family portraits with grandparents in the center. One woman I spoke with, Regina, decided that when her mother, the children's only living grandparent, was turning eighty, she wanted to document the milestone: "We wanted something as a takeaway for our kids so 40 years from now they could say there's a picture of me and my nanny." At first, her mother reacted unfavorably to the idea, but she finally agreed to join the photo shoot. The photographer worked with her limitations, allowing her to sit down for many of the shots. It turned out that the photo shoot itself was an important experience for the family, with multiple generations gathered together. Photographers now advertise the grandparent photo shoot as a part of family packages, and a way to reunite families.

Families are now also finding special ways to include grandparents as participants in wedding ceremonies. Traditionally, siblings and close friends serve as bridesmaids and ushers, and parents engage in the practice of walking their child down the aisle, but beyond being escorted to their seat, there has not been a special ritual for the grandparent. As more grandparents live long enough to attend the weddings of their grandchildren, and as more grandchildren want to acknowledge their affection for their grandparents, they are beginning to ask their grandparents to serve as "flower grandparents." Two such instances received popular attention in *People* magazine: twenty-two-year-old Maggie Wakefield and her husband Josh asked their grandmothers to be flower "girls" at their wedding in recognition for all they meant to them. "She's like my second mother," Maggie said about her grandmother.[74] Likewise, twenty-nine-year-old Jennifer Briskin asked her grandfather to be a "flower grandpa" at her wedding. She said that the idea started off as a joke, but she realized it was a great way to include him in the ceremony.[75]

PRESERVING GRANDPARENTS' STORIES

People are inventing new ritualized practices to preserve more of their grandparents' experiences and memories. Though these memories often are assembled as a memorial, increasingly they are undertaken when the grandparent is still alive, and grandparents themselves participate in the process. Grandparents can buy brag books, keepsake books, and books designed to elicit their stories and memories. Books such as *Grandma Tell Me Your Story* or *Letters to My Grandchild: Write Now, Read Later, Treasure Forever* encourage grandparents to engage in storytelling, prompted by questions like, "Did you have a television?" or "What is a special meal you made for your parent?"

In addition to grandparents writing down their stories, grandchildren are preserving their memories, life stories, and rituals associated with their grandparents. One woman preserved her grandmother's stories by using her old notebooks to create a graphic novel about her life growing up in the Soviet Union.[76] Passing down a grandmother recipe has long been a tradition in families. Now, more formalized processes are sharing recipes beyond the family to a global network. Jessica Theroux created the website *Cooking with Grandmothers*, designed to share the "wisdom of female elders from around the world." A main goal of the website is to preserve the food of "everyday women who would otherwise not be documented." Children have the ability to "add their grandmother" to the website.[77] Similarly, a French filmmaker created an online collective where people can preserve their grandmothers' recipes.[78] The Jewish Food Society has set a goal of saving recipes of grandparents, seeing food as a type of "cultural DNA."[79] The preservation of the lives and stories of grandparents has moved beyond words, as in the case of the woman who turned her grandparents' World War II love letters into jewelry.[80]

Grandparent stories were once the key to the survival of a family's legacy, passed down from generation to generation in a tenuous fashion. Now, as their stories are less needed for utility purposes, they have become valued for emotional reasons. These books, online media, and jewelry are built around the preservation of affection, stories, and memories. New technologies have enhanced the ability to preserve, and this has helped to assure many families that their memories are archived safely in print and digital forms. However, the practice of preservation has become commodified. What was typically an informal practice of teaching grandchildren how to survive and their place in the world is now a more structured process, one which grandparents sometimes feel is a forced and unnecessary obligation as products are marketed to them in this effort. Ironically, now that the need for the practical wisdom of grandparents largely has been replaced with a more generalized cultural knowledge, their own stories become less required for survival, and their telling simply creates additional roles for the grandparents to fill. For many, it's a wonderful chance to pass on their legacy, but for others it's simply another task for them as part of the grandparenting stage of life. As the stories move to the online environment, they also move from the family's possession to a larger global collective. Yes, families can share their stories with the world, but once they become part of the digital economy, they move beyond the control of the family, becoming another market to target.

CHANGES IN SPACE

Grandparents as an everyday part of a family's household were once common before World War II, but in the postwar period, many Americans embraced the idea of the nuclear family and moved away from grandparents. During this period, retiring Americans moved into communities of older adults that promoted a leisure lifestyle, and warmer climates in states like Florida and Arizona attracted many retirees. Rather than focusing on grandparents sharing the living space of a nuclear family, architects are now designing homes that include communal spaces for grandparents and the rest of the family while preserving separate private spaces for both. These homes recognize the greater roles grandparents are playing as part of the extended family.

A trend toward "aging in place" reflects people who choose to stay in their homes or move to smaller homes—close to the home where they raised their children—rather than retire to places that cater to the elderly.[81] This shift is changing markets in real estate, and agents are taking into account the accommodation of grandparents. In New York City, some adult children are setting up homes for their parents so that they can be near their grandchildren. Instead of moving to warm retirement communities, they find themselves in cities, renting studio apartments down the street or even down the hall from their grandchildren.[82] Florida has incentivized these types of arrangements, offering a "Granny Flat Exemption," which allows property owners to pay less property tax when their home additions are designated as living spaces for grandparents.[83]

When grandparents choose to retire, they are not often rushing off to sunny locations distant from their children. Some older couples are choosing to downsize or modify their house to fit their needs. Many prefer to be closer to their grandchildren or future grandchildren. Grandparents are reconfiguring spaces to encourage their grandchildren to spend more time with them. Some who can afford it create elaborate playgrounds and basements filled with entertainment that appeals to teenagers.[84] Retirement communities that restrict younger residents have faced conflicts when residents become the unexpected primary caretakers of their grandchildren. However, some retirement communities now recognize that they need to adapt to evolving relationships between grandparents and their grandchildren.[85] They are building recreational areas and pools for use when grandchildren visit.[86] A typical retirement community, though, may need to do more than make small adaptions to their communal living spaces to attract new residents. More families are considering living arrangements that bring grandparents into the nuclear family.

Architectural firms are responding to the needs of these families and see an opportunity to move into a new sector of design.[87] Pardee Homes offers "GenSmart Suites," which they describe as "A home within your home." The suites can be used for temporary guests or permanent residents such as grandparents.[88] Architectural firms are responding to a growing demand for intergenerational housing by offering competing and creative options. For example, living spaces may be connected to a main house but have separate entrances, "ensuring both togetherness and autonomy."[89] *Metropolis*, an architectural magazine, challenged firms to offer competing designs of what future intergenerational homes could look like, and it published the results. One architectural group, Terreform One, made the cover of the magazine with a proposal for a feature home that was "comprised of fixed and mobile elements, as well as a variety of architectural types, to accommodate the changing desires and lifestyles of multiple generations living together." Designs like these account for various life changes, including times when family members head off to school or when there is a change of marital status. Portions of some houses can become mobile as needed. In the future, a house might move with the family, and a family can be redefined as needed.[90] A housing complex in Irvine, California, offers options for different types of multigenerational living, including two homes sharing a backyard.[91] Others are trying even more innovative arrangements. On its website, Pioneer Valley Cohousing declares, "We are multi-generational and continuously striving to maintain a robust waiting list that includes young families, retiring boomers, and the full spectrum of our diverse culture." Their spaces include children's rooms, meditation rooms, and a home-office building, as well as areas for crafts and woodworking.[92] Some extended families move in together to communities like these, while others seek a sense of community by living close to other families in arrangements like these.[93] Businesses also see the opportunities within these new family arrangements to create new products, such as applications that manage family budgets and meals that appeal to all generations of the family.[94]

It is important to acknowledge that the phenomenon of extended families living together in the United States is not at all new to some cultures, particularly immigrant families. For example, Latin and Asian cultures often have multiple generations living together. The traditions of these groups are moving now to larger segments of the US population. While some groups are experiencing this phenomenon for the first time, they often do not realize that this has always been a living arrangement for many other groups. Among many cultures, intergenerational living is tied to ritual, cultural immersion, and family loyalty. The new living arrangements and designs are created and targeted often to a white middle class just beginning to embrace this trend, rather than groups that have long embraced intergenerational living arrangements as an inherent family structure.

For some families, it's not choice but circumstance that pushes them into extended family arrangements. Sometimes grandparents are needed to provide financial support and homes for their children and grandchildren. Adapting to the trend of what's been labeled "grandfamilies," public housing planners are designing homes in consideration of the needs of extended families, including wider hallways for wheelchairs and playgrounds for children.[95] Guadalupe House, a community near Phoenix, was designed to offer affordable housing that could fit the needs of several generations of families living together.[96]

Intergenerational living is a concept with a long heritage, particularly among immigrant groups in the United States and many cultures outside of the country. Among lower socioeconomic groups, and in particular African American families, grandparents, often the matriarch, play an important role in ensuring the economic survival of the family. Now that the middle and upper classes are reclaiming the practice of intergenerational living, they are doing so without any of those ties. It has become a consumer choice for them, and families pick or leave components as they see fit. These arrangements have the potential to bring families closer together. Gunhild Hagestad and Peter Uhlenberg have noted the problems that age segregation can cause for older adults. They write, "Spatial segregation by age occurs when individuals of different ages do not occupy the same space and hence cannot engage in face-to-face interactions."[97] Multigenerational housing arrangements that value the closeness of families can prevent isolation among the elderly and enhance the lives of the entire family. However, families will need to consider the goals and purposes of these new living arrangements, which may be different from traditional intergenerational families that had clear survival and cultural purposes in mind. Oftentimes, when trends are appropriated from other cultures, they leave behind those who originated them.

THE NEW FAMILY VACATION

Visiting grandparents for the summer became a popular tradition as more families moved away and were not able to have regular contact with them. Now many grandparents are trading in these visits for more exciting travel experiences. Some rent houses for their grandchildren to stay at when they visit, while others plan extended family vacations. Industry reports cite multigenerational travel as a top travel trend in 2016.[98] A travel agent I interviewed, Cindi, works in a travel agency in New York, where she specializes in multigenerational travel. She finds that different families have varying desires for their trips. Some prefer a relaxing experience, often choosing an all-inclusive resort or a cruise. Others like to take a cultural approach, taking a trip to Italy, for example, to share their heritage. Cindi coordinates the travel, including scavenger hunts in the Vatican. She said, "When the grandparents book travel, they want to have an experience that their children and their grandchildren will be able to remember for the rest of their lives." Some grandparents have described to me wonderful camping trips with their grandchildren, often taking them to destinations their parents never could have afforded.

In addition to arranging trips for their entire families, some grandparents are part of a growing trend to travel with their grandchildren without their parents.[99] One grandfather I interviewed, Marty, describes taking his grandchildren someplace special on their tenth birthdays. Another, David, said that when each of his grandchildren was old enough, around fourteen or fifteen, he would offer them a trip to any place in the world. David and his wife have taken their grandchildren individually to London, Paris, Rome, and Chicago, and they currently are planning a trip to Japan. They have experienced the joy of ensuring that their grandchildren see a wider world, and they say they are lucky enough to provide their grandchildren with something their parents do not necessarily have the time or money to do. They also benefit from the trips, saying that when they travel with someone much younger than themselves, they "see it through their eyes."

Grandparents are being targeted for travel and discounts for travel with their grandchildren.[100] Candlewood Suites offers grandparents one night free when checking in to select hotels during holidays. The Generations Riviera Maya in Miami offers a "Grandparents Stay Free" promotion, in which guests can add a free suite for grandparents when they book accommodations.[101] Michigan State University offers Grandparent University, a summer camp where grandparents and their grandchildren can stay in campus dorms and enjoy exciting activities. Their website describes the camp as a "fun-filled experience that actively engages kids in Michigan State academics while creating lasting family memories."[102]

Clearly recognizing the potential of this new trend, Disney has created a section on its website marketing directly to grandparents. Disney promises "Grandparents + Grandkids = A Grand Adventure."[103] Grandparents can consult with other "grands" on the website to share advice or talk about their experiences. Disney has even produced a television commercial that features grandparents enjoying the company's destinations with their grandchildren.

Road Scholar has over 150 options for intergenerational travel among the trips it organizes. Included in their offerings is a grandparent/grandchild summer camp in the Adirondacks. While some trips involve visiting historic or traditional vacation destinations, such as Berlin or the Grand Canyon, others focus on a specific type of experience. For example, included in their options is a "CSI" camp where visitors can learn how to investigate crime scenes, or a camp at the International Wolf Center in Minnesota where campers can learn about local wildlife. They even have set up a dinosaur scavenger hunt for amateur paleontologists.[104] Another option for grandparents is grandparent/grandchild summer camp in Stratford Hall, Virginia, where grandparents can spend three days re-creating life on an eighteenth-century Virginia plantation.[105] At Grands Camp at Great Camp Sagamore, grandparents and their grandchildren can choose from options that involve as many activities as they wish.

For some grandparents, taking trips poses an opportunity to share their values and passions with their grandchildren. The Sierra Club organizes trips "Just for Grandparents and Grandkids." Linda, who has been leading Sierra Club trips for over twenty-five years, said that when she began having grandchildren, she began to help coordinate multigenerational trips. On the service trips that she sets up, the families work together on projects like painting, landscaping, and working to help the environment. Linda describes the motivation she believes may be in it for the participants: "Because of the service component, you get that giving back. It is a great opportunity for grandkids to instill that kind of mentality, dedication and commitment to giving back." It's not only good for the families but for the Sierra Club as well. Linda explains the importance of making sure young people become involved in order to secure "the longevity and the continuity of the organization." She remembers one trip when the grandparents were celebrating their fiftieth wedding anniversary. They brought all their children and grandchildren on the trip, ensuring the three generations participated in their activities.

Many grandparents want the values they possess to be passed down to their descendants. One study reports that "almost half (49%) of grandparents are currently or interested in passing down their value for volunteering."[106] The same study indicates that grandparents also value an understanding and appreciation of their heritage and ancestry, with 41 percent deeming it very important.[107] Organizing family trips becomes a way of passing on to their grandchildren an appreciation of the larger world, their family history, and the values they hold.

CONCLUSION

Grandparenting may once have been a simple stage of life one went through without much fanfare or notice. In the twenty-first century, grandparenting practices are shifting. Particularly in the middle class, grandparents are reinventing grandparenting as a life stage in new and unexpected ways. Companies and marketers are promoting the grandparent life stage by creating more experiences associated with grandparenting. New advertising campaigns are marketed to or feature grandparents, and grandparenting itself is emerging as a brand.

In many ways, these products, brands, and activities can contribute to new feelings of value among the elderly. Potentially useful services, such as organized travel that makes accommodations for grandparents, can help them share experiences with their grandchildren. However, as these services become something to purchase and desire, not everyone may want to, or even can, participate in them. Often, these consumer experiences are targeted to an idealized white, middle-class grandparent who has the luxury to afford these purchases. Roma Stovall Hanks, who researches how businesses market to grandparents, warns that little can be done to prevent companies from distorting the grandparent experience as they market to them. However, she indicates the importance of making certain that "grandparents can accurately describe their experiences and articulate their needs. The construction of extraneous realities about grandparenting can be prevented if both business and academe remain committed to understanding grandparents' lived experiences."[108] Even when they are well intentioned, when marketers and businesses define the grandparent experience, their visibility in the marketplace lends power more to the marketers than to grandparents themselves. Becoming a consumer group gives grandparents new attention. Yet, this identity comes at a cost in that the marketers ultimately desire to reach only those who can buy their products and services. Focusing on only the grandparents who can participate in these consumer transactions closes off access to those who cannot or have other needs. Those who do not have the money to buy into this experience remain invisible to the marketers, and ultimately, to the public.

NOTES

1. Fred Brock, "Seniority: Catering to the Elderly Can Pay Off," *New York Times*, February 2, 2002, http://www.nytimes.com/2002/02/03/business/seniority-catering-to-the-elderly-can-pay-off.html.

2. Dionne Searcey and Robert Gebeloff, "America's Seniors Find Middle-Class 'Sweet Spot,'" *New York Times*, June 14, 2015, http://www.nytimes.com/2015/06/15/business/economy/american-seniors-enjoy-the-middle-class-life.html.

3. "Grandparents Spend $27.5 Billion per Year on Grandkids," *Grandboomers.com* (web page), accessed October 13, 2016, http://www.grandboomers.com/page/grandparents-spend-275-billion.

4. Kelli B. Grant, "Ka-ching! Here's What It Costs to Be a Grandparent," *CNBC* (web page), January 13, 2017, http://www.cnbc.com/2017/01/12/ka-ching-heres-what-it-costs-to-be-a-grandparent.html.

5. Dennis H. Tootelian and Sanjay B. Varshney, "The Grandparent Consumer: A Financial 'Goldmine' with Gray Hair?" *Journal of Consumer Marketing* 27, no. 1 (January 2010): 62.

6. Tootelian and Varshney, 63.

7. Lori K. Bitter, *The Grandparent Economy: How Baby Boomers Are Bridging the Generation Gap* (Ithaca, NY: Paramount Market Publishing, 2015), 4.

8. Pamela Paul, "Make Room for Granddaddy," *AdAge*, April 1, 2002, 42–43, http://adage.com/article/american-demographics/make-room-granddaddy/43877/.

9. Derek Dunham, "Why You Should Be Targeting Grandparents This Holiday Season," *Media Post* (web page), November 25, 2013, http://www.mediapost.com/publications/article/214147/why-you-should-be-targeting-grandparents-this-holi.html.

10. Lori Bitter, "The Psychology of Marketing to Grandparents," *Media Post* (web page), December 21, 2015, http://www.mediapost.com/publications/article/265183/the-psychology-of-marketing-to-grandparents.html.

11. Beth Snyder, "Margeotes Wins Effort for Grandparents' Site," *AdAge* (web page), February 7, 2000, http://adage.com/article/news/margeotes-wins-effort-grandparents-site/59500/.

12. *Grand* (March/April 2017), http://www.grandmagazine.com/.

13. Laura Stampler, "How a Company Targeting Grandparents Became the Most Popular Thing on Facebook You've Never Heard Of," *Business Insider* (web page), December 6, 2012, http://www.businessinsider.com/grandparentscom-is-the-most-popular-facebook-page-that-youve-never-heard-of-2012-12.

14. Christy Fisher, "Grandparents Give of Themselves," *American Demographics* 18, no. 6 (June 1996).

15. Nancy Ann Jeffrey and Sarah Collins, "Family: The Grandparent Industry," *Wall Street Journal*, November 2, 2001.

16. CoCo Key Water Park Boston North Shore (web page), accessed February 19, 2018, http://www.cocokeyboston.com/day-passes/.

17. Kylie, "How to Get a Great Deal at Carter's," *The How to Mom* (web page), August 26, 2013, https://www.thehowtomom.com/2013/08/how-to-get-great-deal-at-carters.html.

18. "Farm Tables for Grandparents Saying 'No' to Downsizing," *Furniture from the Barn* (web page), accessed February 20, 2018, https://furniturefromthebarn.com/farm-tables-for-grandparents-saying-no-to-downsizing/.

19. AnnaMaria Andriotis, "When Grandparents and 529 Plans for College Savings Clash," *Wall Street Journal*, August 22, 2014, https://www.wsj.com/articles/when-grandparents-and-529-plans-for-college-savings-clash-1408747176.

20. Jennifer Levitz, "The New Gift-Givers: Grandparents," *Wall Street Journal*, November 19, 2013, https://www.wsj.com/articles/no-headline-available-1384104115?tesla=y.

21. Neil Howe, "Brands Now Market to the Extended Family," *Forbes*, May 17, 2016, https://www.forbes.com/sites/neilhowe/2016/05/17/brands-now-market-to-the-extended-family/#7c57dbc6c4df.

22. Cheryl L. Lampkin, "Insights and Spending Habits of Modern Grandparents" (Washington, DC: AARP Research, March 2012): 11, http://www.aarp.org/content/dam/aarp/research/surveys_statistics/general/2012/Insights-and-Spending-Habits-of-Modern-Grandparents-AARP.pdf.

23. Beth Snyder Bulik, "Boom in Multigenerational Households Has Wide Implications for Ad Industry," *Ad Age*, August 23, 2010, http://adage.com/article/news/multigenerational-households-implications-marketers/145506/.

24. Jinny Gudmundsen, "Best Apps for Connecting with Distant Relatives," *USA Today*, January 19, 2014, https://www.usatoday.com/story/tech/columnist/gudmundsen/2014/01/19/apps-relatives-ustyme-kindoma-storytime/4475253/.

25. "2017 Essential Facts about the Computer and Video Game Industry" (Washington, DC: Entertainment Software Association), accessed February 24, 2018, http://www.theesa.com/article/2017-essential-facts-computer-video-game-industry/.

26. G. Oscar Anderson, "Video Games: Attitudes and Habits of Adults Age 50-plus" (Washington, DC: AARP Research, June 2016), https://www.aarp.org/research/topics/technology/info-2016/electronic-gaming-research-adults-50plus.html.

27. Brian Stelter, "For Xbox, Focus Shifts from Game to Video," *New York Times*, January 19, 2010, http://www.nytimes.com/2010/01/19/business/media/19xbox.html.

28. Bulik, "Boom in Multigenerational Households."

29. Kelly Servick, "Videogame May Help Rejuvenate Elderly Brains," *Wired*, September 5, 2013, https://www.wired.com/2013/09/video-game-elderly/.

30. Joseph Knoop, "Games for Grandparents," *Polygon* (web page), July 21, 2016, https://www.polygon.com/features/2016/7/21/12239568/games-for-grandparents.

31. Simone Hausknecht, Carman Neustaedter, and David Kaufman, "Blurring the Lines of Age: Intergenerational Collaboration in Alternate Reality Games," *Game-Based Learning across the Lifespan: Cross-Generational and Age-Oriented Topics*, ed. Margarida Romero et al. (Switzerland: Springer, 2017), 49.

32. Mike Monticello, "Best Cars for Families with Grandparents," *Consumer Reports*, September 28, 2016, https://www.consumerreports.org/cars-best-cars-for-families-with-grandparents/.

33. Susan Adcox, "Eye of My Heart: 27 Writers Dish about Being a Grandmother," *The Spruce* (web page), accessed October 24, 2015, https://www.thespruce.com/eye-of-my-heart-being-grandmother-1695580.

34. Sloane Tanen, "16 Great Books about Grandparents," *Grandparents.com* (web page), accessed September 4, 2017, http://www.grandparents.com/grandkids/toys-books-and-entertainment/best-childrens-books-about-grandparents.

35. Pauline Davey Zeece, "Grandparents and Grand Books," *Early Childhood Education Journal* 35, no. 2 (October 2007): 128.

36. Richard A. Settersten and Gunhild O. Hagestad, "Subjective Aging and New Complexities of the Life Course," *Annual Review of Gerontology and Geriatrics* 35, no. 1 (February 2015): 44, https://doi.org/10.1891/0198-8794.35.29.

37. Sheila Johnson, "The Golden Age of Marketing: Our Favorite Ads for Grandparents," *Branding Beat* (blog), accessed February 23, 2018, https://www.qualitylogoproducts.com/blog/ads-for-grandparents/.

38. Dianna Pearl, "12 Holiday Commercials That Will Make You Feel All the Feels," *People.com* (web page), December 7, 2016, http://people.com/tv/best-holiday-commercials-2016/-/.

39. Tim Nudd, "Heathrow Airport's Christmas Ad with Two Old Teddy Bears Makes Britain Feel Happy Again," *Adweek*, November 17, 2016, http://www.adweek.com/creativity/heathrow-airports-christmas-ad-two-old-teddy-bears-makes-britain-feel-happy-again-174681/.

40. "United Healthcare—Medicare Advantage Plan—Grand Kids Come to Visit Grandparents for Weekend—We Can Make It a Little Less Painful—Full Version," *TV Commercial Spots*, accessed March 22, 2017, http://www.tvcommercialspots.com/insurance-and-services/united-healthcare-medicare-advantage-plan-grand-kids-come-to-visit-grandparents-we-can-make-it-a-little-less-painful-full-version-unitedhealthcare-healthcare-united-medicare/.

41. E. J. Schultz, "Meet the Grandma behind VW's New Family-Oriented Marketing for Bigger Vehicles," *AdAge*, May 1, 2017, http://adage.com/article/cmo-strategy/meet-grandma-vw-s-family-oriented-marketing-bigger-atlas/308871/.

42. Gretchen Livingston, "At Grandmother's House We Stay" (Washington, DC: Pew Research Studies, September 4, 2013), http://www.pewsocialtrends.org/2013/09/04/at-grandmothers-house-we-stay/.

43. Jack Neff, "See the Spot: Angel Soft Tearjerker Takes Family Focus to Grandparents in New Ad," *AdAge*, November 16, 2016, http://adage.com/article/see-the-spot/angel-soft-takes-family-focus-grandparents/301356/.

44. This is in part due to factors such as the opiate epidemic in the United States, military deployment, and incarceration. Alejandra Cancino, "More Grandparents Raising Their Grandchildren," *PBS News Hour* (web page), February 16, 2016, http://www.pbs.org/newshour/rundown/more-grandparents-raising-their-grandchildren/.

45. Shyon Baumann and Kim de Laat, "Aspiration and Compromise: Portrayals of Older Adults in Television Advertising," in *Aging, Media and Culture*, ed. C. Lee Harrington, Denise Bielby, and Anthony R. Bardo (Lanham, MD: Lexington Books, 2014), 22.

46. Lisa Wade, "Liu Xianping, Fashionable Grandpa, Models for Teen Clothing Line," *Huffington Post* (blog), December 6, 2012, http://www.huffingtonpost.com/lisa-wade/liu-xianping-model-teen-clothing-line_b_2247586.html.

47. Rachael Allen, "Reebok's New Ad Campaign Features 'China's Hottest Grandpa,'" *FN* (web page), March 30, 2017, http://footwearnews.com/2017/focus/athletic-outdoor/reebok-be-more-human-chinas-hottest-grandpa-331775/.

48. Patrick Coffee, "Anyone Can Be Your Grandma in These Funny, Awkward Ads for Grandma's Cookies," *Adweek* (web page), May 3, 2016, http://www.adweek.com/creativity/anyone-can-be-your-grandma-these-funny-awkward-ads-grandmas-cookies-171189/.

49. Enoteca Maria (web page), accessed October 19, 2017, http://www.enotecamaria.com/wp/our-story/.

50. Arielle Dollinger, "At This Staten Island Restaurant, a Kitchen Run by Grandmas," *New York Times*, March 2, 2017, https://www.nytimes.com/2017/03/02/nyregion/at-this-staten-island-restaurant-a-kitchen-run-by-grandmas.html?_r=0.

51. Katherine Martinko, "Meet WOOLN, the Fashion Company That Hires Grandmas to Do Its Knitting," *Treehugger.com* (web page), November 25, 2016, http://www.treehugger.com/sustainable-fashion/meet-wooln-fashion-company-hires-grandmas-do-its-knitting.html.

52. WOOLN (web page), accessed March 31, 2017, http://www.wooln-ny.com/about-2/.

53. Elaine Durbach, "Meet the 90-Year-Old Great-Grandmother Who Is the New Face of JDate," *The Times of Israel* (web page), February 1, 2018, https://www.timesofisrael.com/meet-the-90-year-old-great-grandmother-who-is-the-new-face-of-jdate/.

54. "Jdate and Hogarth Worldwide Launch Funny New Campaign You Can Kvetch About," *The San Francisco Egotist* (blog), January 11, 2018, http://www.thesfegotist.com/news/local/2018/january/11/jdate-and-hogarth-worldwide-launch-funny-new-campaign-you-can-kvetch-about.

55. Jerry Useem, "How Online Shopping Makes Suckers of Us All," *The Atlantic*, May 2017, https://www.theatlantic.com/magazine/archive/2017/05/how-online-shopping-makes-suckers-of-us-all/521448/.

56. Alyssa Ralston, "Rent-a-Grandma Update 2017—See What Happened after Shark Tank," *Gazette Review* (blog), January 25, 2016, http://gazettereview.com/2016/01/rent-grandma-update-see-happened-shark-tank/.

57. Alexandra Jardine, "Mother London Is Rebranding as 'Grandmother' for Christmas," *AdAge* (web page), December 2, 2016, http://creativity-online.com/work/mother-london-grandmother/50159.

58. Simon Gwynn, "Mother Rebrands to Start Discussion about Old Age," *Campaign* (web page), December 1, 2016, http://www.campaignlive.co.uk/article/mother-rebrands-start-discussion-old-age/1417144.

59. Susie Shy Thompson, "Mamaw Got Run Over by a Combine: Grandparent Naming Practices in the Rural South," *International Association for Intercultural Communication Studies* 10, no. 1 (2000): 185.

60. Thompson, "Mamaw Got Run Over," 186.

61. "Lionel Richie Loves It as a Pop-Pop Star," *Express.co.uk* (web page), May 28, 2013, http://www.express.co.uk/celebrity-news/403003/Lionel-Richie-loves-it-as-a-Pop-Pop-star.

62. Lesley Messer, "Martha Stewart Is a Grandma!" *People.com*, March 11, 2011, http://people.com/babies/martha-stewart-is-a-grandma/.

63. Megan Holohan, "Goodbye Grandma, Hello Honey: Modern Grandparents Embrace Creative Names," *Today.com*, September 3, 2014, http://www.today.com/parents/goodbye-granny-hello-honey-modern-grandparents-embrace-creative-names-t75476.

64. Goldie Hawn, with Wendy Holden, *A Lotus Grows in the Mud* (New York: G. P. Putnam's Sons, 2005), 445.

65. "Glam ma," *Urban Dictionary*, (web page), accessed December 12, 2017, http://www.urbandictionary.com/define.php?term=glam%20ma&utm_source=search-action

66. Clare Ansberry, "Grandfather's Dilemma: Am I a PopPop or a Skipper?" *Wall Street Journal*, May 24, 2016, https://www.wsj.com/articles/grandfathers-dilemma-am-i-a-poppop-or-a-skipper-1464119401.

67. Lin Wellford, *The New Grandparents Name Book* (Green Forest, AZ: ArtStone Press, 2009).

68. "Find Out Your Ultimate Grandparent Name," *Grandparents.com* (web page), accessed October 20, 2017, http://www.grandparents.com/grandparents-name-generator/.

69. "Grandma Puzzled by Grandkids' 'Great' Pregnancy Surprise," *ABC News* (web page), March 3, 2016, http://abcnews.go.com/Lifestyle/great-grandma-puzzled-grandkids-pregnancy-announcement/story?id=37368270.

70. Nicole Pelletiere, "Couple Keeps Pregnancy a Secret for 9 Months, Surprises Grandma," *ABC News* (web page), February 23, 2017, http://abcnews.go.com/Lifestyle/couple-pregnancy-secret-months-surprises-grandma/story?id=45684015.

71. "Grandparents Day Gifts: 17 Pregnancy Reveal Ideas to Surprise New Grandparents," *Kasasa blog*, August 28, 2014, https://blog.kasasa.com/2014/08/grandparents-day-gifts-17-pregnancy-reveal-ideas-surprise-grandparents/.

72. A. Pawlowski, "A Baby Shower of Their Very Own: Grandma Showers Take Off," *Today.com* (web page), May 27, 2014, http://www.today.com/parents/grandma-baby-showers-celebrate-fun-stage-life-2D79695466.

73. Yagana Shah, "Trendy Baby Showers for Grandmas: Sweet or Selfish," *Huffington Post* (blog), January 31, 2014, http://www.huffingtonpost.com/2014/01/31/grandma-baby-showers-_n_4681552.html.

74. "Bride and Groom Invite Their Grandmas to Be Flower Girls," *People.com* (web page), July 19, 2016, http://people.com/celebrity/bride-and-groom-invite-their-grandmas-to-be-flower-girls/.

75. "85-Year-Old 'Flower Grandpa' at Georgia Wedding Is the Best Thing You'll See All Day," *People.com* (web page), November 3, 2016, http://people.com/human-interest/85-year-old-flower-grandpa-at-georgia-wedding-is-the-best-thing-youll-see-all-day/.

76. "'Soviet Daughter': How a Great-Grandmother's Diary Became a Graphic Novel," *NPR.com* (web page), January 22, 2017, http://www.npr.org/2017/01/22/509158334/soviet-daughter-how-a-great-grandmothers-diary-became-a-graphic-novel.

77. Jessica Theroux, *Cooking with Grandmothers* (blog), accessed July 14, 2017, http://www.cookingwithgrandmothers.com/about/jessica-theroux/.

78. Bridget De Maine, "A French Filmmaker Has Created the Perfect Place to Preserve Your Grandmother's Recipes," *Collective Hub* (blog), June 30, 2016, http://collectivehub.com/2016/06/a-french-filmmaker-has-created-the-perfect-place-to-preserve-your-grandmothers-recipes/.

79. Larissa Zimberoff, "The Jewish Food Society Wants to Save the Recipes of Grandmas Everywhere," *NPR.org* (web page), April 3, 2017, http://www.npr.org/sections/thesalt/2017/04/03/520973202/the-jewish-food-society-wants-to-save-the-recipes-of-grandmas-everywhere.

80. Erin Hill, "Woman Turns Her Grandparents' WWII Love Letters into Jewelry Author Interviews," *People.com* (web page), http://people.com/human-interest/woman-turns-grandparents-wwii-love-letters-into-jewelry/.

81. Robert Strauss, "Careers Over, a Growing Number Are Retiring in Place," *New York Times*, May 14, 2013, http://www.nytimes.com/2013/05/15/business/retirementspecial/careers-over-a-growing-number-are-retiring-in-place.html.

82. Ronnie Koenig, "Accidental New Yorkers: Grandparents Relocate," *New York Times*, October 2, 2015, https://www.nytimes.com/2015/10/04/realestate/accidental-new-yorkers-grandparents-relocate.html.

83. Pedro J. Garcia, "Granny Flat Assessment Reduction—Miami-Dade County," *Miami-Dade Property Appraiser* (web page), accessed February 18, 2018, http://www.miamidade.gov/pa/exemptions_granny_flat.asp.

84. Alina Dizik, "For Kids, the Ultimate Play Room…at Grandma's House, *Wall Street Journal*, March 20, 2013, https://www.wsj.com/articles/SB10001424127887324532004578358262626005682.

85. Moira McGarvey, "The Very Best Places to Retire If You Want Your Grandkids to Visit," *Huffington Post*, May 15, 2014, http://www.huffingtonpost.com/moira-mcgarvey-/retirement-with-grandkids-_b_5274764.html.

86. Christina Valhouli, "If You Retire Rich, This Is Where You'll Want to Live," *Fortune Magazine*, April 10, 2015, http://fortune.com/2015/04/10/luxury-retirement-homes/.

87. Kavita Daswani, "Multigenerational Homes for Modern Families," *Los Angeles Times*, June 3, 2016, http://www.latimes.com/business/realestate/hot-property/la-fi-hp-multigenerational-homes-20160604-snap-story.html.

88. "New Homes for Sale with Private Guest Suites," *Pardee Homes* (blog), December 17, 2013, https://www.pardeehomes.com/trends-and-design/gensmart-suites-make-ah-mazing-guest-rooms/.

89. Amy Albert, "Case Study: Three Inspired Houses Respond to Surge in Multigenerational Households," *Builder*, September 12, 2012, http://www.builderonline.com/design/three-inspired-houses-respond-to-surge-in-multigenerational-households_o.

90. Christian Hubert and Mitchell Joachim, "Terreform One Proposes 'Walking City' of Housing for American Families," *Metropolis*, June 25, 2014, http://www.metropolismag.com/architecture/residential-architecture/futurists-propose-walking-city-of-configurable-housing-units/.

91. Jonathan Lansner, "Will Multigenerational Homes Sell in Irvine?" *The Orange County Register*, March 7, 2012, http://www.ocregister.com/2012/05/07/will-multigenerational-homes-sell-in-irvine/.

92. Pioneer Valley Cohousing (web page), accessed February 20, 2018, https://www.cohousing.com/welcome.

93. Tom Verde, "There's Community and Consensus. But It's No Commune," *New York Times*, January 20, 2018, https://www.nytimes.com/2018/01/20/business/cohousing-communities.html.

94. Bulik, "Boom in Multigenerational Households."

95. Steve Inskeep and Jennifer Ludden, "When Grandma's House Is Home: The Rise of Grandfamilies," *NPR.org*, Heard on Morning Edition (web page), December 15, 2014, http://www.npr.org/2014/12/15/369366596/when-grandmas-house-is-home-the-rise-of-grandfamilies.

96. Albert, "Case Study: Three Inspired Houses Respond."

97. Gunhild O. Hagestad and Peter Uhlenberg, "The Social Separation of Old and Young: A Root of Ageism," *Journal of Social Issues* 61, no. 2 (June 2005): 347.

98. "2016 Virtuoso® Luxe Report Shares Five Must-Have Travel Experiences in the Coming Year," *PR Newswire* (web page), November 5, 2015, https://www.prnewswire.com/news-releases/2016-virtuoso-luxe-report-shares-five-must-have-travel-experiences-in-the-coming-year-300173644.html.

99. Alina Dizik, "Grand Tours with Grandparents Are the Growth Area in Travel," *Wall Street Journal*, October 2, 2013, https://www.wsj.com/articles/grand-tours-with-grandparents-are-the-growth-area-in-travel-1380668691.

100. Kitty Bean Yancey, "Grandkids Mean a Great Deal—As in Discounts," *USA Today*, September 19, 2003, LexisNexis, 1D.

101. "Grandparents Stay Free at Generations Riviera Maya by Karisma," *Travelweek* (web page), January 19, 2017, http://www.travelweek.ca/news/grandparents-stay-free-generations-riviera-maya-karisma/.

102. "Grandparents University," *MSU Alumni Association* (web page), accessed February 20, 2018, https://alumni.msu.edu/learn/on-campus/grandparents-university/index.cfm.

103. "Grandparents + Grandkids = A Grand Adventure," *Walt Disney World Resort* (web page), accessed November 5, 2017, https://disneyworld.disney.go.com/grandparents-grandkids/.

104. "Scavenger Hunt," *Road Scholar* (web page), accessed April 15, 2017, https://www.roadscholar.org/find-an-adventure ?query=grandparents&page=1&pagesize=12.

105. "Grandparent Grandchild Summer Camp," *Stratford Hall* (web page), accessed April 16, 2017, http://www.stratfordhall.org/events/grandparent-grandchild-summer-camp-2/.

106. "Grandparents Investing in Grandchildren: The MetLife Study on How Grandparents Share Their Time, Values, and Money" (New York: MetLife Mature Market Institute and Generations United, September 2012), 19, https://www.metlife.com/assets/cao/mmi/publications/studies/2012/studies/MMIGrandparentsStudy_Web.pdf.

107. *Grandparents Investing*, 20.

108. Roma Stovall Hanks, " 'Grandma, What Big Teeth You Have!': The Social Construction of Grandparenting in American Business and Academe," *Journal of Family Issues* 22, no. 5 (July 2001): 670, https://doi.org/10.1177/019251301022005007.

Conclusion

The Grandparent Paradox

THE GRANDPARENT LIFESTYLE

One day, I walked into my kitchen to find my son and my father both looking puzzled over a *New Yorker* magazine. The cover of the magazine featured a cartoon of Kanye West with the caption "Trump Defeats Kanye," alluding to the "Dewey Defeats Truman" newspaper headline in 1948. My son asked my father, "Who is Dewey?" My father laughed and replied, "I can tell you that, but who is Kanye?"

Their grandparent-grandchild relationship, at that moment and throughout their lifetime, mirrors the cyclical shifting of grandparenting in our culture today. When puzzling out the cartoon they were on equal footing, each with knowledge from their own world that would help them together find the meaning. As in past periods, they have a symbiotic relationship; they depend on each other's skill sets to move through the world. My father and mother, like many grandparents today, are active participants in childcare, not just shuttling my children to and from activities, but also taking an interest in the everyday details of their lives. At the same time, my children involve their grandparents in fun activities and assist them in chores, like carrying their laundry and showing them how to download pictures (usually of their many other grandchildren) off their phones. But, more than building a symbiotic relationship, they have developed an affection and companionship through this experience.

My parents, like many grandparents, treat their grandparenting experience as part of a new life stage, filled with novel rituals to participate in with their grandchildren. They spend money on their grandchildren, live close enough to my children to experience a second stage of parenting, and bridge the distance with their grandchildren who live further away through regular texts and video chats. Surely, this is an improvement over previous periods, when the elderly were less visible or valued only for what they could offer their family in terms of inheritance or financial assistance. A realignment that promotes warm relationships between grandparents and their grandchildren is helpful for families. The benefits of these relationships are reciprocal, as grandparents have much to offer by sharing their practical knowledge and world view. Many studies in this book have documented the benefits of having a grandparent and being a grandparent. For many, grandparenting has become more enjoyable and perhaps even more meaningful. However, as a new grandparenting lifestyle develops, it becomes an opportunity for businesses to move in and market products and brands around it. This consumerization of the grandparent lifestyle leaves out people who are not able to participate due to economic status, family conflict, or other reasons. Others simply do not want to engage in a second stage of parenting through grandparenting. By extending opportunities to celebrate this life stage, grandparenting can deliver power and attention to a group previously overlooked, but it can also transform into an ideal that may be out of reach for many.

THE GRANDPARENTING STAGE

As people live longer, grandparenting becomes a complex life phase. What was once a homogenized group is now separated into several distinct stages, as younger grandparents continue to have active lifestyles. Grandparents now join worlds they were previously excluded from, like a grandfather recruited to play for a college golf team,[1] or grandmas and grandpas playing Dungeons & Dragons.[2] Recent studies indicate that playing video games can help improve memory for the elderly.[3] In all these cases, grandparents are becoming more visible. Even Pope Francis talks about grandparents regularly; he recently offered a special prayer for them, highlighting their significance. Pope Francis warned, "A people that does not take care of grandparents, that does not treat them well, has no future. . . . The elderly have wisdom."[4]

There are additional signs that younger generations, such as Millennials, are strengthening ties with their grandparents. They share similar hobbies, values, and increasingly lavish attention on each other. Their relationships are reified as significant when shared repeatedly on social media and admired by news media. For example, one woman received national attention for gifting her grandparents a house so they could live their later years in a modern home after spending their lifetimes without running water or electricity.[5] Generation X soon will be the next set of grandparents. They are less likely than Boomers to see themselves as "old" at a young age. One study indicates that many Gen Xers will not think of themselves as "old" until they are approximately sixty-three years old.[6] The way they grandparent in part will be determined by the expectations set up by the Baby Boomers, many of whom already are actively defying the stereotypes associated with aging. A public relations company even partnered with the video game company Nintendo to create the "Ageless Awards." The event recognized "the unique achievements of Americans who push the traditional boundaries of age and performance" while promoting Nintendo's products that claim to enhance the brain.[7] Scholar Deborah Jermyn writes about the "girling" of older women as "symptomatic of postfeminist culture and indicative of a move to push back the boundaries of ageing."[8] On the one hand, engaging in more youthful activities may allow grandparents to feel more active, but it also reinforces the idea that aging itself is bad and something to resist.

CONSUMING GRANDPARENTS

Businesses and marketers have moved in to both serve and profit off of this new group of grandparents. The travel industry offers specialized vacations for grandparents to embark on with their grandchildren. Amusement parks and museums discount products and experiences for grandparents and grandchildren to enjoy together. For many grandparents, these consumer options present a chance to engage in fun. My own mother loves to take my children to days at children's museums when grandparents get in for free. Grandparent price discounts on baby products assist some grandparents in setting up mini-nurseries in their own homes to help care for their grandchildren.

The consumer experience makes grandparenting itself a brand. In addition to products and activities marketed to grandparents, the image of the grandparent lifestyle becomes a commodity. Whether it is offering grandmothers as babysitters or building a grandma-themed restaurant, using grandparents to sell an ideal of grandparenting is becoming more popular. Sometimes those involved in these enterprises are not even grandparents but simply elderly people, who are used for attributes of nurturing, wisdom, or nostalgia that are usually associated with aging adults. The increasing diversity of popular media images of grandparents contributes to changing the way that grandparents are seen. More people may recognize grandparents as worthwhile, contributing members of society, which impacts how they may value their own grandparents and other elderly people. However, this consumer world is out of reach for many. Madonna Harrington Meyer and Yooumi Lee point out that the type of grandparenting people can do depends upon their access to resources: "It may be more difficult to provide support to younger generations for grandparents who have less income, less education, and worse health."[9] Thus, the consumer market brings forth an idealized standard of grandparenting that generates new pressures on consumers who internalize these representations.

THE GRANDPARENTING SHIFT

Scholars have deconstructed the mommy myth and the concept of new momism. Susan Douglas and Meredith Michaels define "new momism" as "a set of ideals, norms, and practices, most frequently and powerfully represented in the media, that seem on the surface to celebrate motherhood, but which in reality promulgate standards of perfection that are beyond your reach."[10] Today, the mommy myth has become even more extreme, as the expectations of parenting have intensified and last over a longer duration. The extreme focus on caregiving for children has extended to fathers, and now to grandparents as well.

The expectations of what grandparents can contribute are changing. As I wrote this book, I spoke to grandparents who felt guilt or even fear in saying no to their children's requests for them to babysit. Others were sad when they were prevented from having their desired grandparent experience. One woman described to me how she misses her granddaughter, who lives far away. She envies her son's in-laws, who are able to spend more time with her grandchild, but she also recognizes the futility of her longing. "It should be my opportunity," she said, "but you can't do that. They got to babysit her recently. I can't do that. These are the things I would love to do. I wouldn't say resentment, just envious. They are so lucky they get to see her on a holiday."

The CDC reports, "Birth rates also declined for women in their 20s to record lows in 2013. Rates rose for women in their 30s and late 40s."[11] As people in the United States delay childbirth, parents of adult children may have to wait longer for the grandparent experience, if they have it at all. In response, some parents are pressuring their children to give them grandchildren, even helping them pay for reproductive measures.[12] When they do become grandparents, they feel pressure to condense many of their activities into a shorter time period to catch up. Some parents feel guilty for not giving their parents grandchildren; they write to advice columns with questions like "Are we being cruel not to give our parents grandchildren?" and "How do your parents handle being told they won't have grandchildren?"[13]

While many people are not able to have the grandparent experience, others are finding themselves more intensely involved than they had hoped. Many grandparents are helping out with childcare for their grandchildren. Studies indicate that some women are retiring less out of a full desire to do so than out of an obligation to help care for their children's children. One study reports that grandmothers choose to reduce their work hours rather than completely retire if they can. Some may need to continue working for economic reasons, but others simply prefer to remain, at least partially, in the workforce.[14] As women gain more equality in the workplace, careers may be appealing for women in their 60s and 70s because they present the first opportunity to find workplace satisfaction.[15] However, grandmothers sometimes have to push aside their own desires to help their children with childcare. In her research on working grandmothers, Madonna Harrington Meyer argues, "Grandmothering is intensifying in part because of the increase in single parenting, economic insecurity and the absences of federal policies that guarantee paid time off for sickness, childbirth, and vacation, or readily affordable child-care options."[16] They do so to help the survival and welfare of the family, despite the fact that this might disrupt their economic security.[17]

Grandparents may be experiencing a new "having-it-all" problem that many women in the workforce have long encountered. This "grandparent shift" presents the same problems that the "second shift" had for women. Grandparents sometimes are forced to choose between their work and caring for their grandchildren. For instance, a grandmother in Florida faced a difficult decision when her daughter, about to give birth, needed her to provide emergency caregiving for the family's young child in Colorado. She chose to travel to Colorado to help her daughter's family, but she was fired from her job.[18] According to the National Association of Child Care Resource and Referral Agencies, in the United States, "about 40 percent of grandparents, who have grandchildren under age 13 and live within an hour from them, are currently providing child care for their grandchildren while parents are at work or school. Another 19 percent have done so in the past. In total, nearly 60 percent of grandparents are either providing child care for their grandchildren or have in the past."[19] Little attention is given to grandparents providing this care.

Recently, some have raised the idea of establishing a more formal acknowledgment of grandparent care, such as grandparent pay.[20] Grandmothers are so embedded within the system of childcare in the United States that, if the nation were to fund paid parental leave, policy makers should consider the fact that many elderly women who are dropping out of the workforce to care for young children might instead choose to remain working longer.[21] Studies assessing job rates and economic growth dispute the popular narrative that aging Baby Boomers are not getting out of the way fast enough for younger workers.[22] However, if structural changes are made to childcare resources, it is possible that more elderly employees may choose to stay working, providing fodder for the fearful rhetoric over the competition for jobs.

It is important to acknowledge that some grandparents resist caregiving not because of a work conflict, but because they feel they have already served their time parenting and do not want to take on the additional "grandparent shift" of childcare. Like adults in the child-free movement, some grandparents may want to have minimal involvement in the lives of their grandchildren. These voices are heard less often, but they exist, like the personal stories of women who simply never desired to be a mother or a grandmother.[23] Recently, the *New York Times* published an article titled "Need a Babysitter? Don't Count on Grandma" about grandmothers who are reluctant to provide childcare for their children.[24] In a blog post, one woman reflected on why she does not envy her friends who are grandparents. She wrote, "Do I want to avoid grandchildren because I'm divorced, which means I'll never grandparent with my former spouse? Am I set in my ways? Am I selfish or even narcissistic? Am I missing the Nana-maternal gene?"[25]

Becoming a grandparent is such a significant stage in people's lives that those who don't achieve it, or do not desire it, are seen as outliers. In addition, parents who are conditioned by images of grandparents assuming a significant burden of childcare often feel confused, puzzled, or resentful that their own parents do not want to help out in the same way. A grandparenting paradox is rising; as grandparents are showered with more attention and opportunities to be active and involved, the expectations of active grandparenting become normalized. As a result, those who are unwilling or unable to participate at that level feel left out or judged.

DIGITAL CULTURES

Just as new markets create the grandparent consumer, and economic pressures put more babysitting responsibilities on grandparents, the current digital media environment sets up ambiguous boundaries for grandparenting in our culture. It used to be that parents gave pictures of their children to grandparents without knowing what they did with them. At the same time, grandparents could share their photos only within their immediate circle of family and friends. In the digital world, grandparents become grandparents to everyone, in the sense that anything they share can be open to the world. Some create a carefully cultivated grandma image, like those who write blogs about their own grandparenting experiences. Others post pictures for the admiring public, but the line over when to share can sometimes be confusing for parents, grandparents, and grandchildren. One study noted that parents sometimes feel the pressure to post more pictures on Facebook than they prefer so that grandparents can see and share them with friends.[26] Another article ponders a grandmother's social etiquette in choosing to share her grandchildren's Instagram posts on Facebook to a wider audience than the grandchildren would like.[27]

The digital world privileges the attributes of youth: newness, mastery of the latest technology, and a familiarity with popular culture. Recognizing this, youngsters are routinely taking videos and images of their grandparents and building an audience around them. Whether it's an angry grandpa, a fashion grandma, or wise grandparents, social media are filled with images of all types of grandparents embracing a digitized youth culture. While at times grandchildren are proudly showing off their grandparents, more often viewers are laughing with (or at) grandparent figures for their lack of knowledge of the digital world that belongs to the young. For example, a shared image went viral of a grandma who punctuated all her Google searches with "please" and "thank you."[28] Viewers laughed at her not understanding that technology doesn't care if she's polite, but they also marveled at the civility she exuded.

As they use digital technologies, grandparents are not just figures to be laughed at, but also to be admired. With so many people connected to and dependent on the digital world, many experience "FOMO" (the fear of missing out). However, the elderly represent one of the last groups untethered to technology and popular culture. As a result, they often are portrayed as providing wisdom to people who are so beholden to digital media. When people need to detox from their digital world, they turn to the recipes, pastimes, and survival tales of their grandparents. Activities and styles once restricted to the elderly, such as knitting, sewing, and fashion trends from earlier periods, are adopted by younger people. Youth become tourists in the elderly world and pull grandparents into their digital world, where the elderly lose some control over how they are portrayed. Their images often are transformed into communal grandparents, widely shared and known.

At times, these figures may seem to have power in these new worlds. They can advocate for a political cause, like the Raging Grannies, or use their popularity with young people to be political influencers. At other times, these grandparent images offer amusement but little tangible power for older people in society. They are appreciated and respected, but these representations often reinforce ageism stereotypes. Age may be valued by youth, but it remains in the service of youth, alternatively to be respected or discarded at will. The glamour of aging often seen in digital culture serves to render invisible once again the harsher realities of aging that older people are forced to confront.

MAKING GRANDPARENTS VISIBLE

Grandparenting once was within the domain of the family, less a stage experienced than one simply achieved (if you were lucky). For some groups, grandparents were simply the elderly members of the tribe, full of wisdom and advice from their many years of living. At other points in history, within specific cultures, families relied on grandparents in a symbiotic relationship.

Today, parents, grandparents, digital culture, and the marketplace all are reviving and transforming the grandparent experience. Families are developing new rituals to bond with grandparents, and the communal grandparent figure is watched and enjoyed from afar. According to the Census Bureau, aging Baby Boomers will contribute to the greying of the population in the United States.[29] Boomers are likely to demand new representations of themselves to match the fact that they are living longer and are more active as grandparents. As more people reach the grandparent stage of life, how we see and understand the grandparent image matters.

These digital technologies have the power to provide grandparents more access to family members and to reconnect them to popular culture. Grandparents can be old and still sexy, old and still stylish, old and still fun. Grandparenting culture as a distinct phase of life is becoming something that is desired and valued. However, when this phase of life is constantly promoted and revered, those who do not participate in the celebration are regarded with suspicion. Some view grandparenting as an opportunity to develop warm relationships, a second chance at parenting, or duty-free parenting. For others, though, grandparenting is yet another burden. Like mother labor, grandparent labor often is invisible, precluding discussion about the economic, political, and personal implications of their caregiving.

Honest discussions about the reality of aging, which sometimes may be unpleasant, are displaced when mediated images promoting the consumption of grandparenting become ubiquitous. As the culture of grandparenting becomes more visible, we must progress beyond merely consuming grandparenting brands and using their images for our amusement to supporting grandparents and meeting their needs as they navigate their third act.

NOTES

1. Jason Sobel, "How Bellevue University Recruited a 61-Year-Old to Its Golf Team," *ESPN.com* (web page), January 9, 2018, http://www.espn.com/golf/story/_/id/22005266/espn-golf-nebraska-college-recruits-61-year-old-golf-team.

2. Bonnie Burton, "Grandparents Roll the Dice, Play Elves in 'D&D AARPG,'" *CNET* (web page), April 10, 2017, https://www.cnet.com/news/d-d-aarpg-dungeons-and-dragons-seniors-geek-sundry-youtube/.

3. Kelly Servick, "Videogame May Help Rejuvenate Elderly Brains," *Wired*, September 5, 2013, https://www.wired.com/2013/09/video-game-elderly/.

4. Quoted in Hannah Brockhaus, "Pope Francis Is Praying for Grandparents This December," *Catholic News Agency*, December 4, 2017, https://www.catholicnewsagency.com/news/pope-francis-is-praying-for-grandparents-this-december-73826.

5. Johanna Li, "Woman, 29, Gifts New Home to Grandparents Who Never Had Electricity or Running Water," *Inside Edition* (web page), March 24, 2017, http://www.insideedition.com/headlines/22394-woman-29-gifts-new-home-to-grandparents-who-never-had-electricity-or-running-water.

6. Amy Goyer, "The MetLife Study of Gen X: The MTV Generation Moves into Mid-Life" (New York: Met Life Mature Market Institute, April 2013), 6–7. https://www.lifehappens.org/wp-content/uploads/2015/02/Research_MetLifeStudyofGenX-TheMTVGenerationMovesIntoMid-Life.pdf.

7. "Grandparent Marketing Group Develops Celebration of 100 'Ageless' Americans for Nintendo," *PR Leap* (web page press release), February 9, 2007, http://www.prleap.com/pr/65042/grandparent-marketing-group-develops.

8. Deborah Jermyn, "'Get a Life, Ladies. Your Old One Is Not Coming Back': Ageing, Ageism and the Lifespan of Female Celebrity," *Celebrity Studies* 3, no. 1 (March 2012): 1, https://doi.org/10.1080/19392397.2012.644708.

9. Madonna Harrington Meyer and Yooumi Lee, "Grandparenting in the United States," in *Grandparenting in the United States*, ed. Madonna Harrington Meyer and Ynesse Abdul-Malak (Amityville, NY: Baywood Publishing Company, 2016), 3.

10. Susan Douglas and Meredith Michaels, *The Mommy Myth: The Idealization of Motherhood and How It Has Undermined All Women* (New York: Free Press, 2005) 4–5.

11. Brady E. Hamilton et al., "Births: Final Data for 2014," National Vital Statistics Reports 64, no. 12 (Hyattsville, MD: National Center for Health Statistics, 2015), 2, https://www.cdc.gov/nchs/data/nvsr/nvsr64/nvsr64_01.pdf.

12. Anne Tergeson, "The Long (Long) Wait to Become a Grandparent," *Wall Street Journal*, March 30, 2014, https://www.wsj.com/articles/SB1000142405270230377550457939550 1172676002.

13. Some examples: Annalisa Barbieri, "Are We Being Cruel Not to Give Our Parents Grandchildren?" *The Guardian*, May 24, 2013, https://www.theguardian.com/lifeandstyle/2013/may/24/cruel-to-give-parents-grandchildren, and: "How Do Your Parents Handle Being Told They Won't Have Grandchildren?" *Reddit* (blog), accessed February 20, 2018, https://www.reddit.com/r/childfree/comments/2he85f/how_do_your_parents_handle_being_told_they_wont/.

14. Robin L. Lumsdaine and Stephanie J. C. Vermeer, "Retirement Timing of Women and the Role of Care Responsibilities for Grandchildren," *Demography* 52, no. 2 (April 2015): 452, https://doi.org/10.1007/s13524-015-0382-5.

15. Claire Cain Miller, "More Women in Their 60s and 70s Are Having 'Way Too Much Fun' to Retire," *New York Times*, February 11, 2017, https://www.nytimes.com/2017/02/11/upshot/more-women-in-their-60s-and-70s-are-having-way-too-much-fun-to-retire.html.

16. Madonna Harrington Meyer, *Grandmothers at Work: Juggling Families and Jobs* (New York: New York University Press, 2014), 65.

17. Meyer, 96, 131.

18. Cynthia Ramnarace, "Caregiving Grandparent Gets Fired," *AARP Bulletin* (web page), April 11, 2011, http://www.aarp.org/politics-society/rights/info-04-2011/caregiving-grandparent-gets-fired.html.

19. "Grandparents: A Critical Child Care Safety Net" (Arlington, VA: National Association of Child Care Resource & Referral Agencies, 2008), https://issuu.com/naccrra/docs/grandparents?layout=white.

20. "Grandparents Babysitting: Should They Get Paid?" *Huffington Post*, March 8, 2013, https://www.huffingtonpost.com/2013/03/08/grandparents-babysitting-payment_n_2812587.html.

21. Lumsdaine and Vermeer, "Retirement Timing of Women," 452–453.

22. Economic Mobility Project, "When Baby Boomers Delay Retirement, Do Younger Workers Suffer?" (Washington, DC: The Pew Charitable Trusts, September 13, 2012), http://www.pewtrusts.org/en/research-and-analysis/issue-briefs/2012/09/13/when-baby-boomers-delay-retirement-do-younger-workers-suffer.

23. Diana Athill,"Why I Never Became a Gran," *The Guardian*, November 16, 2012, https://www.theguardian.com/lifeandstyle/2012/nov/16/diana-athill-why-never-grandparent.

24. Sharon Jayson, "Need a Babysitter? Don't Count on Grandma," *New York Times* (Well blog), August 9, 2016, https://well.blogs.nytimes.com/2016/08/09/need-a-babysitter-dont-count-on-grandma/.

25. Nancy Wurtzel, "Why I Don't Want Grandchildren," *Next Avenue* (blog), September 18, 2014, https://www.nextavenue.org/why-i-dont-want-grandchildren/.

26. Priya Kumar, "A Digital Footprint from Birth: New Mothers' Decisions to Share Baby Pictures Online" (master's thesis, University of Michigan, 2014), 58, https://deepblue.lib.umich.edu/bitstream/handle/2027.42/106577/Priya_Kumar_Thesis.pdf?sequence=1&isAllowed=y.

27. Woodrow Hartzog and Evan Selinger, "Why Grandma Shouldn't Have Posted Instagram Pics on Facebook," *Forbes*, January 7, 2014, https://www.forbes.com/sites/privacynotice/2014/01/07/why-grandma-shouldnt-have-posted-instagram-pics-on-facebook-2/#512d136a5cbd.

28. Camila Domonoske, "A Bit of Afternoon Cheer: Google Charmed by Grandma's Polite Searches," *NPR* (web page), June 16, 2016, https://www.npr.org/sections/thetwo-way/2016/06/16/482343107/a-bit-of-afternoon-cheer-google-charmed-by-grandmas-polite-searches.

29. Sandra L. Colby and Jennifer M. Ortman, "Projections of the Size and Composition of the U.S. Population: 2014 to 2060," (Washington, DC: United States Census Bureau, March 2015), https://www.census.gov/content/dam/Census/library/publications/2015/demo/p25-1143.pdf.

Works Cited

"2017 Essential Facts about the Computer and Video Game Industry." Washington, DC: Entertainment Software Association. Accessed February 24, 2018. http://www.theesa.com/article/2017-essential-facts-computer-video-game-industry/.

Aarsand, Pål André. "Computer and Video Games in Family Life: The Digital Divide as a Resource in Intergenerational Interactions." *Childhood* 14, no. 2 (May 2007): 235–56. https://doi.org/10.1177/0907568207078330.

Albrecht, Ruth. "The Parental Responsibilities of Grandparents." *Marriage and Family Living* 16, no. 3 (1954): 201–4. https://doi.org/10.2307/348486.

Anderson, Oscar G. "Video Games: Attitudes and Habits of Adults Age 50-Plus." Washington, DC: AARP Research, June 1, 2016. https://doi.org/10.26419/res.00125.001.

Baumann, Shyon, and Kim de Laat. "Aspiration and Compromise: Portrayals of Older Adults in Television Advertising." In *Aging, Media, and Culture*, edited by C. Lee Harrington, Denise Bielby, and Anthony R. Bardo, 13–24. Lanham, MD: Lexington Books, 2014.

Baxandall, Rosalyn, and Elizabeth Ewen. *Picture Windows: How the Suburbs Happened.* New York: Basic Books, 2000.

Beland, Robert M., and Terry L. Mills. "Positive Portrayal of Grandparents in Current Children's Literature." *Journal of Family Issues* 22, no. 5 (July 1, 2001): 639–51. https://doi.org/10.1177/019251301022005006.

Ben-Ari, Orit Taubman-, Shirley Ben Shlomo, and Liora Findler. "Personal Growth and Meaning in Life among First-Time Mothers and Grandmothers." *Journal of Happiness Studies* 13, no. 5 (October 1, 2012): 801–20. https://doi.org/10.1007/s10902-011-9291-5.

Bennetts, Leslie. *The Feminine Mistake: Are We Giving Up Too Much?* New York: Hyperion, 2007.

Bernstein, Mary. "Celebration and Suppression: The Strategic Uses of Identity by the Lesbian and Gay Movement." *American Journal of Sociology* 103, no. 3 (November 1997): 531–65. https://doi.org/10.1086/231250.

Bertera, Elizabeth M., and Sandra Edmonds Crewe. "Parenthood in the Twenty-First Century: African American Grandparents as Surrogate Parents." *Journal of Human Behavior in the Social Environment* 23, no. 2 (February 2013): 178–92. https://doi.org/10.1080/10911359.2013.747348.

Binstock, Robert H. "The Prolonged Old, the Long-Lived Society, and the Politics of Age." *Public Policy & Aging Report* 14, no. 2 (March 1, 2004): 1–31. https://doi.org/10.1093/ppar/14.2.1a.

Bitter, Lori K. *The Grandparent Economy: How Baby Boomers Are Bridging the Generation Gap.* Ithaca, NY: Paramount Market Publishing, 2015.

Bittner, Jane C. "Insights and Spending Habits of Modern Grandparents: A Look at African American and Hispanic/Latino Grandparents." Washington, DC: AARP, 2012. https://www.aarp.org/content/dam/aarp/research/surveys_statistics/general/2012/Insights-and-Spending-Habits-of-Modern-Grandparents-A-Look-at-African-American-and-Hispanic-Latino-Grandparents-AARP.pdf.

Bordone, Valeria, and Bruno Arpino. "Do Grandchildren Influence How Old You Feel?" *Journal of Aging and Health* 28, no. 6 (September 2016): 1055–72. https://doi.org/10.1177/0898264315618920.

Brookfield, Katherine, Claire Fitzsimons, Iain Scott, Gillian Mead, John Starr, Neil Thin, Anthea Tinker, and Catherine Ward Thompson. "The Home as Enabler of More Active Lifestyles among Older People." *Building Research & Information* 43, no. 5 (June 4, 2015): 616–30. https://doi.org/10.1080/09613218.2015.1045702.

Burn, Katherine F., Victor W. Henderson, David Ames, Lorraine Dennerstein, and Cassandra Szoeke. "Role of Grandparenting in Postmenopausal Women's Cognitive Health: Results from the Women's Healthy Aging Project." *Menopause* 21, no. 10 (October 2014): 1069–74. https://doi.org/10.1097/GME.0000000000000236.

Bygren, Lars O., Petter Tinghög, John Carstensen, Sören Edvinsson, et al. "Change in Paternal Grandmothers' Early Food Supply Influenced Cardiovascular Mortality of the Female Grandchildren." *BMC Genetics* 15, no. 12 (February 2014): https://doi.org/10.1186/1471-2156-15-12.

Carlin, Diana B., and Kelly L. Winfrey. "Have You Come a Long Way, Baby? Hillary Clinton, Sarah Palin, and Sexism in 2008 Campaign Coverage." *Communication Studies* 60, no. 4 (2009): 326–43. https://doi.org/10.1080/10510970903109904.

Carstensen, Laura L., Bulent Turan, Susanne Scheibe, Nilam Ram, Hal Ersner-Hershfield, Gregory R. Samanez-Larkin, Kathryn P. Brooks, and John R. Nesselroade. "Emotional Experience Improves with Age: Evidence Based on over 10 Years of Experience Sampling." *Psychology and Aging* 26, no. 1 (March 2011): 21–33. https://doi.org/10.1037/a0021285.

Chazan, May, and Stephanie Kittmer. "Defying, Producing, and Overlooking Stereotypes? The Complexities of Mobilizing 'Grandmotherhood' as Political Strategy." *Journal of Women & Aging* 28, no. 4 (July 3, 2016): 297–308. https://doi.org/10.1080/08952841.2015.1017428.

Chen, Feinian, Guangya Liu, and Christine A. Mair. "Intergenerational Ties in Context: Grandparents Caring for Grandchildren in China." *Social Forces* 90, no. 2 (December 1, 2011): 571–94. https://doi.org/10.1093/sf/sor012.

Chen, Hao-Min, and Denise C. Lewis. "A Changing Relationship: Visiting Chinese Grandparents and Their Adult Children in the United States." *Journal of Ethnographic & Qualitative Research* 11, no. 2 (2016): 87–98.

Chen, Yao-Chu, Cheng-Chiang Chen, Jean Decety, and Yawei Cheng. "Aging Is Associated with Changes in the Neural Circuits Underlying Empathy." *Neurobiology of Aging* 35, no. 4 (April 1, 2014): 827–36. https://doi.org/10.1016/j.neurobiolaging.2013.10.080.

Cherlin, Andrew J. "On Single Mothers 'Doing' Family." *Journal of Marriage and Family* 68, no. 4 (2006): 800–803.

Cherlin, Andrew J., and Frank F. Furstenberg Jr. *The New American Grandparent: A Place in the Family, a Life Apart*. Cambridge, MA: Harvard University Press, 1992.

Coall, David A., and Ralph Hertwig. "Grandparental Investment: Past, Present, and Future." *Behavioral and Brain Sciences* 33, no. 1 (February 2010): 1–40. https://doi.org/10.1017/S0140525X09991105.

Cogan, Brian, and Thom Gencarelli, eds. *Baby Boomers and Popular Culture: An Inquiry into America's Most Powerful Generation*. Santa Barbara, CA: Praeger, 2015.

Colby, Sandra L., and Jennifer M. Ortman. "Projections of the Size and Composition of the U.S. Population: 2014 to 2060." Current Population Reports. Washington, DC: United States Census Bureau, March 2015. https://www.census.gov/content/dam/Census/library/publications/2015/demo/p25-1143.pdf.

Collins, Patricia Hill. *Black Feminist Thought: Knowledge, Consciousness, and the Politics of Empowerment*. 2nd ed. New York: Routledge, 2009.

Collins, Patricia Hill. "The Meaning of Motherhood in Black Culture and Mother-Daughter Relationships." In *Maternal Theory: Essential Readings*, edited by Andrea O'Reilly. Toronto: Demeter Press, 2015.

Coontz, Stephanie. *The Way We Never Were: American Families and the Nostalgia Trap*. New York: Basic Books, 2005.

Copen, Casey, and Merril Silverstein. "Transmission of Religious Beliefs across Generations: Do Grandparents Matter?" *Journal of Comparative Family Studies* 38, no. 4 (Autumn 2007): 497–510.

Covey, Herbert C., and Paul T. Lockman Jr. "Narrative References to Older African Americans Living under Slavery." *Social Science Journal* 33, no. 1 (January 1, 1996): 23–37. https://doi.org/10.1016/S0362-3319(96)90003-8.

Coyne, Sarah M., Jennifer Ruh Linder, David A. Nelson, and Douglas A. Gentile. "'Frenemies, Fraitors, and Mean-Em-Aitors': Priming Effects of Viewing Physical and Relational Aggression in the Media on Women." *Aggressive Behavior* 38, no. 2 (March 1, 2012): 141–49. https://doi.org/10.1002/ab.21410.

Craig, Lyn, and Bridget Jenkins. "The Composition of Parents' and Grandparents' Child-Care Time: Gender and Generational Patterns in Activity, Multi-Tasking and Co-Presence." *Ageing & Society* 36, no. 4 (April 2016): 785–810. https://doi.org/10.1017/S0144686X14001548.

Crewe, Sandra Edmonds. "Guardians of Generations: African American Grandparent Caregivers for Children of HIV/AIDS Infected Parents." *Journal of Family Strengths* 12, no. 1 (2012): 1–20.

Dannefer, Dale, and Karie Feldman. "Age Integration, Age Segregation, and Generation X: Life-Course Perspectives." *Generations* 41, no. 3 (October 2017): 20–26.

Danowski, Jesica L. "The Portrayal of Older Characters in Popular Children's Books: A Content Analysis from 2000 to 2010." Brigham Young University BYU ScholarsArchive, March 15, 2011. https://scholarsarchive.byu.edu/cgi/viewcontent.cgi?referer=&httpsredir=1&article=3468&context=etd.

Dohle, Simone, and Brian Wansink. "Fit in 50 Years: Participation in High School Sports Best Predicts One's Physical Activity after Age 70." *BMC Public Health* 13 (December 1, 2013): 6. https://doi.org/10.1186/1471-2458-13-1100.

Donlon, Margie M., Ori Ashman, and Becca R. Levy. "Re-Vision of Older Television Characters: A Stereotype-Awareness Intervention." *Journal of Social Issues* 61, no. 2 (June 2005): 307–19. https://doi.org/10.1111/j.1540-4560.2005.00407.x.

Douglas, Susan J., and Meredith W. Michaels. *The Mommy Myth: The Idealization of Motherhood and How It Has Undermined All Women*. New York: Free Press, 2005.

Economic Mobility Project. "When Baby Boomers Delay Retirement, Do Younger Workers Suffer?" Washington, DC: Pew Charitable Trusts, September 13, 2012. http://pew.org/2yITEvM.

Ellis, Renee R., and Tavia Simmons. "Coresident Grandparents and Their Grandchildren: 2012." Washington, DC: United States Census Bureau, October 2014. https://www.census.gov/content/dam/Census/library/publications/2014/demo/p20-576.pdf.

Fairclough, Kirsty. "Nothing Less Than Perfect: Female Celebrity, Ageing and Hyper-Scrutiny in the Gossip Industry." *Celebrity Studies* 3, no. 1 (March 2012): 90–103. https://doi.org/10.1080/19392397.2012.644723.

Falk, Ursula A., and Gerhard Falk. *Grandparents: A New Look at the Supporting Generation*. Amherst, NY: Prometheus Books, 2002.

"Family Law—Grandparent Visitation—California Supreme Court Finds No Infringement of Custodial Mother's Due Process Parenting Interest When Noncustodial Father Supports Grandparent Visitation Petition—*Butler v. Harris (In re Marriage of Harris)*, 96 P.3d 141 (Cal. 2004)." *Harvard Law Review* 118, no. 3 (2005): 1046–53.

Fingerman, Karen L. "The Role of Offspring and In-Laws in Grandparents' Ties to Their Grandchildren." *Journal of Family Issues* 25, no. 8 (November 2004): 1026–49. https://doi.org/10.1177/0192513X04265941.

Fingerman, Karen, and Megan Dolbin-MacNab. "The Baby Boomers and Their Parents: Cohort Influences and Intergenerational Ties." In *The Baby Boomers Grow Up: Contemporary*

Perspectives on Midlife, edited by Susan Krauss Whitbourne and Sherry L. Willis. Mahwah, NJ: Lawrence Erlbaum, 2006.

Fingerman, Karen L., Karl A. Pillemer, Merril Silverstein, and J. Jill Suitor. "The Baby Boomers' Intergenerational Relationships." *The Gerontologist* 52, no. 2 (April 1, 2012): 199–209. https://doi.org/10.1093/geront/gnr139.

Fingerman, Karen L., and J. Jill Suitor. "Millennials and Their Parents: Implications of the New Young Adulthood for Midlife Adults." *Innovation in Aging* 1, no. 3 (November 1, 2017). https://doi.org/10.1093/geroni/igx026.

Fischer, David Hackett. *Growing Old in America*. Oxford: Oxford University Press, 1978.

Fisher, Christy. "Grandparents Give of Themselves." *American Demographics* 18, no. 6 (June 1996).

"Fourth International Conference on Periodontal Research, June 26–28, 1978—Stockholm, Sweden. Research Reports." *Journal of Periodontal Research* 14, no. 3 (May 1979): 245–68.

Francese, Peter. "The MetLife Report on American Grandparents: New Insights for a New Generation of Grandparents." New York: MetLife Mature Market Institute, July 2011. https://www.metlife.com/assets/cao/mmi/publications/studies/2011/mmi-american-grandparents.pdf.

Frazier, E. Franklin. *The Negro Family in the United States*. Chicago: University of Chicago Press, 1939.

Frissen, Valerie A. J. "ICTs in the Rush Hour of Life." *The Information Society* 16, no. 1 (March 2000): 65–75. https://doi.org/10.1080/019722400128338.

Fry, Richard. "For First Time in Modern Era, Living with Parents Edges Out Other Living Arrangements for 18- to 34-Year-Olds." Washington, DC: Pew Research Center, May 24, 2016. http://www.pewsocialtrends.org/2016/05/24/for-first-time-in-modern-era-living-with-parents-edges-out-other-living-arrangements-for-18-to-34-year-olds/.

Fuller-Thomson, Esme, and Meredith Minkler. "Central American Grandparents Raising Grandchildren." *Hispanic Journal of Behavioral Sciences* 29, no. 1 (February 1, 2007): 5–18. https://doi.org/10.1177/0739986306293680.

Ge, William, and Andrew Adesman. "Grandparents Raising Grandchildren: A Primer for Pediatricians." *Current Opinion in Pediatrics* 29, no. 3 (June 2017): 379. https://doi.org/10.1097/MOP.0000000000000501.

Gerbner, George, Larry Gross, Nancy Signorielli, and Michael Morgan. "Aging with Television: Images on Television Drama and Conceptions of Social Reality." *Journal of Communication* 30, no. 1 (Winter 1980): 37–47. https://doi.org/10.1111/j.1460-2466.1980.tb01766.x.

Gerstel, Naomi. "Rethinking Families and Community: The Color, Class, and Centrality of Extended Kin Ties: Rethinking Families and Community." *Sociological Forum* 26, no. 1 (March 2011): 1–20. https://doi.org/10.1111/j.1573-7861.2010.01222.x.

Gianturco, Paola. *Grandmother Power: A Global Phenomenon*. Brooklyn, NY: PowerHouse Books, 2012.

Gibson, Mhairi A., and Ruth Mace. "Helpful Grandmothers in Rural Ethiopia: A Study of the Effect of Kin on Child Survival and Growth." *Evolution and Human Behavior* 26, no. 6 (November 2005): 469–82. https://doi.org/10.1016/j.evolhumbehav.2005.03.004.

Goh, Esther C. L., and Leon Kuczynski. "Agency and Power of Single Children in Multi-Generational Families in Urban Xiamen, China." *Culture & Psychology* 15, no. 4 (December 2009): 506–32. https://doi.org/10.1177/1354067X09344881.

Golly, Carol Hosmer. "Pruning the Family Tree: The Plight of Grandparents Who Are Alienated from Their Grandchildren." *The International Journal of Aging and Society* 7, no. 2 (2016): 21–31. https://doi.org/10.18848/2160-1909/CGP/v07i02/21-31.

Goodman, Catherine Chase, and Merril Silverstein. "Grandmothers Who Parent Their Grandchildren: An Exploratory Study of Close Relations across Three Generations." *Journal of Family Issues* 22, no. 5 (July 1, 2001): 557–78. https://doi.org/10.1177/019251301022005002.

Goodman, Melanie R., and Satya P. Rao. "Grandparents Raising Grandchildren in a US-Mexico Border Community." *Qualitative Health Research* 17, no. 8 (October 1, 2007): 1117–36. https://doi.org/10.1177/1049732307308457.

Gourdon, Vincent. "Are Grandparents Really Absent from Family Tradition?: Forbears in the Region of Vernon (France) around 1800." *The History of the Family* 4, no. 1 (January 1, 1999): 77–91. https://doi.org/10.1016/S1081-602X(99)80266-8.

Goyer, Amy. "The MetLife Study of Gen X: The MTV Generation Moves into Mid-Life." MetLife Mature Market Institute, April 2013.

"Grandparents: A Critical Child Care Safety Net." Arlington, VA: National Association of Child Care Resource & Referral Agencies, 2008. https://www.researchconnections.org/childcare/resources/14636.

"Grandparents Investing in Grandchildren: The MetLife Study on How Grandparents Share Their Time, Values, and Money." New York: MetLife Mature Market Institute and Generations United, September 2012. https://www.metlife.com/assets/cao/mmi/publications/studies/2012/studies/MMIGrandparentsStudy_Web.pdf.

Gratton, Brian, and Carole Haber. "Three Phases in the History of American Grandparents: Authority, Burden, Companion." *Generations* 20, no. 1 (Spring 1996).

Grenier, Amanda, and Jill Hanley. "Older Women and 'Frailty': Aged, Gendered and Embodied Resistance." *Current Sociology* 55, no. 2 (March 2007): 211–28. https://doi.org/10.1177/0011392107073303.

Haber, Carole. *Beyond Sixty-Five: The Dilemma of Old Age in America's Past*. Cambridge: Cambridge University Press, 1983.

Haber, Carole. "Historians' Approach to Aging in America." In *Handbook of the Humanities and Aging*, 2nd ed., edited by Thomas R. Cole, Robert Kastenbaum, and Ruth E. Ray, 25–40. New York: Springer, 2000.

Hagestad, Gunhild O., and Mary E. Lang. "The Transition to Grandparenthood: Unexplored Issues." *Journal of Family Issues* 7, no. 2 (June 1, 1986): 115–30. https://doi.org/10.1177/019251386007002001.

Hagestad, Gunhild O., and Peter Uhlenberg. "The Social Separation of Old and Young: A Root of Ageism." *Journal of Social Issues* 61, no. 2 (June 2005): 343–60. https://doi.org/10.1111/j.1540-4560.2005.00409.x.

Hamilton, Brady E., Joyce A. Martin, Michelle J. K. Osterman, Sally C. Curtin, and M. S. Matthews. "Births: Final Data for 2014." National Vital Statistics Reports. Hyattsville, MD: National Center for Health Statistics, 2015. https://www.cdc.gov/nchs/data/nvsr/nvsr64/nvsr64_12.pdf.

Hanks, Roma Stovall. "'Grandma, What Big Teeth You Have!' The Social Construction of Grandparenting in American Business and Academe." *Journal of Family Issues* 22, no. 5 (July 1, 2001): 652–76. https://doi.org/10.1177/019251301022005007.

Harari, Yuval N. *Sapiens: A Brief History of Humankind*. New York: Harper Collins, 2015.

Hareven, Tamara K. "Aging and Generational Relations: A Historical and Life Course Perspective." *Annual Review of Sociology* 20 (August 1994): 437–61. https://doi.org/10.1146/annurev.so.20.080194.002253.

Hausknecht, Simone, Carman Neustaedter, and David Kaufman. "Blurring the Lines of Age: Intergenerational Collaboration in Alternate Reality Games." In *Game-Based Learning across the Lifespan: Cross-Generational and Age-Oriented Topics*, edited by Margarida Romero, Josep Blat, Kim Sawchuk, and Hubert Ouellet, 47–64. Switzerland: Springer, 2017.

Hawkes, Kristen. "Human Longevity: The Grandmother Effect." *Nature* 428, no. 6979 (March 2004): 128–29. https://doi.org/10.1038/428128a.

Hawn, Goldie, with Wendy Holden. *A Lotus Grows in the Mud*. New York: G. P. Putnam's Sons, 2005.

Hayslip, Bert, Heidemarie Blumenthal, and Ashley Garner. "Health and Grandparent-Grandchild Well-Being: One-Year Longitudinal Findings for Custodial Grandfamilies." *Journal of Aging and Health* 26, no. 4 (2014): 559–582. doi: 10.1177/0898264314525664.

He, Wan, Daniel Goodkind, and Paul Kowal. "An Aging World: 2015." Washington, DC: U.S. Census Bureau, March 2016. https://www.census.gov/library/publications/2016/demo/P95-16-1.html.

"The Health and Retirement Study: Aging in the 21st Century: Challenges and Opportunities for Americans." University of Michigan: Survey Research Center, Institute for Social Research, University of Michigan, 2006. http://hrsonline.isr.umich.edu/sitedocs/databook/inc/pdf/HRS-Aging-in-the-21St-Century.pdf.

"Health and Retirement Study: A Longitudinal Study of Health, Retirement, and Aging." Institute for Social Research, University of Michigan, National Institute on Aging, January 2017. http://hrsonline.isr.umich.edu/sitedocs/databook/inc/pdf/HRS-Aging-in-the-21St-Century.pdf.

Henderson, Tammy L., and Patricia B. Moran. "Grandparent Visitation Rights: Testing the Parameters of Parental Rights." *Journal of Family Issues* 22, no. 5 (July 1, 2001): 619–38. https://doi.org/10.1177/019251301022005005.

Hilbrand, Sonja, David A. Coall, Denis Gerstorf, and Ralph Hertwig. "Caregiving within and beyond the Family Is Associated with Lower Mortality for the Caregiver: A Prospective Study." *Evolution and Human Behavior* 38, no. 3 (May 2017): 397–403. https://doi.org/10.1016/j.evolhumbehav.2016.11.010.

Hill, Twyla J. "What's a Grandparent to Do? The Legal Status of Grandparents in the Extended Family." *Journal of Family Issues* 22, no. 5 (July 1, 2001): 594–618. https://doi.org/10.1177/019251301022005004.

Hill-Lubin, Mildred A. "The African-American Grandmother in Autobiographical Works by Frederick Douglass, Langston Hughes, and Maya Angelou." *International Journal of Aging and Human Development* 33, no. 3 (October 1991): 173–85. https://doi.org/10.2190/4XJ4-42N4-LD4J-12ER.

Hilt, Michael L., and Jeremy Harris Lipschultz. *Mass Media, an Aging Population, and the Baby Boomers*. New York: Routledge, 2013.

Hochschild, Arlie Russell. *The Outsourced Self: Intimate Life in Market Times*. New York: Metropolitan Books, 2012.

Hochschild, Arlie Russell, and Anne Machung. *The Second Shift*. New York: Penguin Books, 2003.

Hrdy, Sarah Blaffer. *Mothers and Others: The Evolutionary Origins of Mutual Understanding*. Cambridge: Harvard University Press, 2011.

Hudson, Robert B., and Judith G. Gonyea. "Baby Boomers and the Shifting Political Construction of Old Age." *The Gerontologist* 52, no. 2 (April 1, 2012): 272–82. https://doi.org/10.1093/geront/gnr129.

Hulbert, Ann. *Raising America: Experts, Parents, and a Century of Advice about Children*. New York: Alfred A. Knopf, 2003.

Hunt, Judith. "Make Room for Daddy…And Mommy: Helicopter Parents Are Here!" *The Journal of Academic Administration in Higher Education* 3, no. 1 (Spring 2008): 10.

Hunt, Michael E., ed. *Retirement Communities: An American Original*. New York: Haworth Press, 1984.

Jermyn, Deborah. "'Get a Life, Ladies. Your Old One Is Not Coming Back': Ageing, Ageism and the Lifespan of Female Celebrity." *Celebrity Studies* 3, no. 1 (March 1, 2012): 1–12. https://doi.org/10.1080/19392397.2012.644708.

Jimenez, Jillian. "The History of Grandmothers in the African-American Community." *Social Service Review* 76, no. 4 (December 2002): 523–51. https://doi.org/10.1086/342994.

Kamo, Yoshinori. "Asian Grandparents." In *Handbook on Grandparenthood*, edited by Maximiliane Szinovácz, 97–112. Westport, CT: Greenwood Press, 1998.

Kaptijn, Ralf, Fleur Thomese, Theo G. van Tilburg, and Aart C. Liefbroer. "How Grandparents Matter: Support for the Cooperative Breeding Hypothesis in a Contemporary Dutch Population." *Human Nature* 21, no. 4 (December 2010): 393–405. https://doi.org/10.1007/s12110-010-9098-9.

Kauffman, Ronald H. "Bleeding Grandparent Visitation Rights." *The Florida Bar Journal* 86, no. 8 (October 2012): 42–47.

Kelly, Janice, and Laura Tropp. "Changing Conceptions of the Good Dad in Popular Culture." In *Deconstructing Dads: Changing Images of Fathers in Popular Culture*, edited by Laura Tropp and Janice Kelly. Lanham, MD: Lexington Books, 2016.

King, Valarie, and Glen H. Elder Jr. "The Legacy of Grandparenting: Childhood Experiences with Grandparents and Current Involvement with Grandchildren." *Journal of Marriage and Family* 59, no. 4 (November 1997): 848–59.

Kinser, Amber E. *Motherhood and Feminism*. Berkeley, CA: Perseus Books, 2010.

Knight, Chris, and Camilla Power. "Grandmothers, Politics, and Getting Back to Science." In *Grandmotherhood: The Evolutionary Significance of the Second Half of Female Life*, edited by Eckart Voland, Athanasios Chasiotis, and Wulf Schiefenhövel, 81–98. New Brunswick, NJ: Rutgers University Press, 2005.

Kochhar, Rakesh, and D'Vera Cohn. "Fighting Poverty in a Bad Economy, Americans Move in with Relatives." Washington, DC: Pew Research Center, October 3, 2011. http://www.pewsocialtrends.org/2011/10/03/fighting-poverty-in-a-bad-economy-americans-move-in-with-relatives/.

Kornhaber, Arthur. *Contemporary Grandparenting*. Thousand Oaks, CA: Sage Publications, 1996.

Kornhaber, Arthur, and Kenneth L. Woodward. *Grandparents/Grandchildren: The Vital Connection*. New Brunswick, NJ: Transaction Books, 1985.

Krogstad, Jens Manuel. "5 Facts about American Grandparents." Washington, DC: Pew Research Center, September 13, 2015. http://www.pewresearch.org/fact-tank/2015/09/13/5-facts-about-american-grandparents/.

Lampkin, Cheryl L. "Insights and Spending Habits of Modern Grandparents." Washington, DC: AARP Research, March 2012. https://www.aarp.org/content/dam/aarp/research/surveys_statistics/general/2012/Insights-and-Spending-Habits-of-Modern-Grandparents-AARP.pdf.

Lancy, David F. *The Anthropology of Childhood: Cherubs, Chattel, Changelings*. 2nd ed. New York: Cambridge University Press, 2015.

Laslett, Peter. *A Fresh Map of Life: The Emergence of the Third Age*. London: Weidenfeld and Nicolson, 1989.

Lee, Eunju, Michael Clarkson-Hendrix, and Yeonggeul Lee. "Parenting Stress of Grandparents and Other Kin as Informal Kinship Caregivers: A Mixed Methods Study." *Children and Youth Services Review* 69 (October 1, 2016): 29–38. https://doi.org/10.1016/j.childyouth.2016.07.013.

Livingston, Gretchen. "At Grandmother's House We Stay." Washington, DC: Pew Research Center, September 4, 2013. http://www.pewsocialtrends.org/2013/09/04/at-grandmothers-house-we-stay/.

Lucas, Susan. "From Levittown to Luther Village: Retirement Communities and the Changing Suburban Dream." *Canadian Journal of Urban Research* 11, no. 2 (2002): 323–42.

Lumsdaine, Robin L., and Stephanie J. C. Vermeer. "Retirement Timing of Women and the Role of Care Responsibilities for Grandchildren." *Demography* 52, no. 2 (April 2015): 433–54. https://doi.org/10.1007/s13524-015-0382-5.

Mann, Robin. "Out of the Shadows?: Grandfatherhood, Age and Masculinities." *Journal of Aging Studies* 21, no. 4 (December 2007): 281–91. https://doi.org/10.1016/j.jaging.2007.05.008.

McKoy, Briana. "Tyler Perry and the Weight of Misrepresentation." *McNair Scholars Research Journal* 5, no. 1 (2012): 127–46.

McLuhan, Marshall. *The Gutenberg Galaxy: The Making of Typographic Man*. Toronto: University of Toronto Press, 1962.

———. *Understanding Media: The Extensions of Man*. Cambridge, MA: MIT Press, 1994.

Mead, Margaret. *Blackberry Winter: My Earlier Years*. New York: Kodansha America, 1995.

Meyer, Madonna Harrington. *Grandmothers at Work: Juggling Families and Jobs*. New York: New York University Press, 2014.

Meyer, Madonna Harrington, and Yooumi Lee. "Grandparenting in the United States." In *Grandparenting in the United States*, edited by Madonna Harrington Meyer and Ynesse

Abdul-Malak. Society and Aging Series. Amityville, NY: Baywood Publishing Company, 2016.

Meyrowitz, Joshua. *No Sense of Place: The Impact of Electronic Media on Social Behavior*. New York: Oxford University Press, 1986.

"Millennials: Confident. Connected. Open to Change." Washington, DC: Pew Research Center, February 24, 2010. http://www.pewinternet.org/2010/02/24/millennials-confident-connected-open-to-change/.

Minkler, Meredith, and Kathleen M. Roe. *Grandmothers as Caregivers: Raising Children of the Crack Cocaine Epidemic*. Newbury Park, CA: Sage, 1993.

Molloy, Raven, Christopher L. Smith, and Abigail Wozniak. "Internal Migration in the United States." Working paper. Washington, DC: National Bureau of Economic Research, August 2011. http://www.nber.org/papers/w17307.pdf.

Monk-Turner, Elizabeth, Mary Heiserman, Crystle Johnson, Vanity Cotton, and Manny Jackson. "The Portrayal of Racial Minorities on Prime Time Television: A Replication of the Mastro and Greenberg Study a Decade Later." *Studies in Popular Culture* 32, no. 2 (Spring 2010): 101–114. https://www.jstor.org/stable/23416158.

Moses, Marlene Eskind, and Jessica J. Uitto. "The Current Status of Tennessee's Grandparent Visitation Law." *Tennessee Bar Journal* 46, no. 1 (January 2010): 24.

Moulton, Vanessa, Eirini Flouri, Heather Joshi, and Alice Sullivan. "The Influence of Grandparents' Social Class on Children's Aspirations." *British Journal of Sociology of Education* 38, no. 4 (May 2017): 500–517. https://doi.org/10.1080/01425692.2015.1093407.

Mulvey, Laura. *Visual and Other Pleasures*. 2nd ed. New York: Palgrave Macmillan, 2009.

Musial, Jennifer. "From 'Madonna' to 'Whore': Sexuality, Pregnancy, and Popular Culture." *Sexualities* 17, no. 4 (June 2014): 394–411. https://doi.org/10.1177/1363460713516335.

Mutchler, Jan E., Lindsey A. Baker, and SeungAh Lee. "Grandparents Responsible for Grandchildren in Native-American Families." *Social Science Quarterly* 88, no. 4 (December 1, 2007): 990–1009. https://doi.org/10.1111/j.1540-6237.2007.00514.x.

Nathanson, Elizabeth. *Knitting, Sewing and Grandma's Retro-Style*. Routledge Advances in Television Studies 3. New York: Routledge/Taylor and Francis Group, 2013.

Nedelcu, Mihaela. "Transnational Grandparenting in the Digital Age: Mediated Co-Presence and Childcare in the Case of Romanian Migrants in Switzerland and Canada." *European Journal of Ageing* 14, no. 4 (December 1, 2017): 375–83. https://doi.org/10.1007/s10433-017-0436-1.

Newman, Sally, ed. *Intergenerational Programs: Past, Present, and Future*. Washington, DC: Taylor and Francis, 1997.

Ong, Walter J. *Orality and Literacy: The Technologizing of the Word*. New York: Routledge, 1991.

Orel, Nancy. "Lesbian and Bisexual Women as Grandparents: The Centrality of Sexual Orientation in the Grandparent-Grandchild Relationship." In *Lesbian, Gay, Bisexual, Transgender Aging: Research and Clinical Perspectives*, edited by Douglas Kimmel, Tara Rose, and Steven David. New York: Columbia University Press, 2006.

Overall, Christine. "Longevity, Identity, and Moral Character: A Feminist Approach." In *The Fountain of Youth: Cultural, Scientific, and Ethical Perspectives on a Biomedical Goal*, edited by Robert H. Binstock and Stephen G. Post. Oxford: Oxford University Press, 2004.

Orit, Taubman-Ben-Ari, and Ben Shlomo Shirley. "Measuring Personal Growth of New Grandparents: A Practical Tool for Social Workers." *Research on Social Work Practice* 26, no. 6 (October 1, 2016): 704–11. https://doi.org/10.1177/1049731514564165.

Parker, Kim, and Gretchen Livingston. "6 Facts about American Fathers." Washington, DC: Pew Research Center, June 15, 2017. http://www.pewresearch.org/fact-tank/2017/06/15/fathers-day-facts/.

Parker, Kim, and Juliana Menasce Horowitz. "Family Support in Graying Societies: How Americans, Germans and Italians Are Coping with an Aging Population." Washington, DC: Pew Research Center, May 21, 2015. http://www.pewsocialtrends.org/2015/05/21/family-support-in-graying-societies/.

Patten, Eileen, and Richard Fry. "How Millennials Today Compare with Their Grandparents 50 Years Ago," March 19, 2015. http://www.pewresearch.org/fact-tank/2015/03/19/how-millennials-compare-with-their-grandparents/.

Patterson, Charlotte J., Susan Hurt, and Chandra D. Mason. "Families of the Lesbian Baby Boom: Children's Contact with Grandparents and Other Adults." *The American Journal of Orthopsychiatry* 68, no. 3 (July 1998): 390–99. https://doi.org/10.1037/h0080348.

Pembrey, Marcus, Lars Olov Bygren, Gunnar Kaati, Sören Edvinsson, et al. "Sex-Specific, Male-Line Transgenerational Responses in Humans." *European Journal of Human Genetics* 14, no. 2 (February 2006): 159–66. doi: 10.1038/sj.ejhg.5201538.

Perlesz, Amaryll, Rhonda Brown, Jo Lindsay, Ruth McNair, David deVaus, and Marian Pitts. "Family in Transition: Parents, Children and Grandparents in Lesbian Families Give Meaning to 'Doing Family.'" *Journal of Family Therapy* 28, no. 2 (May 2006): 175–99. https://doi.org/10.1111/j.1467-6427.2006.00345.x.

Pittman, LaShawnDa. "How Well Does the 'Safety Net' Work for Family Safety Nets? Economic Survival Strategies among Grandmother Caregivers in Severe Deprivation." *The Russell Sage Foundation Journal of the Social Sciences* 1, no. 1 (November 2015): 78–97.

Pittman, LaShawnDa, and Deirdre Oakley. "'It Was Love in All the Building They Tore Down': How Caregiving Grandmothers Create and Experience a Sense of Community in Chicago Public Housing." *City & Community* 17, no. 2 (June 2018): 461–484. doi: 10.1111/cico.12280.

Postman, Neil. *The Disappearance of Childhood*. New York: Random House, 1982.

———. *Technopoly: The Surrender of Culture to Technology*. New York: Vintage Books, 1993.

Putnam, Robert D. *Our Kids: The American Dream in Crisis*. New York: Simon & Schuster, 2015.

Robinson, Tom, and Caitlin Anderson. "Older Characters in Children's Animated Television Programs: A Content Analysis of Their Portrayal." *Journal of Broadcasting & Electronic Media* 50, no. 2 (June 1, 2006): 287–304. https://doi.org/10.1207/s15506878jobem5002_7.

Robinson, Tom, Mark Callister, Dawn Magoffin, and Jennifer Moore. "The Portrayal of Older Characters in Disney Animated Films." *Journal of Aging Studies* 21, no. 3 (August 2007): 203–13. https://doi.org/10.1016/j.jaging.2006.10.001.

Romero, Margarida, Kimberly Sawchuk, Josep Blat, Sergio Sayago, and Hubert Ouellet. *Game-Based Learning across the Lifespan: Cross-Generational and Age-Oriented Topics*. Switzerland: Springer, 2017.

Rosenberg, Bruce A. "The Complexity of Oral Tradition." *Oral Tradition* 2, no. 1 (1987): 73–90.

Ruddick, Sara. "Maternal Thinking: Toward a Politics of Peace." In *Maternal Theory: Essential Readings*, edited by Andrea O'Reilly. Toronto: Demeter Press, 2007.

Ruiz, Sarah A., and Merril Silverstein. "Relationships with Grandparents and the Emotional Well-Being of Late Adolescent and Young Adult Grandchildren." *Journal of Social Issues* 63, no. 4 (December 1, 2007): 793–808. https://doi.org/10.1111/j.1540-4560.2007.00537.x.

Samms-Vaughan, M., and P. B. Gray. "Investigating Potential Hormonal Associations of Grandmaternal Care in Jamaica." *The Internet Journal of Biological Anthropology* 4, no. 1 (January 2010). https://doi.org/10.5580/104c.

Sangree, Walter H. "Grandparenthood and Modernization: The Changing Status of Male and Female Elders in Tiriki, Kenya, and Irigwe, Nigeria." *Journal of Cross-Cultural Gerontology* 7, no. 4 (October 1992): 331–61. https://doi.org/10.1007/BF01848698.

Sasse, Benjamin E. *The Vanishing American Adult: Our Coming-of-Age Crisis—and How to Rebuild a Culture of Self-Reliance*. New York: St. Martin's Press, 2017.

Sawchuk, Dana. "The Raging Grannies: Defying Stereotypes and Embracing Aging through Activism." *Journal of Women & Aging* 21, no. 3 (2009): 171–85. https://doi.org/10.1080/08952840903054898.

Sawchuk, Kim, and Barbara Crow. "'I'm G-Mom on the Phone.'" *Feminist Media Studies* 12, no. 4 (December 1, 2012): 496–505. https://doi.org/10.1080/14680777.2012.741863.

Seltzer, Judith A., and Jenjira J. Yahirun. "Diversity in Old Age: The Elderly in Changing Economic and Family Contexts." American Communities Project of Brown University.

New York: Russell Sage Foundation, November 6, 2013. https://s4.ad.brown.edu/Projects/Diversity/Data/Report/report11062013.pdf.

Senior, Jennifer. *All Joy and No Fun: The Paradox of Modern Parenthood*. New York: HarperCollins Publishers, 2014.

Settersten, Richard A., Jr. "The New Landscape of Adult Life: Road Maps, Signposts, and Speed Lines." *Research in Human Development* 4, no. 3–4 (July 1, 2007): 239–52. https://doi.org/10.1080/15427600701663098.

Settersten, Richard A. "The New Landscape of Adult Life: Road Maps, Signposts, and Speed Lines." *Research in Human Development* 4, no. 3–4 (2017): 239–52. https://doi.org/10.1080/15427600701663098.

Settersten, Richard A., Jr. and Gunhild O. Hagestad. "Subjective Aging and New Complexities of the Life Course." *Annual Review of Gerontology and Geriatrics* 35, no. 1 (February 2015): 29–53. https://doi.org/10.1891/0198-8794.35.29.

Sicherman, Nachum, George Loewenstein, Teresa Tavassoli, et al. "Grandma Knows Best: Family Structure and Age of Diagnosis of Autism Spectrum Disorder." *Autism* 22, no. 3 (February 2018): 368–376. doi: 10.1177/1362361316679632.

Sigad, Laura I., and Rivka A. Eisikovits. "Grandparenting across Borders: American Grandparents and Their Israeli Grandchildren in a Transnational Reality." *Journal of Aging Studies* 27, no. 4 (December 2013): 308–16. https://doi.org/10.1016/j.jaging.2013.06.002.

Smith, Aaron. "15% of American Adults Have Used Online Dating Sites or Mobile Dating Apps." Washington, DC: Pew Research Center, February 11, 2016. http://www.pewinternet.org/2016/02/11/15-percent-of-american-adults-have-used-online-dating-sites-or-mobile-dating-apps/.

Stahl, Lesley. *Becoming Grandma: The Joys and Science of the New Grandparenting*. New York: Blue Rider Press, 2016.

Stepler, Renee. "Led by Baby Boomers, Divorce Rates Climb for America's 50+ Population," Washington, DC: Pew Research Center, March 9, 2017. http://www.pewresearch.org/fact-tank/2017/03/09/led-by-baby-boomers-divorce-rates-climb-for-americas-50-population/.

Sussman, Marvin B. "Relationships of Adult Children with Their Parents in the United States." In *Social Structure and the Family: Generational Relations*, edited by Ethel Shanas and Gordon F. Streib. Durham, NC: Duke University Press, 1967.

Sussman, Marvin B, and Lee Burchinal. "Kin Family Network: Unheralded Structure in Current Conceptualizations of Family Functioning." In *Middle Age and Aging: A Reader in Social Psychology*, edited by Bernice Levin Neugarten, 246–54. Chicago: University of Chicago Press, 1968.

Suzman, Richard, and John Beard. "Global Health and Aging." Washington, DC: National Institute on Aging, National Institutes of Health and World Health Organization, October 2011. https://www.nia.nih.gov/sites/default/files/2017-06/global_health_aging.pdf.

Sze, Jocelyn A., Anett Gyurak, Madeleine S. Goodkind, and Robert W. Levenson. "Greater Emotional Empathy and Prosocial Behavior in Late Life." *Emotion* 12, no. 5 (October 2012): 1129–40. https://doi.org/10.1037/a0025011.

Tehrani, Jamshid J. "The Phylogeny of Little Red Riding Hood." *PLOS ONE* 8, no. 11 (November 13, 2013): e78871. https://doi.org/10.1371/journal.pone.0078871.

Thane, Pat. "The History of Aging in the West." In *Handbook of the Humanities and Aging*, edited by Thomas R. Cole, Robert Kastenbaum, and Ruth E. Ray, 2nd ed., 3–24. New York: Springer, 2000.

Thane, Pat, and J. Paul Getty Museum, eds. *A History of Old Age*. Los Angeles: J. Paul Getty Museum, 2005.

Thompson, Susan Shy. "Mamaw Got Run Over by a Combine: Grandparent Naming Practices in the Rural South." *International Association for Intercultural Communication Studies* 10, no. 1 (2000): 177–88.

Thurer, Shari L. *The Myths of Motherhood: How Culture Reinvents the Good Mother*. New York: Penguin Books, 1995.

Tootelian, Dennis H., and Sanjay Varshney. "The Grandparent Consumer: A Financial 'Goldmine' with Gray Hair?" *Journal of Consumer Marketing* 27, no. 1 (January 26, 2010): 57–63. https://doi.org/10.1108/07363761011012958.

Tourjeman, Kobi, Israel Doron, and Miri Cohen. "Losing a Grandchild: The Mourning Experience of Grandparents in Israel." *Death Studies* 39, no. 8 (September 2015): 491–99. https://doi.org/10.1080/07481187.2014.970298.

Traister, Rebecca. *All the Single Ladies: Unmarried Women and the Rise of an Independent Nation*. New York: Simon & Schuster, 2016.

Treas, Judith. "Transnational Older Adults and Their Families." *Family Relations* 57, no. 4 (October 1, 2008): 468–78. https://doi.org/10.1111/j.1741-3729.2008.00515.x.

Tropp, Laura. "Off Their Rockers: Representations of Post-Partum Depression." In *MTV and Teen Pregnancy: Critical Essays on 16 and Pregnant and Teen Mom*, edited by Letizia Guglielmo. Lanham: Scarecrow Press, 2013.

———. "What's a Baby Daddy to Do: Fathers on the Fringe in MTV's *16 and Pregnant*." In *MTV and Teen Pregnancy: Critical Essays on* 16 and Pregnant *and* Teen Mom, edited by Letizia Guglielmo, 161–76. Lanham, MD: Scarecrow Press, 2013.

———. "Who's Your Daddy: Sperm Donation and the Cultural Construction of Fatherhood." In *Deconstructing Dads: Changing Images of Fathers in Popular Culture*, edited by Laura Tropp and Janice Kelly. Lanham, MD: Lexington Books, 2016.

———. *A Womb with a View: America's Growing Public Interest in Pregnancy*. Santa Barbara, CA: Praeger, 2013.

Tukachinsky, Riva."Where We Have Been and Where We Can Go from Here: Looking to the Future in Research on Media, Race, and Ethnicity." *Journal of Social Issues* 71, no. 1 (2015): 186–199, doi: 10.1111/josi.12104.

Uslaner, Eric M. "Where You Stand Depends Upon Where Your Grandparents Sat: The Inheritability of Generalized Trust." *Public Opinion Quarterly* 72, no. 4 (January 2008): 725–40. https://doi.org/10.1093/poq/nfn058.

Vaillant, George E. *Aging Well: Surprising Guideposts to a Happier Life from the Landmark Harvard Study of Adult Development*. Reprint edition. New York: Little, Brown and Company, 2003.

Van den Bulck, Hilde. "Growing Old in Celebrity Culture." In *Aging, Media, and Culture*, edited by C. Lee Harrington and Denise Bielby. Lanham, MD: Rowman & Littlefield, 2014.

Vernon, JoEtta A., J. Allen Williams Jr., Terri Phillips, and Janet Wilson. "Media Stereotyping: A Comparison of the Way Elderly Women and Men Are Portrayed on Primetime Television." *Journal of Women & Aging* 2, no. 4 (1990): 55–68. https://doi.org/10.1300/J074v02n04_05.

Weinberg, John. "The Great Recession and Its Aftermath." Federal Reserve History. Federal Reserve Board, November 22, 2013. https://www.federalreservehistory.org/essays/great_recession_and_its_aftermath.

Wellford, Lin. *The New Grandparents Name Book*. Green Forest, AZ: ArtStone Press, 2009.

Williams, Joan. *Unbending Gender: Why Family and Work Conflict and What to Do about It*. New York: Oxford University Press, 2000.

Yahnke, Robert E. "Intergeneration and Regeneration: The Meaning of Old Age in Films and Videos." In *Handbook of the Humanities and Aging*, edited by Thomas R. Cole, Robert Kastenbaum, and Ruth E. Ray, 2nd ed., 293–323. New York: Springer Publishing, 2000.

Yarbrough, Marilyn, and Crystal Bennett. "Cassandra and the Sistahs: The Peculiar Treatment of African American Women in the Myth of Women as Liars." *Journal of Gender, Race and Justice* 3 (Spring 2000): 625–57.

Zeece, Pauline Davey. "Grandparents and Grand Books." *Early Childhood Education Journal* 35, no. 2 (October 2007): 127–30. https://doi.org/10.1007/s10643-007-0171-x.

Index

About the Author

Dr. Laura Tropp is a scholar on pregnancy, motherhood, and fatherhood studies with a doctoral degree from New York University. The focus of her work is on connections between popular culture, media technology, and families and parenting. Her first book, *A Womb with a View: America's Growing Public Interest in Pregnancy*, was published in 2013. Her co-edited collection, *Deconstructing Dads: Images of Fathers in Popular Culture*, was published by Lexington Books in 2016. She is currently a professor at Marymount Manhattan College, where she teaches courses on media studies, gender studies, and popular culture. She has been featured in the media in many different popular publications, including, most recently, *Smithsonian Magazine, Salon*, and the *Huffington Post*. She currently lives intergenerationally with her parents, husband, and children.

www.ingramcontent.com/pod-product-compliance
Lightning Source LLC
LaVergne TN
LVHW101447200926
848483LV00001B/74